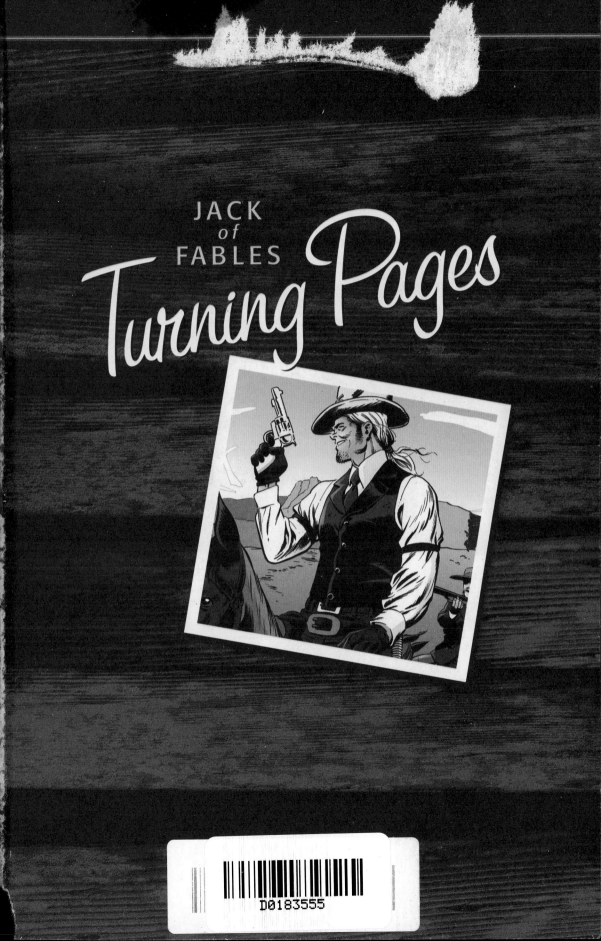

JACK
of
FABLES
Turning Pages

BILL WILLINGHAM **MATTHEW STURGES**
Writers

RUSS BRAUN **TONY AKINS**
Pencillers

JOSÉ MARZÁN, JR. **ANDREW PEPOY**
STEVE LEIALOHA
Inkers

DANIEL VOZZO
Colorist

TODD KLEIN
Letterer

BRIAN BOLLAND *Original Series Covers*
JACK OF FABLES created by **BILL WILLINGHAM**

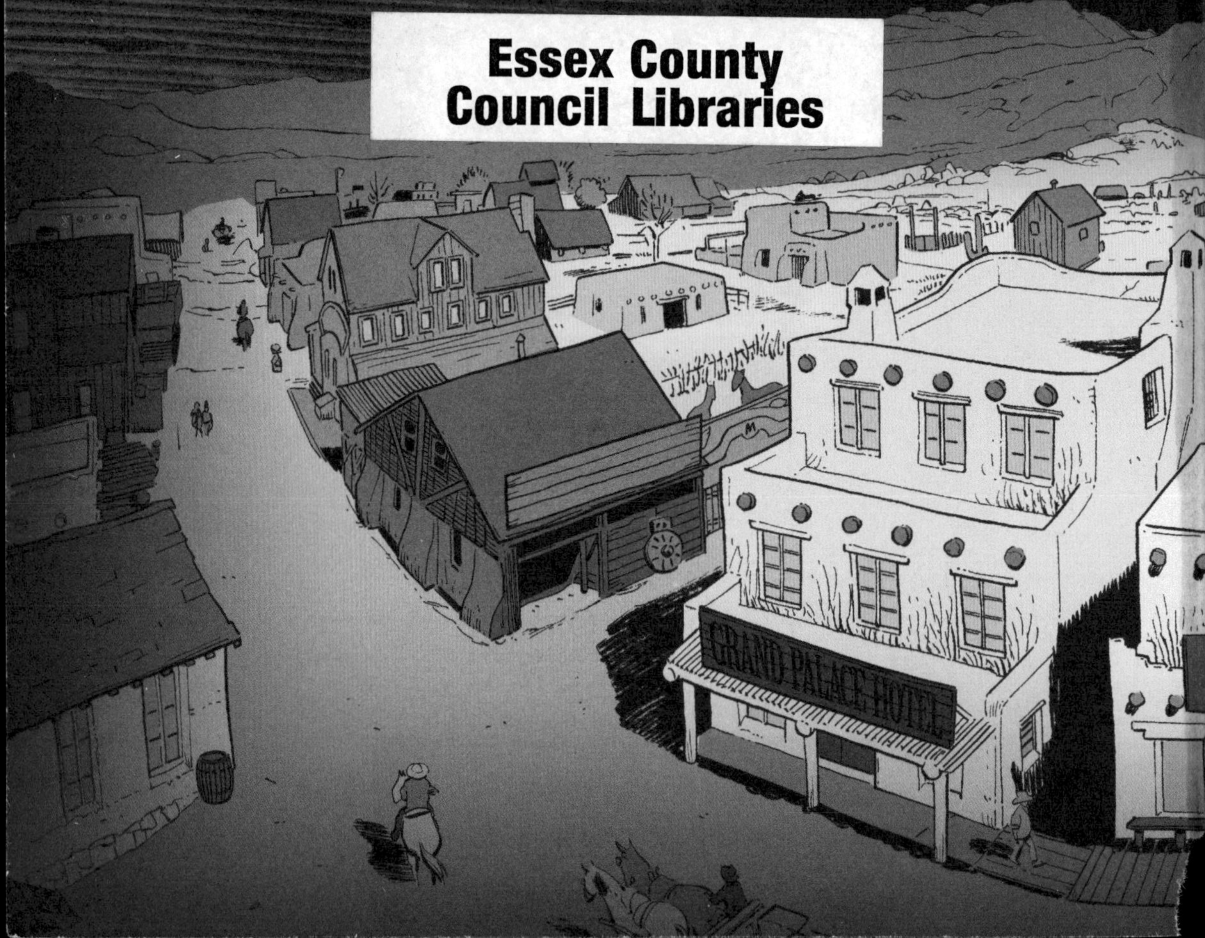
GRAND PALACE HOTEL

JACK of FABLES
Turning Pages

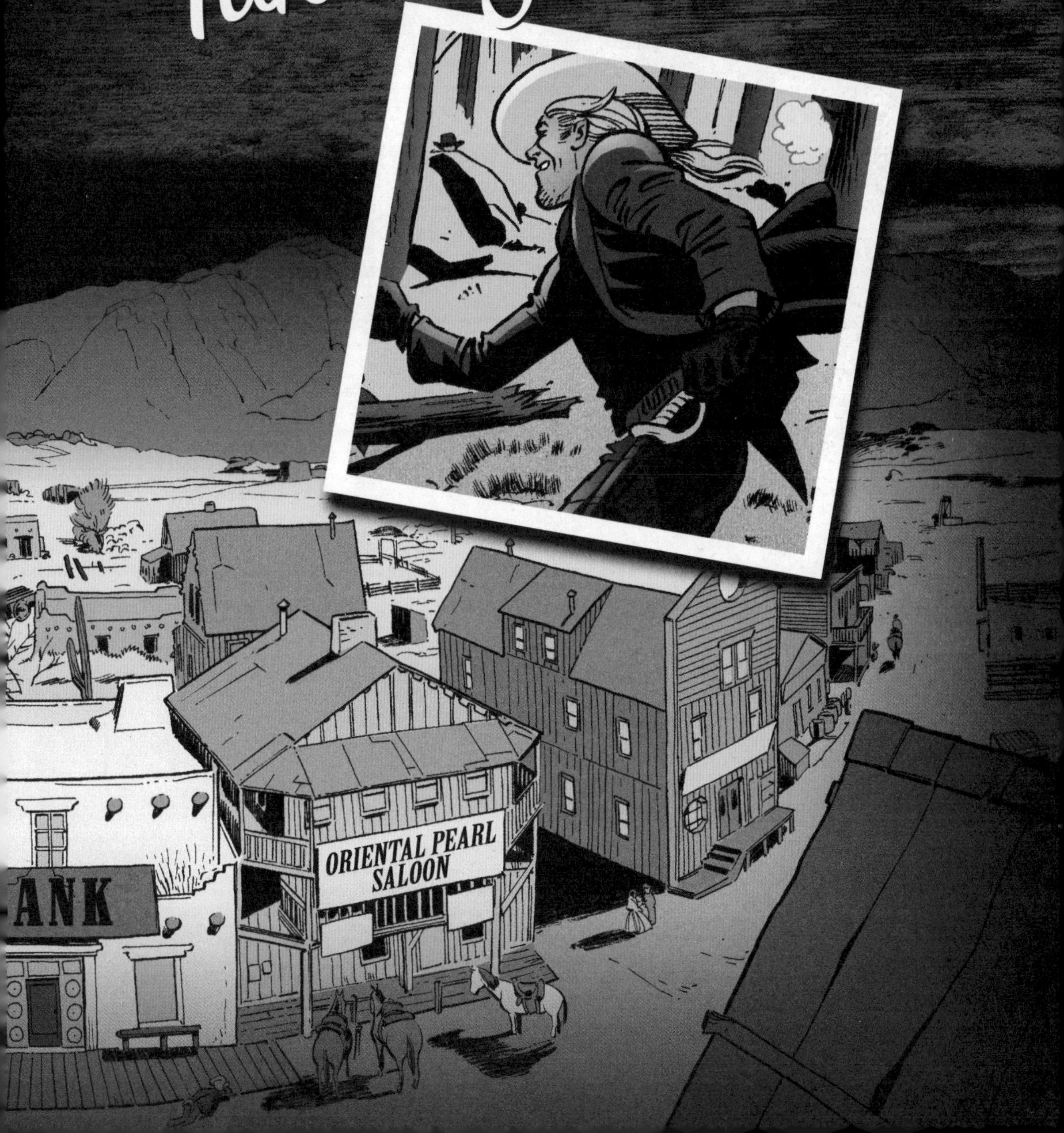
ORIENTAL PEARL SALOON
ANK

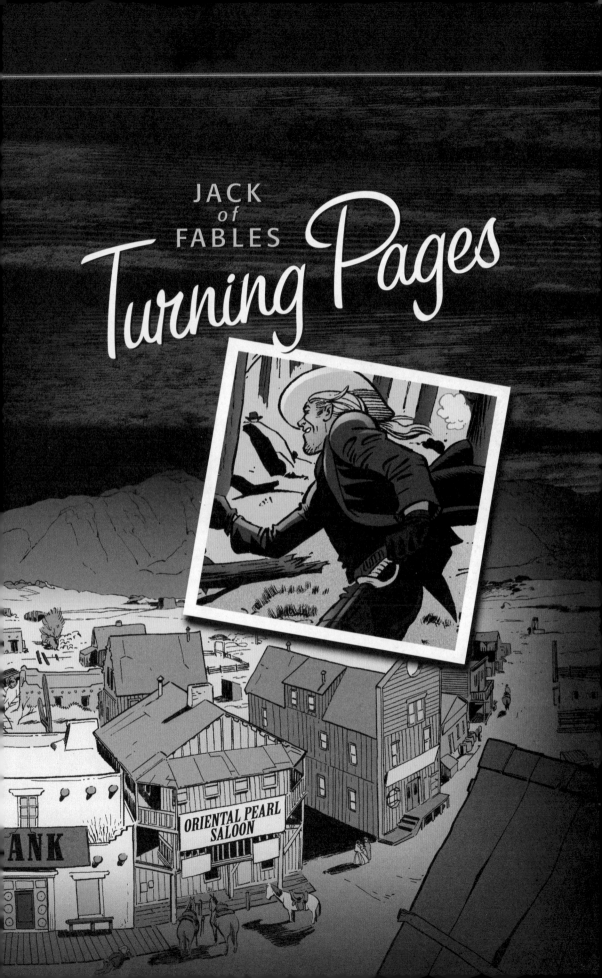

Cover illustration by Brian Bolland. Logo design by James Jean. Publication design by Brainchild Studios/NYC.

DC Comics, 1700 Broadway, New York, NY 10019
A Warner Bros. Entertainment Company.
Printed in Canada. First Printing.
ISBN: 978-1-4012-2138-6

SFI CERTIFIED SOURCING Fiber used in this product line meets the sourcing requirements of the SFI program. www.sfiprogram.org PWC-SFICOC-260

Table of Contents

DRAMATIS PERSONAE **6**

1883

Chapter One: **THE LEGEND OF SMILIN' JACK** **7**
Pencils by Tony Akins • Inks by Andrew Pepoy

Chapter Two: **MOON OF THE WOLF** **29**
Pencils by Tony Akins • Inks by Andrew Pepoy (pages 29-32, 42-50)
and José Marzán, Jr. (pages 33-41)

Chapter Three: **THE SHOWDOWN** **51**
Pencils by Tony Akins (pages 51-66) and Russ Braun (pages 67-72)
Inks by José Marzán, Jr.

TURNING PAGES

Chapter One: **ROBIN** **73**
Pencils by Russ Braun • Inks by José Marzán, Jr. (pages 73-78, 80-82,
84, 86-89, 91-94) and Steve Leialoha (pages 79, 83, 85, 90)

Chapter Two: **PRISCILLA** **95**
Pencils by Russ Braun • Inks by José Marzán, Jr.

Chapter Three: **HILLARY** **117**
Pencils by Russ Braun • Inks by José Marzán, Jr.

COVER GALLERY **139**

Dramatis Personae

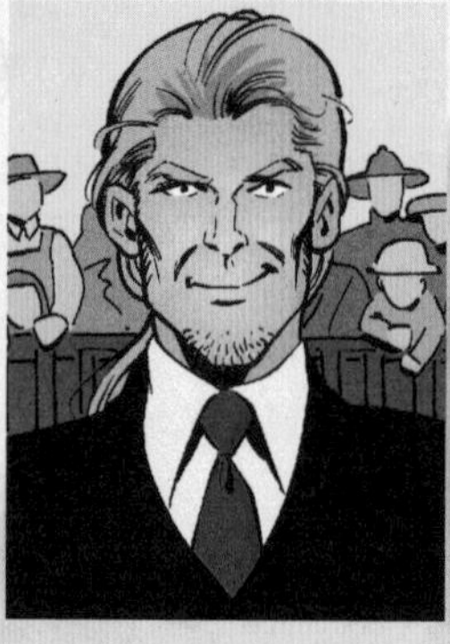

JACK
Also known as Little Jack Horner, Jack B. Nimble, Jack the Giant Killer and by countless other aliases, our hero Jack of the Tales embodies the archetype of the lovable rogue (minus, according to many, the lovability).

BIGBY WOLF
The biggest, baddest sheriff ever to wear the tin star, and one of Fabletown's staunchest defenders.

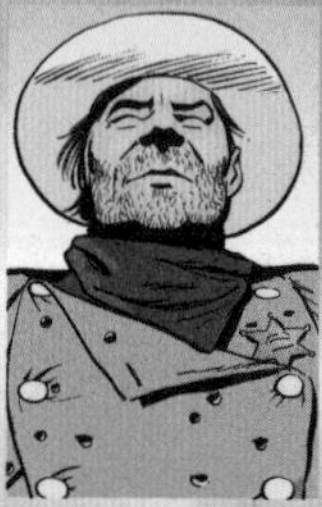

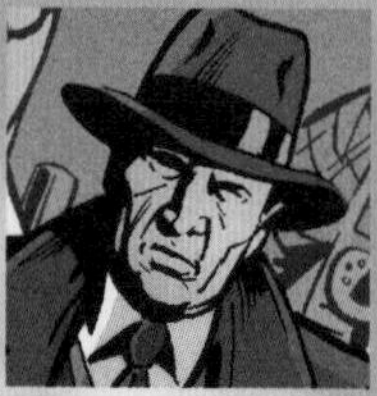

THE BOOKBURNER
The head librarian of Americana, and the Fables' worst nightmare.

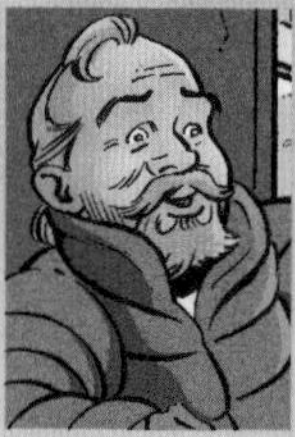

GARY, THE PATHETIC FALLACY
A timid, impressionable and warm-hearted fellow whose power over inanimate objects is matched only by his love of Sousa marches.

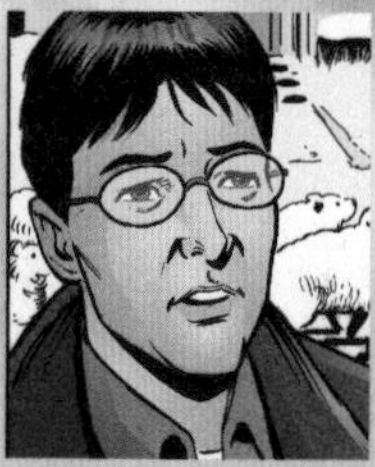

KEVIN THORN
Newly revealed as the father of Mr. Revise and the son of the Pathetic Fallacy, he is currently a "guest" of the Golden Boughs.

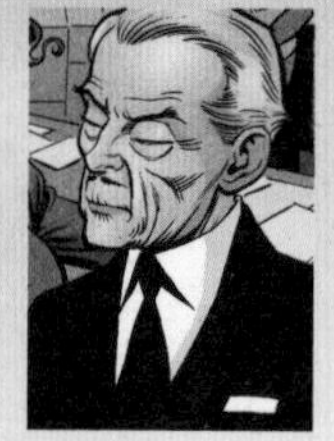

MR. REVISE
Jack's untiring antagonist, dedicated to trapping Fables and draining their power in pursuit of a magic-free world.

HUMPTY DUMPTY
A stout fellow from Colchester, his ferocious bark belies his brittle nature.

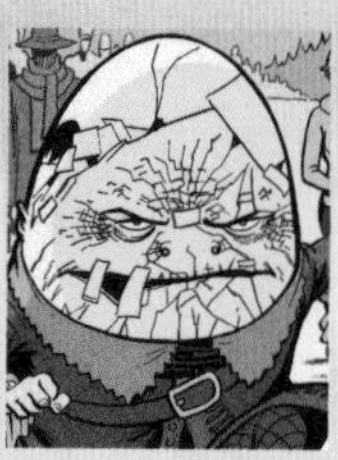

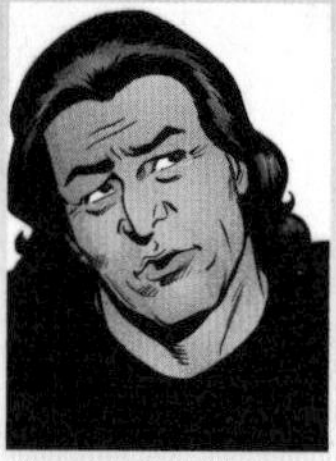

RAVEN
Jack's new Native American companion, blessed with a contrary nature and some surprising abilities.

THE PAGE SISTERS
Right-hand women to Mr. Revise and the chief librarians at his Fable prison, the Golden Boughs Retirement Village.

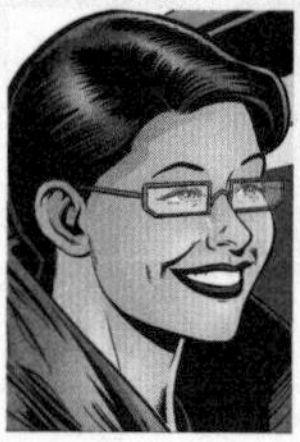

Robin Page

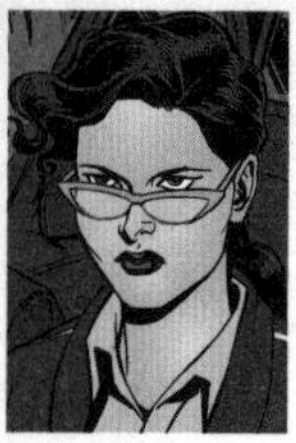

Priscilla Page

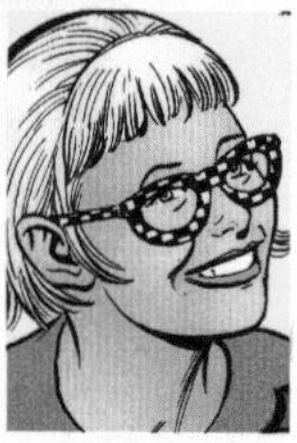

Hillary Page

GOLDILOCKS
A self-styled revolutionary whose narcissism is almost equal to Jack's own.

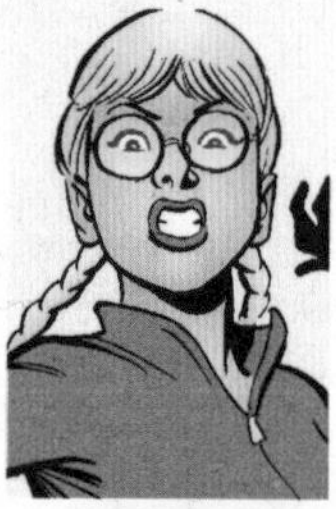

LADY LUCK
A capricious tyrant, given to rhyming and brain-eating.

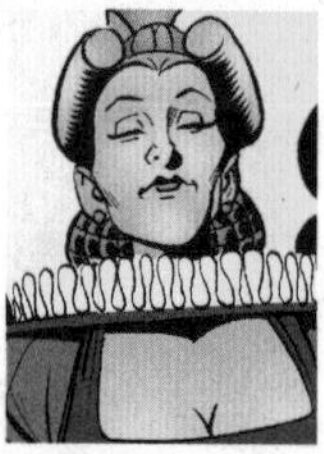

BABE
A blue ox with a gift for self-invention.

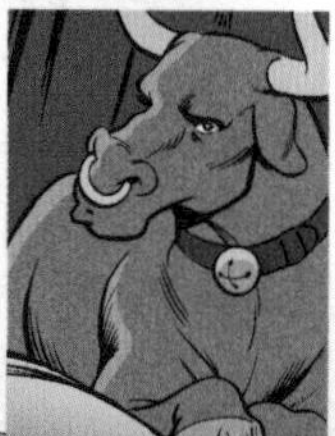

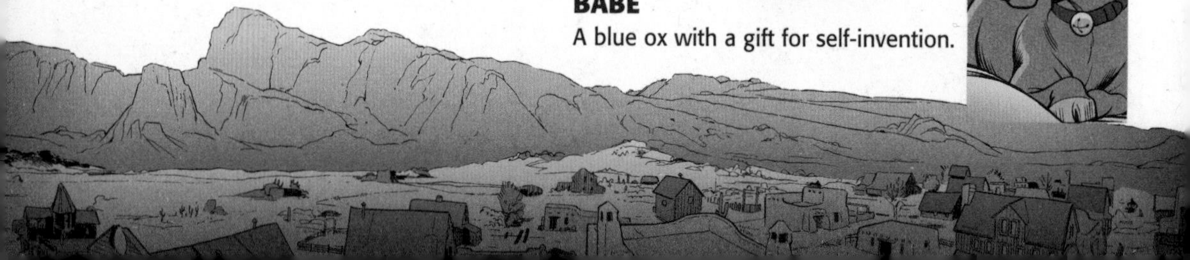

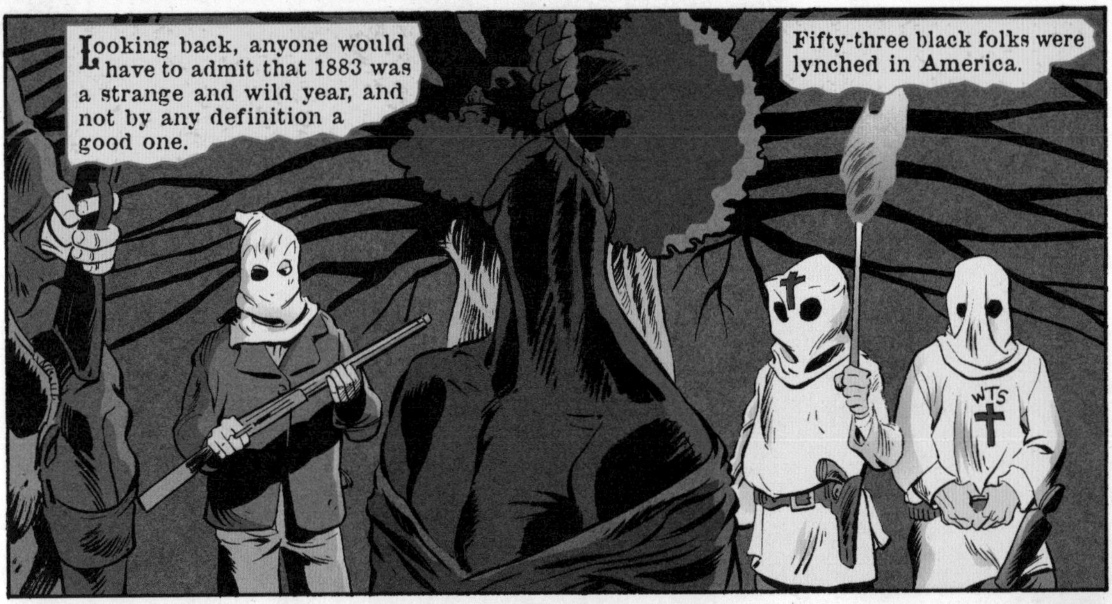
Looking back, anyone would have to admit that 1883 was a strange and wild year, and not by any definition a good one.
Fifty-three black folks were lynched in America.
WTS

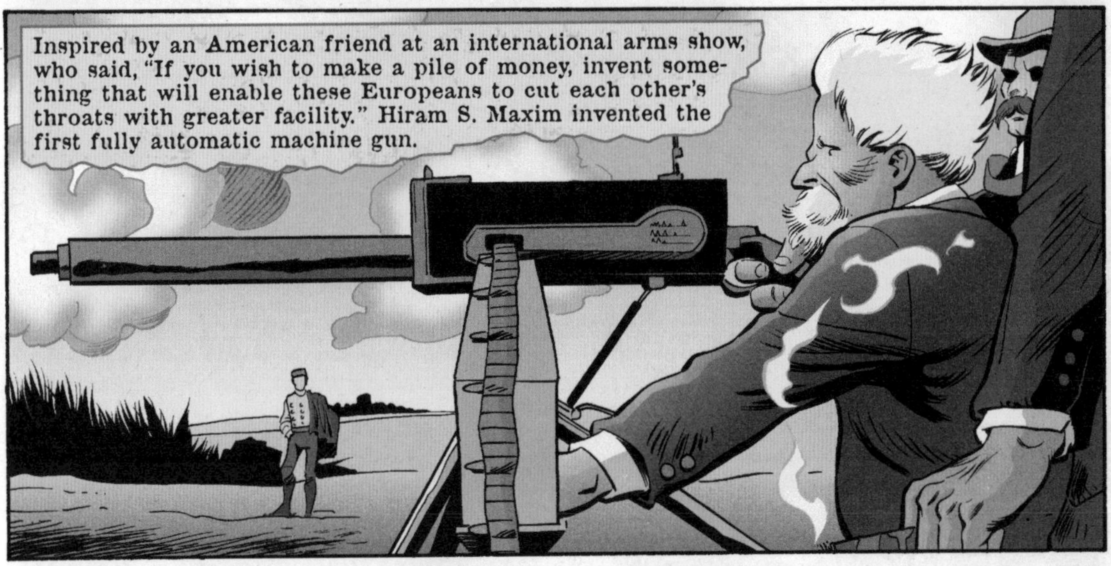
Inspired by an American friend at an international arms show, who said, "If you wish to make a pile of money, invent something that will enable these Europeans to cut each other's throats with greater facility." Hiram S. Maxim invented the first fully automatic machine gun.

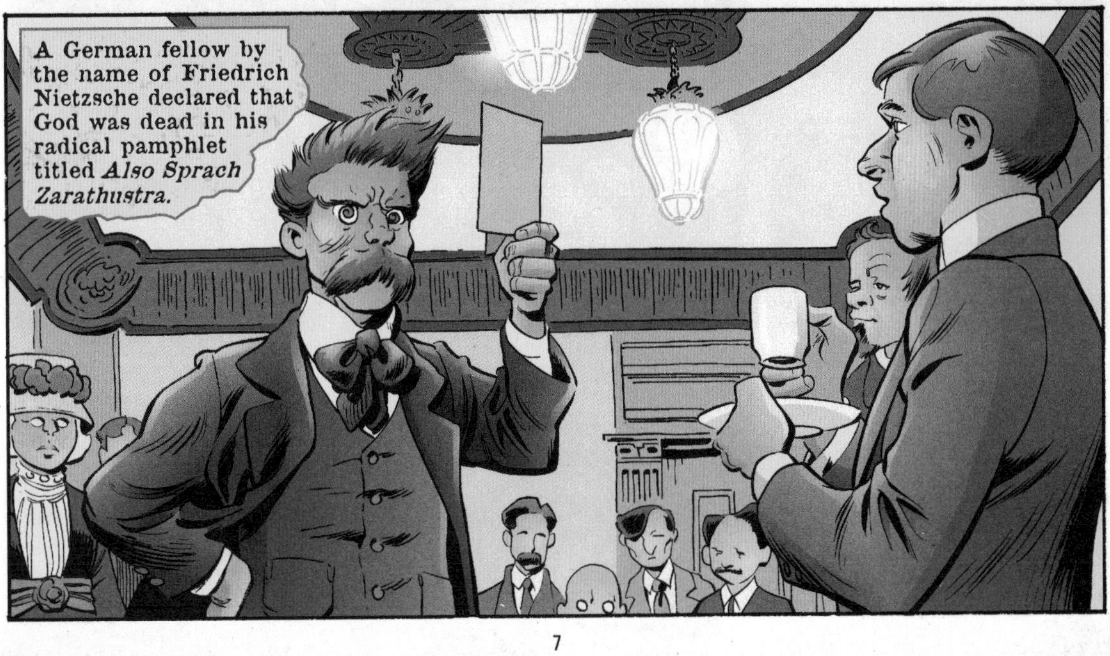
A German fellow by the name of Friedrich Nietzsche declared that God was dead in his radical pamphlet titled *Also Sprach Zarathustra.*

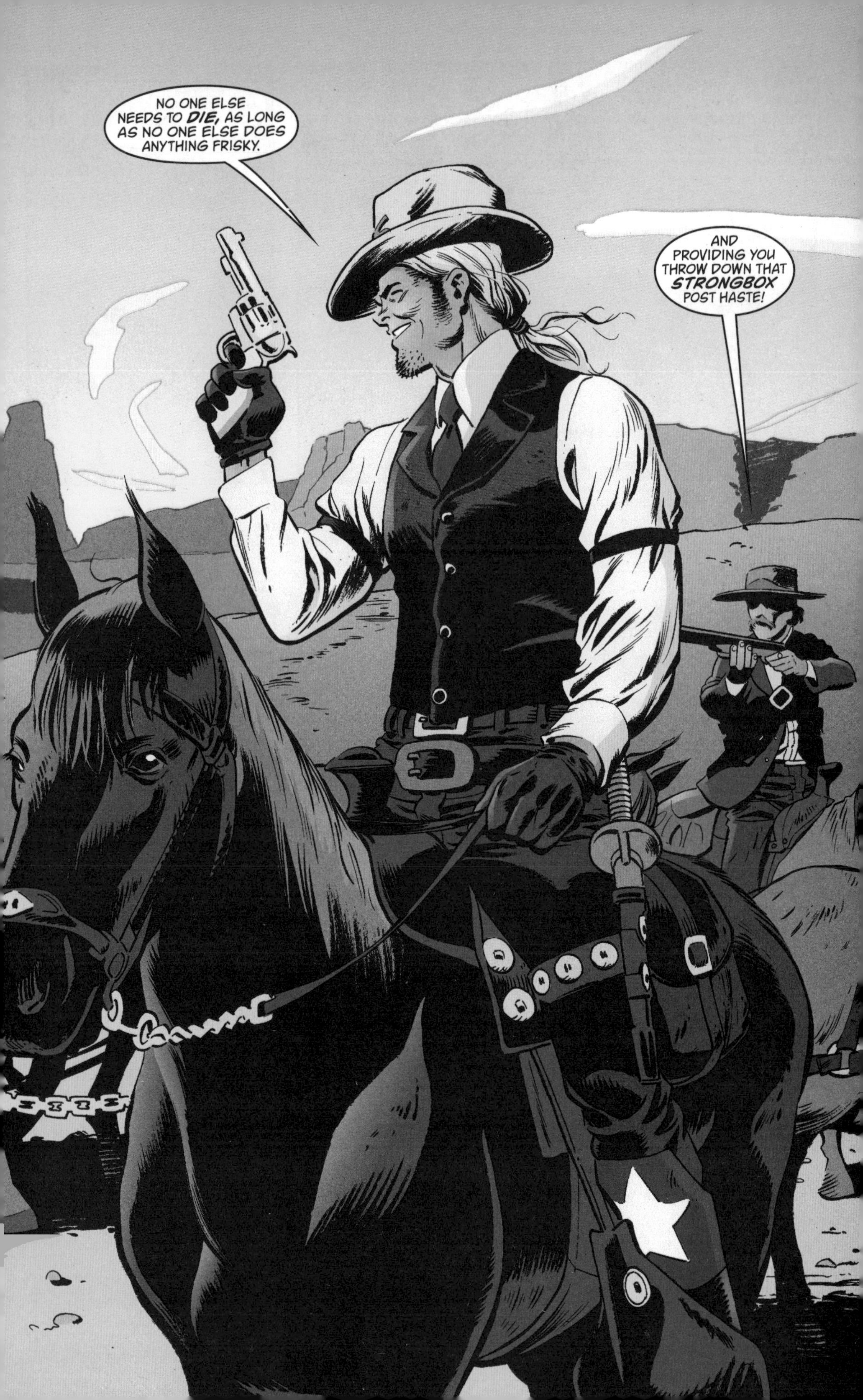
NO ONE ELSE NEEDS TO DIE, AS LONG AS NO ONE ELSE DOES ANYTHING FRISKY.
AND PROVIDING YOU THROW DOWN THAT STRONGBOX POST HASTE!

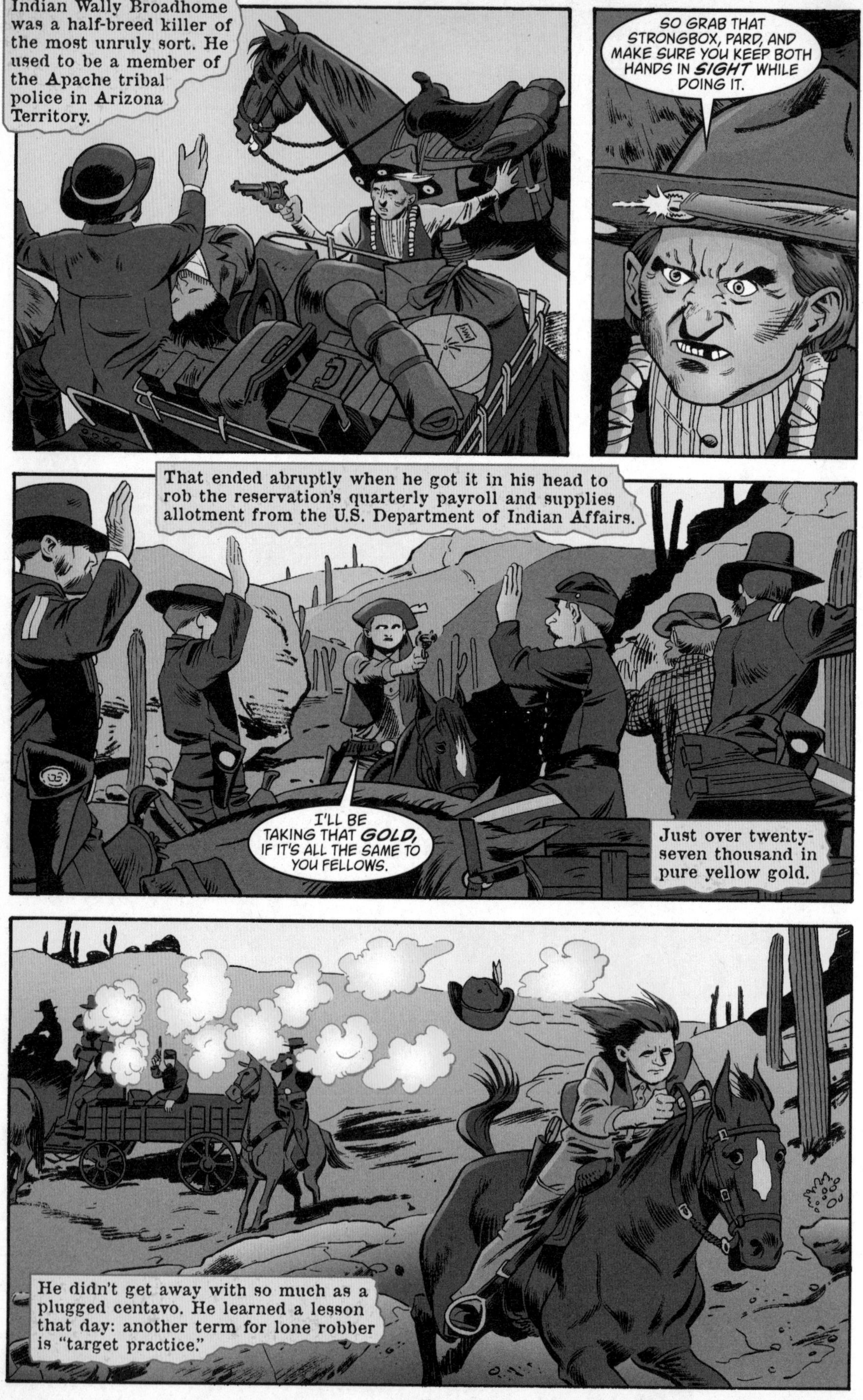
Indian Wally Broadhome was a half-breed killer of the most unruly sort. He used to be a member of the Apache tribal police in Arizona Territory.
SO GRAB THAT STRONGBOX, PARD, AND MAKE SURE YOU KEEP BOTH HANDS IN SIGHT WHILE DOING IT.
That ended abruptly when he got it in his head to rob the reservation's quarterly payroll and supplies allotment from the U.S. Department of Indian Affairs.
I'LL BE TAKING THAT GOLD, IF IT'S ALL THE SAME TO YOU FELLOWS.
Just over twenty-seven thousand in pure yellow gold.
He didn't get away with so much as a plugged centavo. He learned a lesson that day: another term for lone robber is "target practice."

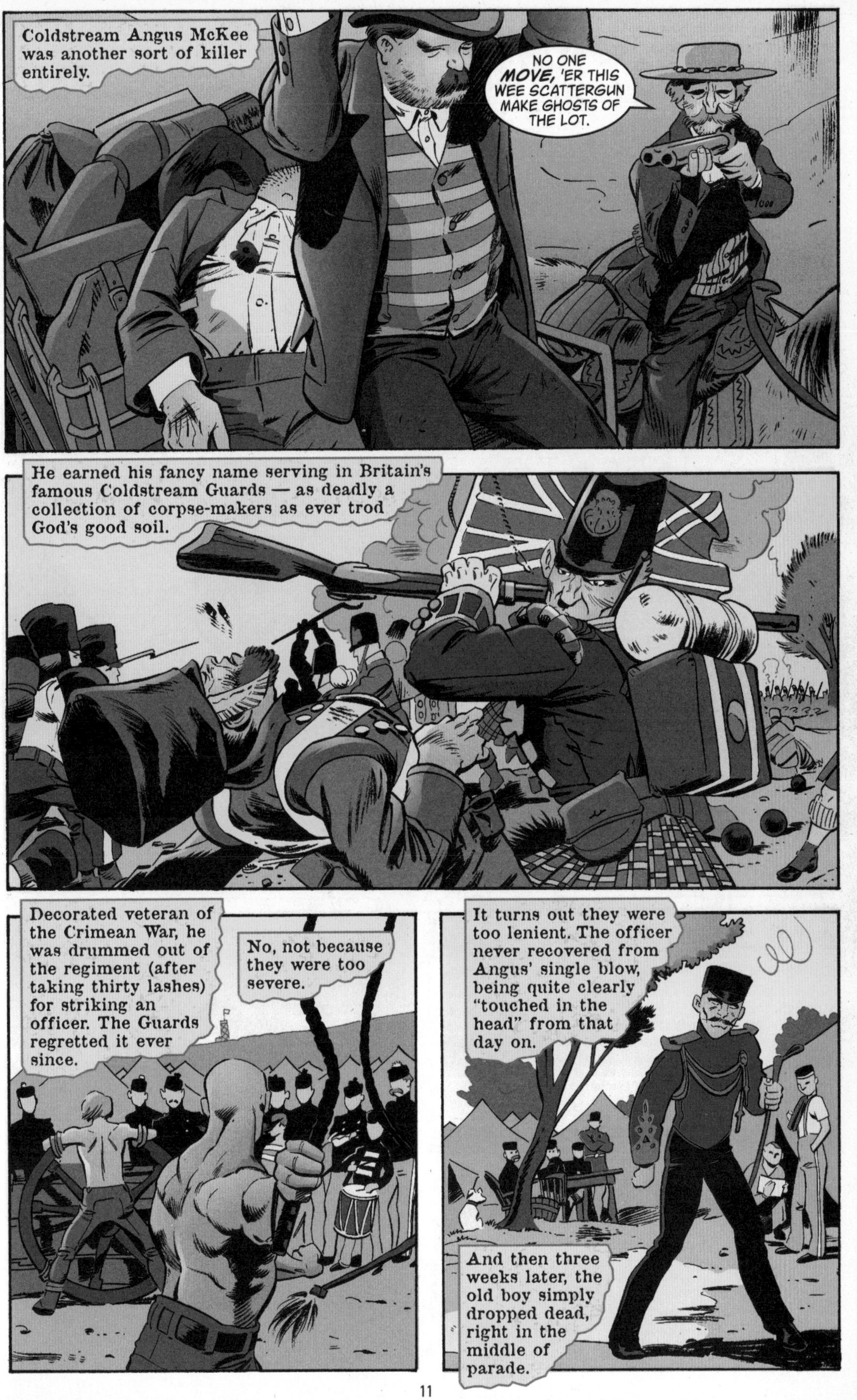
Coldstream Angus McKee was another sort of killer entirely.
NO ONE MOVE, 'ER THIS WEE SCATTERGUN MAKE GHOSTS OF THE LOT.
He earned his fancy name serving in Britain's famous Coldstream Guards — as deadly a collection of corpse-makers as ever trod God's good soil.
Decorated veteran of the Crimean War, he was drummed out of the regiment (after taking thirty lashes) for striking an officer. The Guards regretted it ever since.
No, not because they were too severe.
It turns out they were too lenient. The officer never recovered from Angus' single blow, being quite clearly "touched in the head" from that day on.
And then three weeks later, the old boy simply dropped dead, right in the middle of parade.

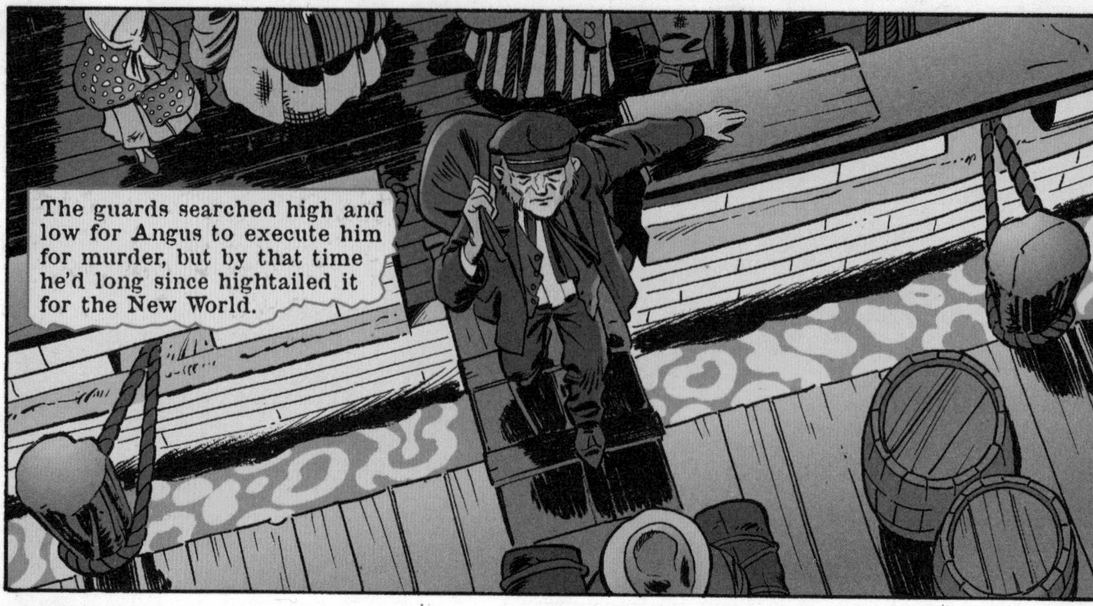
The guards searched high and low for Angus to execute him for murder, but by that time he'd long since hightailed it for the New World.

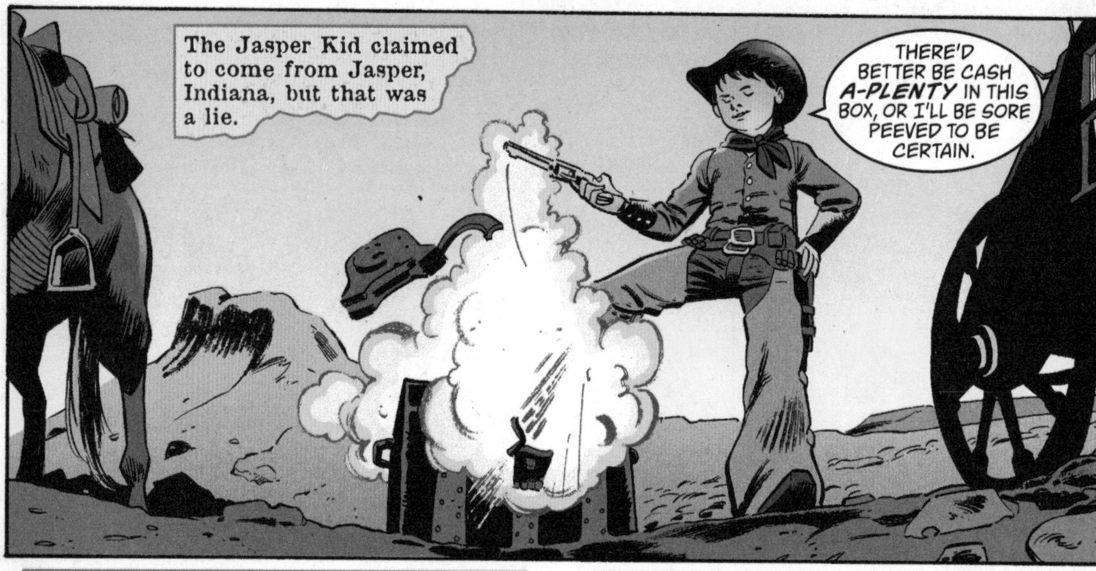
The Jasper Kid claimed to come from Jasper, Indiana, but that was a lie.
THERE'D BETTER BE CASH A-PLENTY IN THIS BOX, OR I'LL BE SORE PEEVED TO BE CERTAIN.

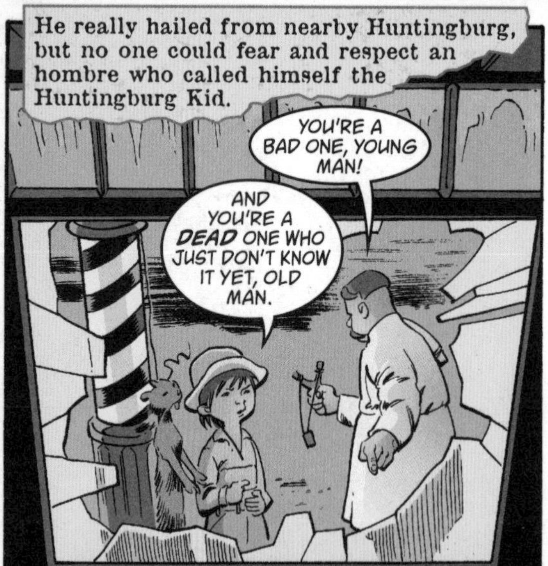
He really hailed from nearby Huntingburg, but no one could fear and respect an hombre who called himself the Huntingburg Kid.
YOU'RE A BAD ONE, YOUNG MAN!
AND YOU'RE A DEAD ONE WHO JUST DON'T KNOW IT YET, OLD MAN.

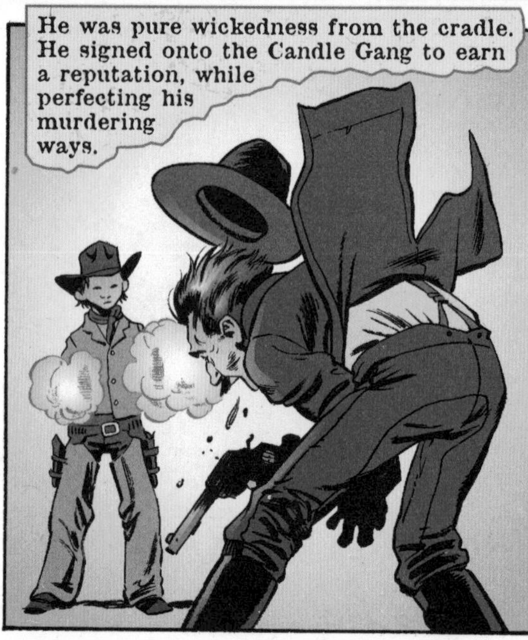
He was pure wickedness from the cradle. He signed onto the Candle Gang to earn a reputation, while perfecting his murdering ways.

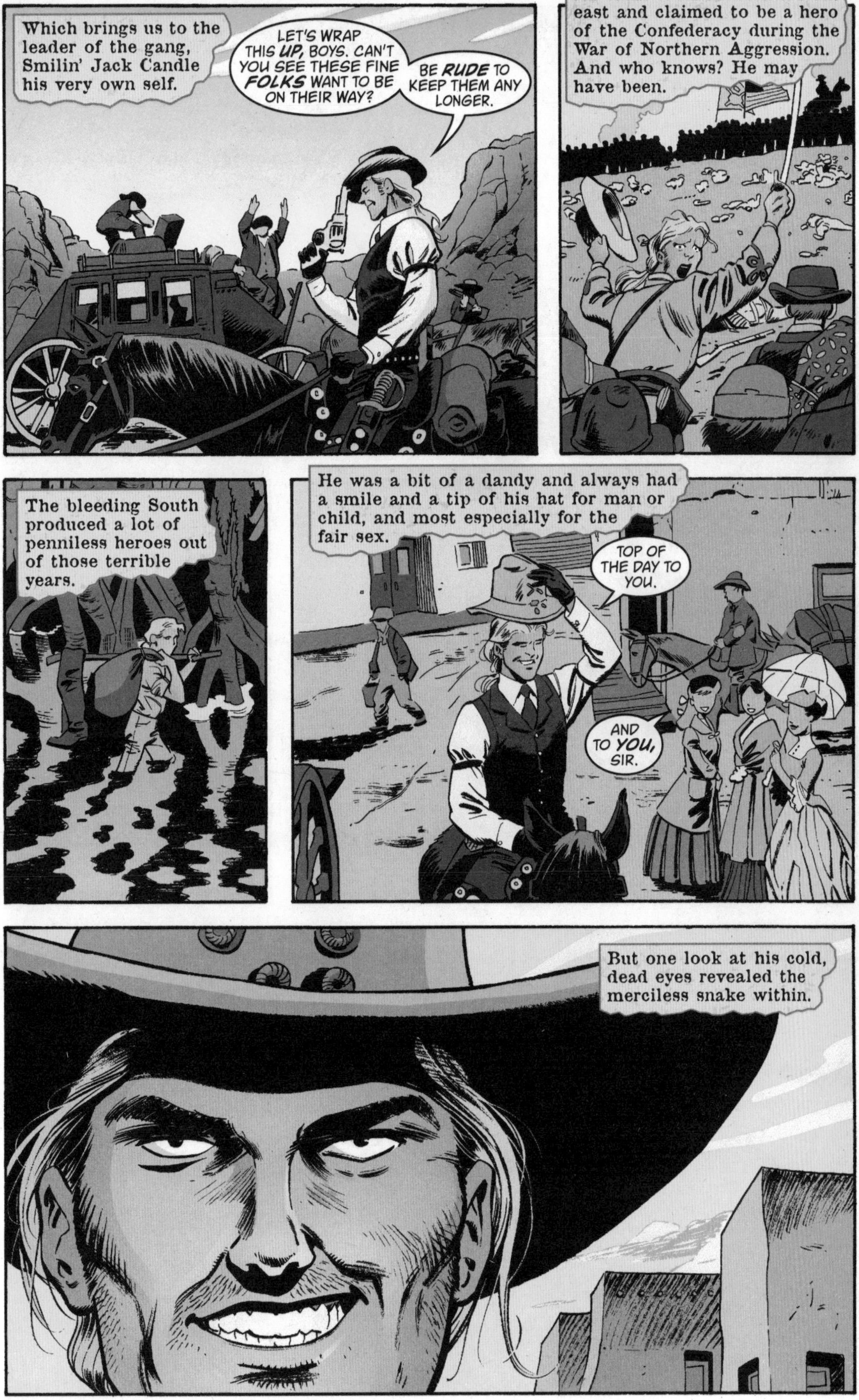

Which brings us to the leader of the gang, Smilin' Jack Candle his very own self.
LET'S WRAP THIS UP, BOYS. CAN'T YOU SEE THESE FINE FOLKS WANT TO BE ON THEIR WAY?
BE RUDE TO KEEP THEM ANY LONGER.
He came from somewhere out east and claimed to be a hero of the Confederacy during the War of Northern Aggression. And who knows? He may have been.
The bleeding South produced a lot of penniless heroes out of those terrible years.
He was a bit of a dandy and always had a smile and a tip of his hat for man or child, and most especially for the fair sex.
TOP OF THE DAY TO YOU.
AND TO YOU, SIR.
But one look at his cold, dead eyes revealed the merciless snake within.

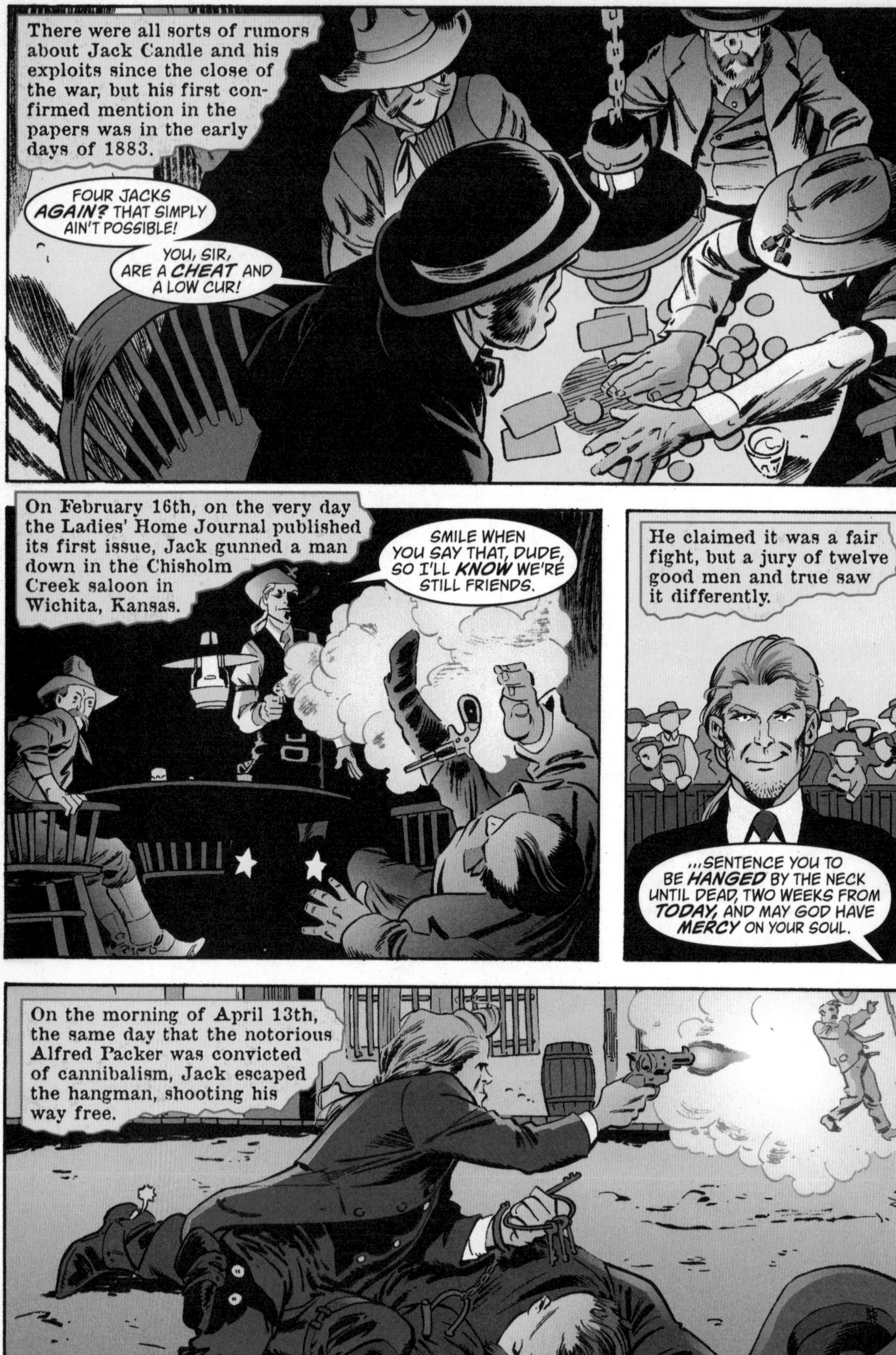
There were all sorts of rumors about Jack Candle and his exploits since the close of the war, but his first confirmed mention in the papers was in the early days of 1883.
FOUR JACKS AGAIN? THAT SIMPLY AIN'T POSSIBLE!
YOU, SIR, ARE A CHEAT AND A LOW CUR!
On February 16th, on the very day the Ladies' Home Journal published its first issue, Jack gunned a man down in the Chisholm Creek saloon in Wichita, Kansas.
SMILE WHEN YOU SAY THAT, DUDE, SO I'LL KNOW WE'RE STILL FRIENDS.
He claimed it was a fair fight, but a jury of twelve good men and true saw it differently.
...SENTENCE YOU TO BE HANGED BY THE NECK UNTIL DEAD, TWO WEEKS FROM TODAY, AND MAY GOD HAVE MERCY ON YOUR SOUL.
On the morning of April 13th, the same day that the notorious Alfred Packer was convicted of cannibalism, Jack escaped the hangman, shooting his way free.

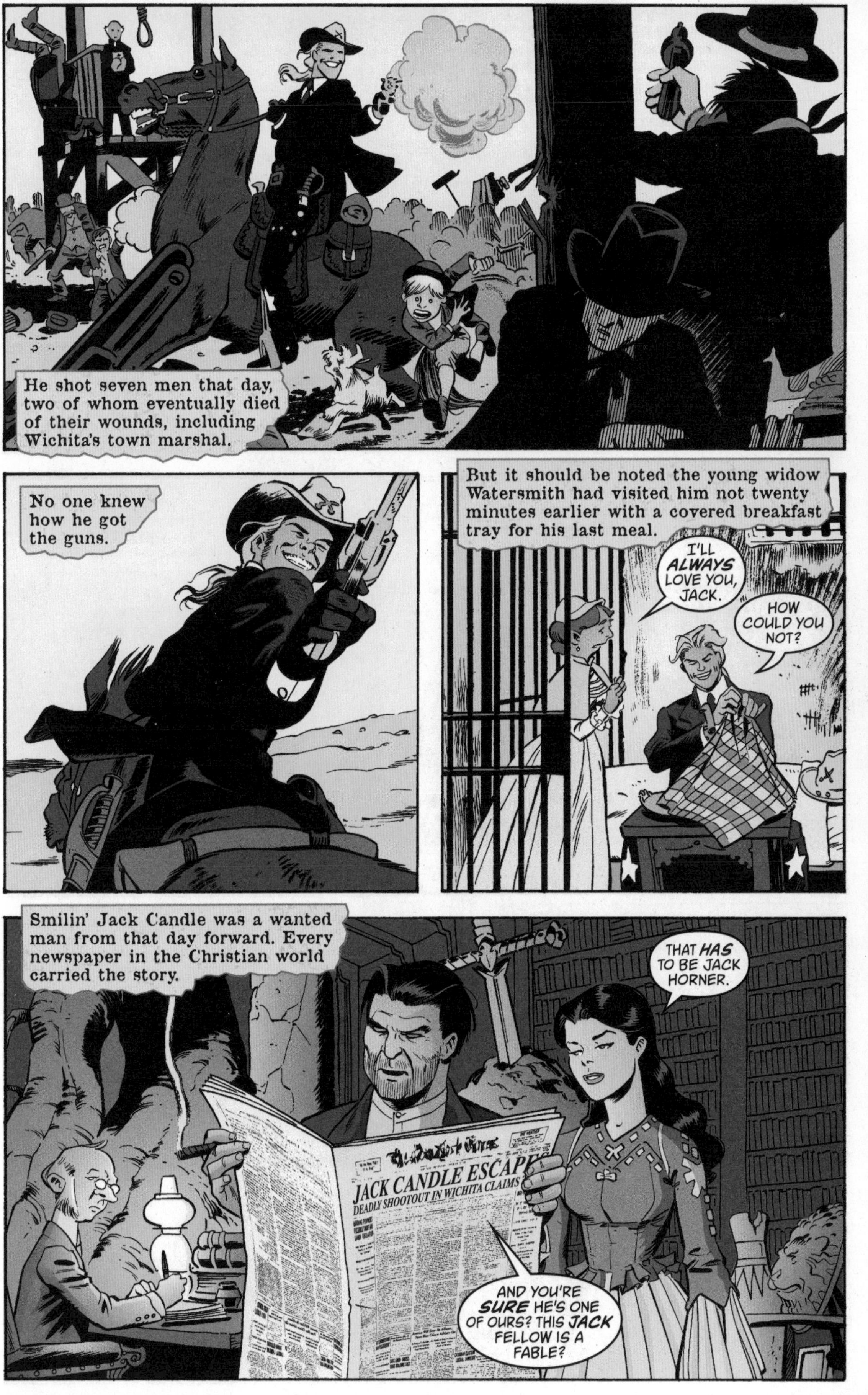
He shot seven men that day, two of whom eventually died of their wounds, including Wichita's town marshal.
No one knew how he got the guns.
But it should be noted the young widow Watersmith had visited him not twenty minutes earlier with a covered breakfast tray for his last meal.
I'LL *ALWAYS* LOVE YOU, JACK.
HOW COULD YOU NOT?
Smilin' Jack Candle was a wanted man from that day forward. Every newspaper in the Christian world carried the story.
THAT *HAS* TO BE JACK HORNER.
JACK CANDLE ESCAP
DEADLY SHOOTOUT IN WICHITA CLAIMS
AND YOU'RE *SURE* HE'S ONE OF OURS? THIS *JACK* FELLOW IS A FABLE?

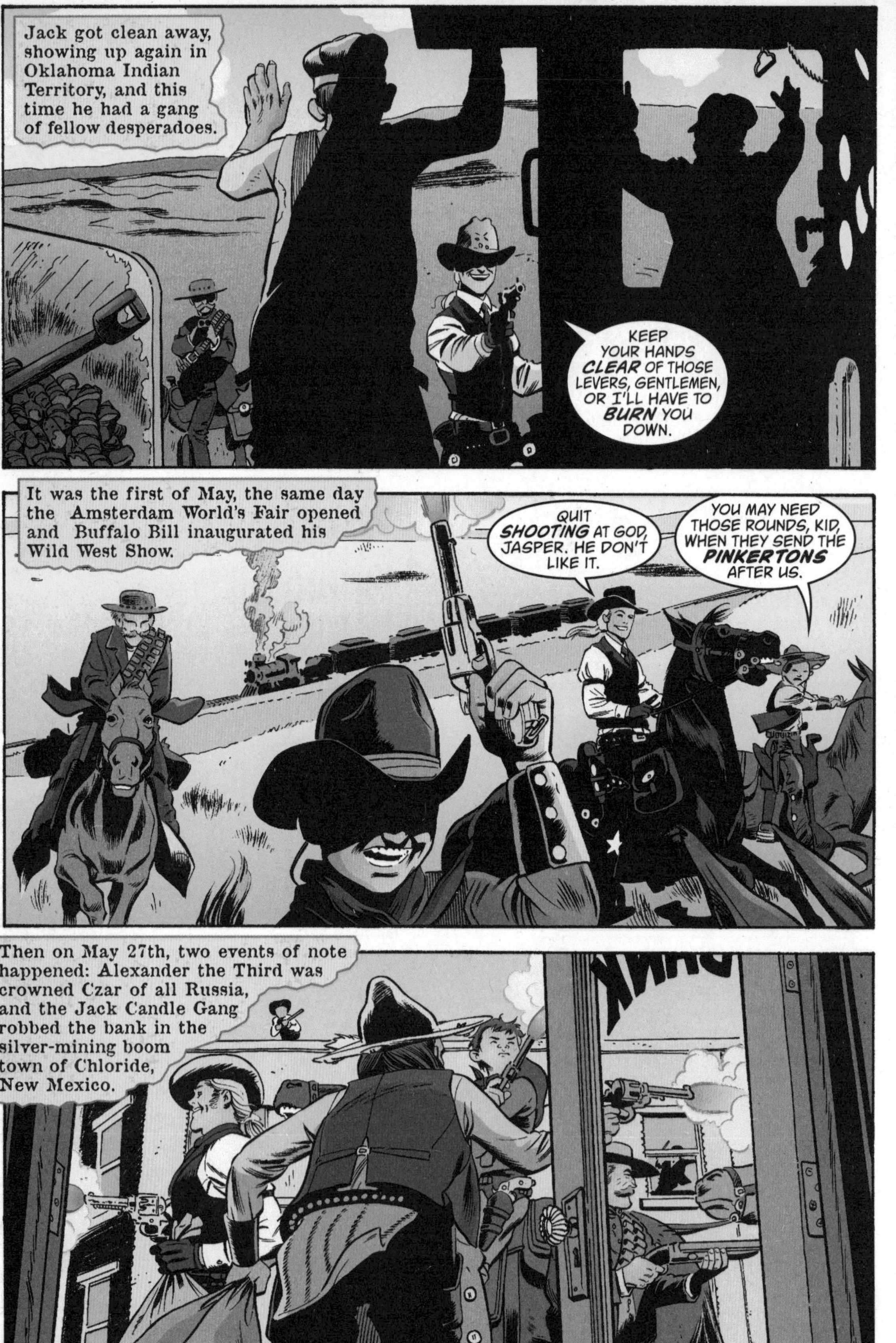

Jack got clean away, showing up again in Oklahoma Indian Territory, and this time he had a gang of fellow desperadoes.
KEEP YOUR HANDS CLEAR OF THOSE LEVERS, GENTLEMEN, OR I'LL HAVE TO BURN YOU DOWN.
It was the first of May, the same day the Amsterdam World's Fair opened and Buffalo Bill inaugurated his Wild West Show.
QUIT SHOOTING AT GOD, JASPER. HE DON'T LIKE IT.
YOU MAY NEED THOSE ROUNDS, KID, WHEN THEY SEND THE PINKERTONS AFTER US.
Then on May 27th, two events of note happened: Alexander the Third was crowned Czar of all Russia, and the Jack Candle Gang robbed the bank in the silver-mining boom town of Chloride, New Mexico.

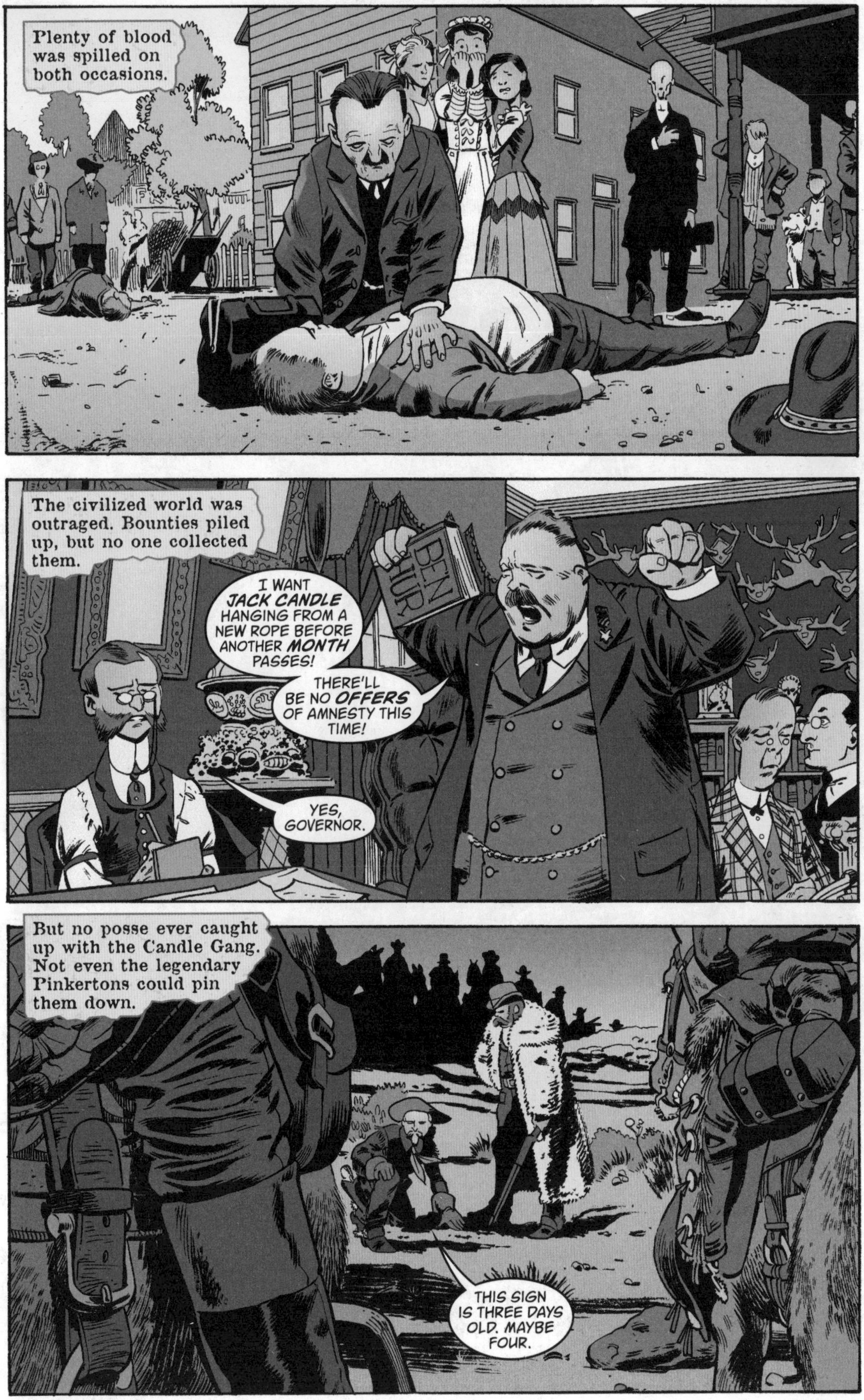

Plenty of blood was spilled on both occasions.
The civilized world was outraged. Bounties piled up, but no one collected them.
BEN HUR
I WANT JACK CANDLE HANGING FROM A NEW ROPE BEFORE ANOTHER MONTH PASSES!
THERE'LL BE NO OFFERS OF AMNESTY THIS TIME!
YES, GOVERNOR.
But no posse ever caught up with the Candle Gang. Not even the legendary Pinkertons could pin them down.
THIS SIGN IS THREE DAYS OLD. MAYBE FOUR.

He claimed to be a sheriff from someplace back east, but never quite specified where.

GOOD EVENING, MARSHAL. WHAT'S THE LATEST REPORT ON THE JACK CANDLE GANG? I'VE BEEN TRAVELING TOO *LONG* TO BE CAUGHT UP ON THE NEWS.

More than one local peace officer had abandoned his post in 1883 to seek after the fat bounty on Jack's head.

YOU'RE A BIT OUT OF YOUR *JURISDICTION,* AREN'T YOU, SHERIFF? PLANNING TO EARN YOUR FORTUNE?

COULD BE. I'LL BE HEADING OUT AT FIRST LIGHT.

He stayed only one night in the hotel, and was quite transformed in the morning.

RIDING OUT ALONE?

YEP.

DAMN *FOOL* THING TO DO, IF YOU ASK ME. BUT I GUESS A MAN HAS A GOD-GIVEN RIGHT TO BE *STUPID.*

HEY! I DON'T SEE YOU SPORTIN' ANY IRON!

NEVER HAD MUCH *USE* FOR FIREARMS.

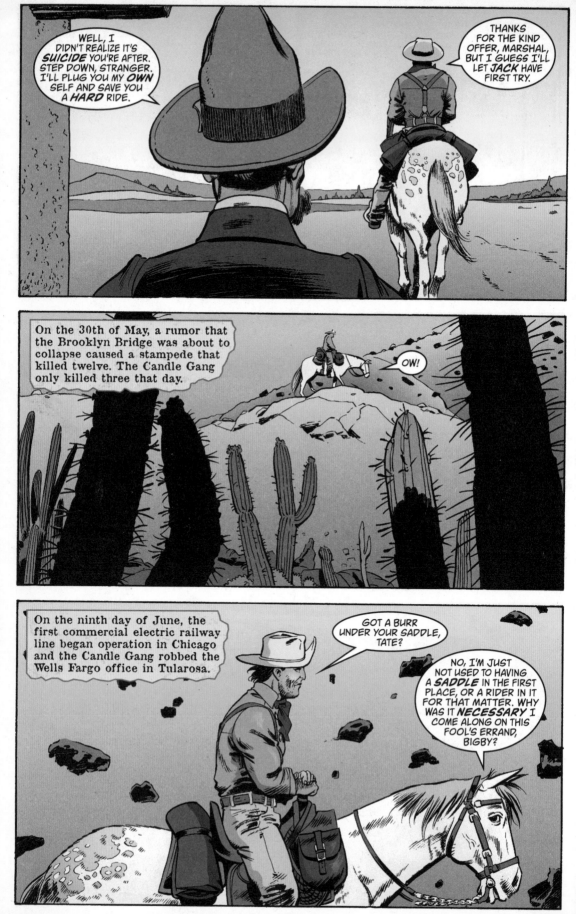

WELL, I DIDN'T REALIZE IT'S *SUICIDE* YOU'RE AFTER. STEP DOWN, STRANGER. I'LL PLUG YOU MY *OWN* SELF AND SAVE YOU A *HARD* RIDE.

THANKS FOR THE KIND OFFER, MARSHAL, BUT I GUESS I'LL LET *JACK* HAVE FIRST TRY.

On the 30th of May, a rumor that the Brooklyn Bridge was about to collapse caused a stampede that killed twelve. The Candle Gang only killed three that day.

OW!

On the ninth day of June, the first commercial electric railway line began operation in Chicago and the Candle Gang robbed the Wells Fargo office in Tularosa.

GOT A BURR UNDER YOUR SADDLE, TATE?

NO, I'M JUST NOT USED TO HAVING A *SADDLE* IN THE FIRST PLACE, OR A RIDER IN IT FOR THAT MATTER. WHY WAS IT *NECESSARY* I COME ALONG ON THIS FOOL'S ERRAND, BIGBY?

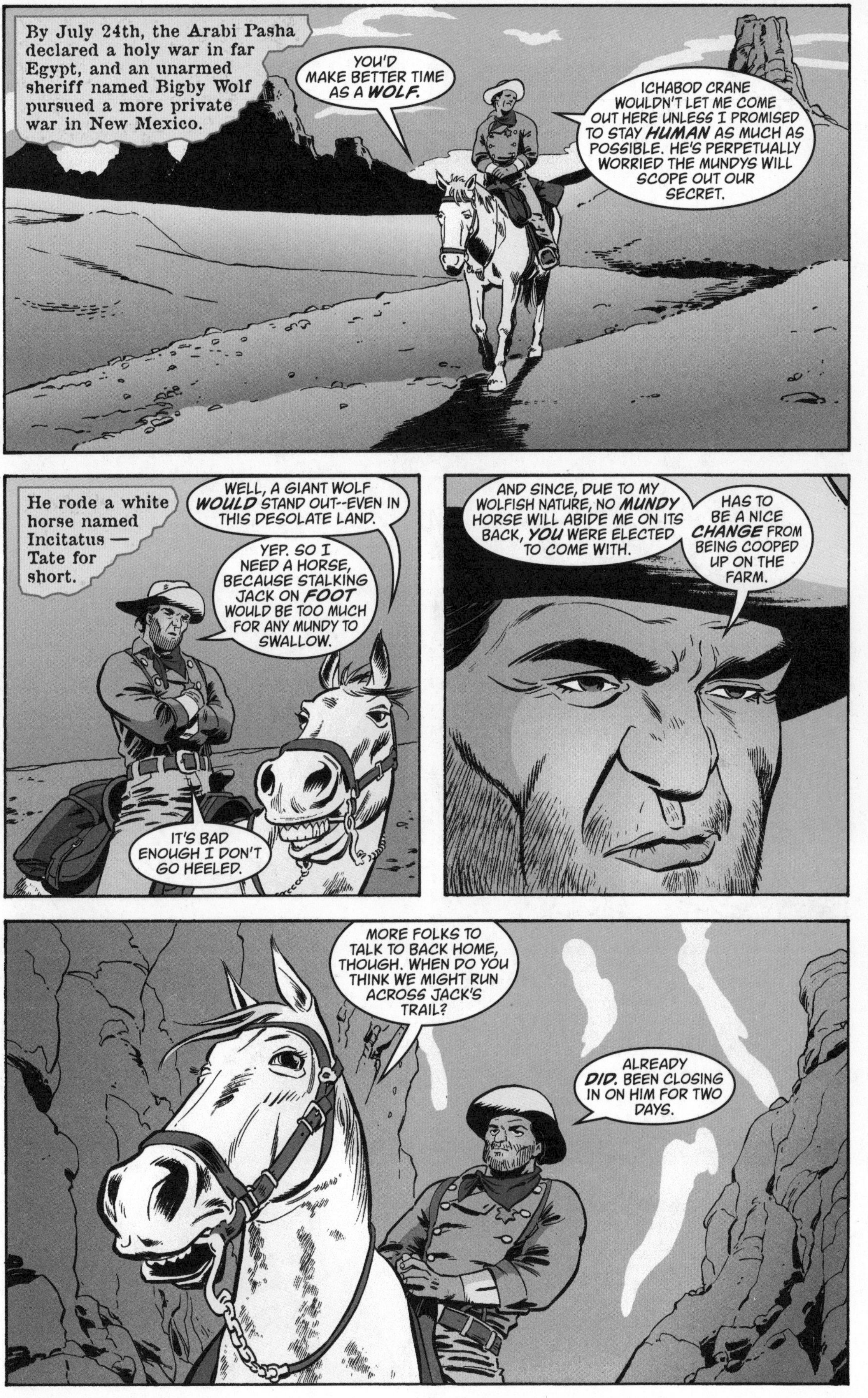
By July 24th, the Arabi Pasha declared a holy war in far Egypt, and an unarmed sheriff named Bigby Wolf pursued a more private war in New Mexico.
YOU'D MAKE BETTER TIME AS A WOLF.
ICHABOD CRANE WOULDN'T LET ME COME OUT HERE UNLESS I PROMISED TO STAY HUMAN AS MUCH AS POSSIBLE. HE'S PERPETUALLY WORRIED THE MUNDYS WILL SCOPE OUT OUR SECRET.
He rode a white horse named Incitatus — Tate for short.
WELL, A GIANT WOLF WOULD STAND OUT--EVEN IN THIS DESOLATE LAND.
YEP. SO I NEED A HORSE, BECAUSE STALKING JACK ON FOOT WOULD BE TOO MUCH FOR ANY MUNDY TO SWALLOW.
IT'S BAD ENOUGH I DON'T GO HEELED.
AND SINCE, DUE TO MY WOLFISH NATURE, NO MUNDY HORSE WILL ABIDE ME ON ITS BACK, YOU WERE ELECTED TO COME WITH.
HAS TO BE A NICE CHANGE FROM BEING COOPED UP ON THE FARM.
MORE FOLKS TO TALK TO BACK HOME, THOUGH. WHEN DO YOU THINK WE MIGHT RUN ACROSS JACK'S TRAIL?
ALREADY DID. BEEN CLOSING IN ON HIM FOR TWO DAYS.

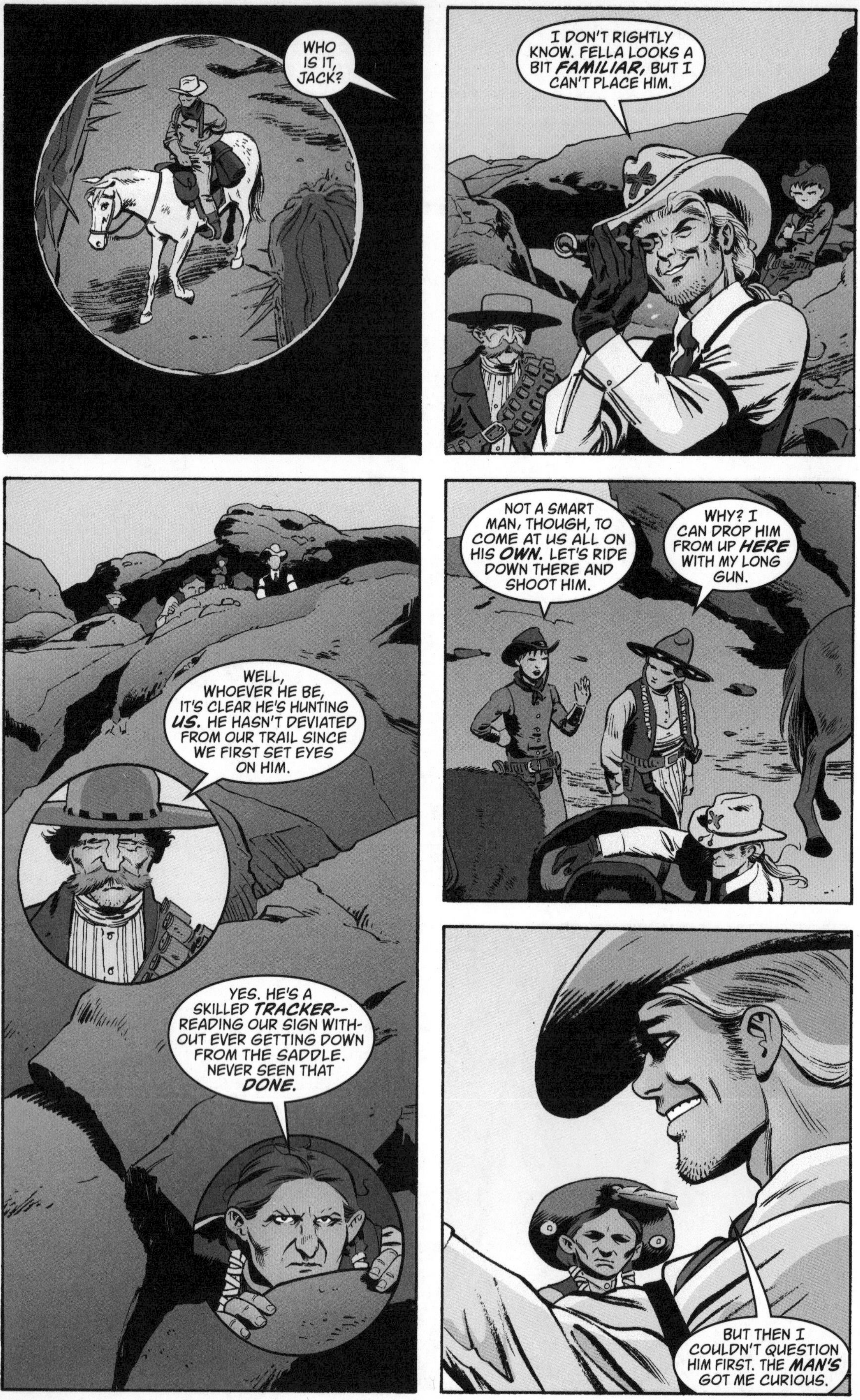
WHO IS IT, JACK?
I DON'T RIGHTLY KNOW. FELLA LOOKS A BIT FAMILIAR, BUT I CAN'T PLACE HIM.
WELL, WHOEVER HE BE, IT'S CLEAR HE'S HUNTING US. HE HASN'T DEVIATED FROM OUR TRAIL SINCE WE FIRST SET EYES ON HIM.
YES. HE'S A SKILLED TRACKER-- READING OUR SIGN WITH-OUT EVER GETTING DOWN FROM THE SADDLE. NEVER SEEN THAT DONE.
NOT A SMART MAN, THOUGH, TO COME AT US ALL ON HIS OWN. LET'S RIDE DOWN THERE AND SHOOT HIM.
WHY? I CAN DROP HIM FROM UP HERE WITH MY LONG GUN.
BUT THEN I COULDN'T QUESTION HIM FIRST. THE MAN'S GOT ME CURIOUS.

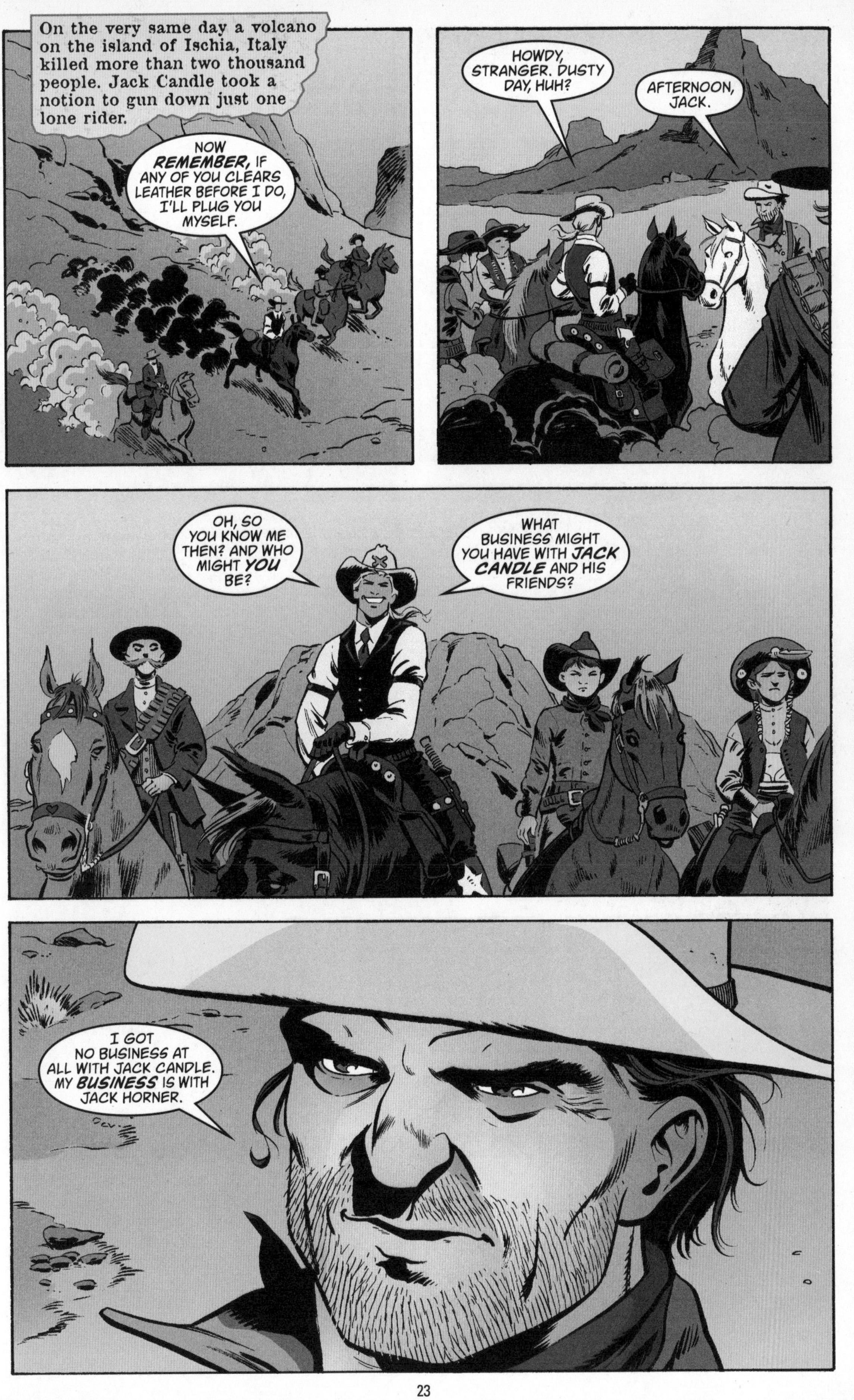
On the very same day a volcano on the island of Ischia, Italy killed more than two thousand people. Jack Candle took a notion to gun down just one lone rider.
NOW REMEMBER, IF ANY OF YOU CLEARS LEATHER BEFORE I DO, I'LL PLUG YOU MYSELF.
HOWDY, STRANGER. DUSTY DAY, HUH?
AFTERNOON, JACK.
OH, SO YOU KNOW ME THEN? AND WHO MIGHT YOU BE?
WHAT BUSINESS MIGHT YOU HAVE WITH JACK CANDLE AND HIS FRIENDS?
I GOT NO BUSINESS AT ALL WITH JACK CANDLE. MY BUSINESS IS WITH JACK HORNER.

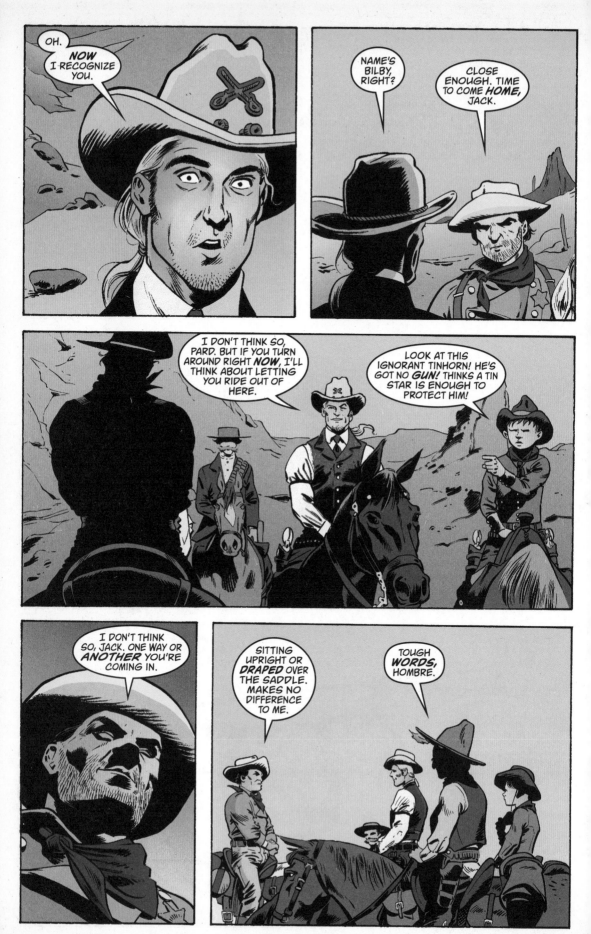

OH. *NOW* I RECOGNIZE YOU.

NAME'S BILBY, RIGHT?

CLOSE ENOUGH. TIME TO COME *HOME*, JACK.

I DON'T THINK SO, PARD. BUT IF YOU TURN AROUND RIGHT *NOW*, I'LL THINK ABOUT LETTING YOU RIDE OUT OF HERE.

LOOK AT THIS IGNORANT TINHORN! HE'S GOT NO *GUN!* THINKS A TIN STAR IS ENOUGH TO PROTECT HIM!

I DON'T THINK SO, JACK. ONE WAY OR *ANOTHER* YOU'RE COMING IN.

SITTING UPRIGHT OR *DRAPED* OVER THE SADDLE. MAKES NO DIFFERENCE TO ME.

TOUGH *WORDS*, HOMBRE.

24

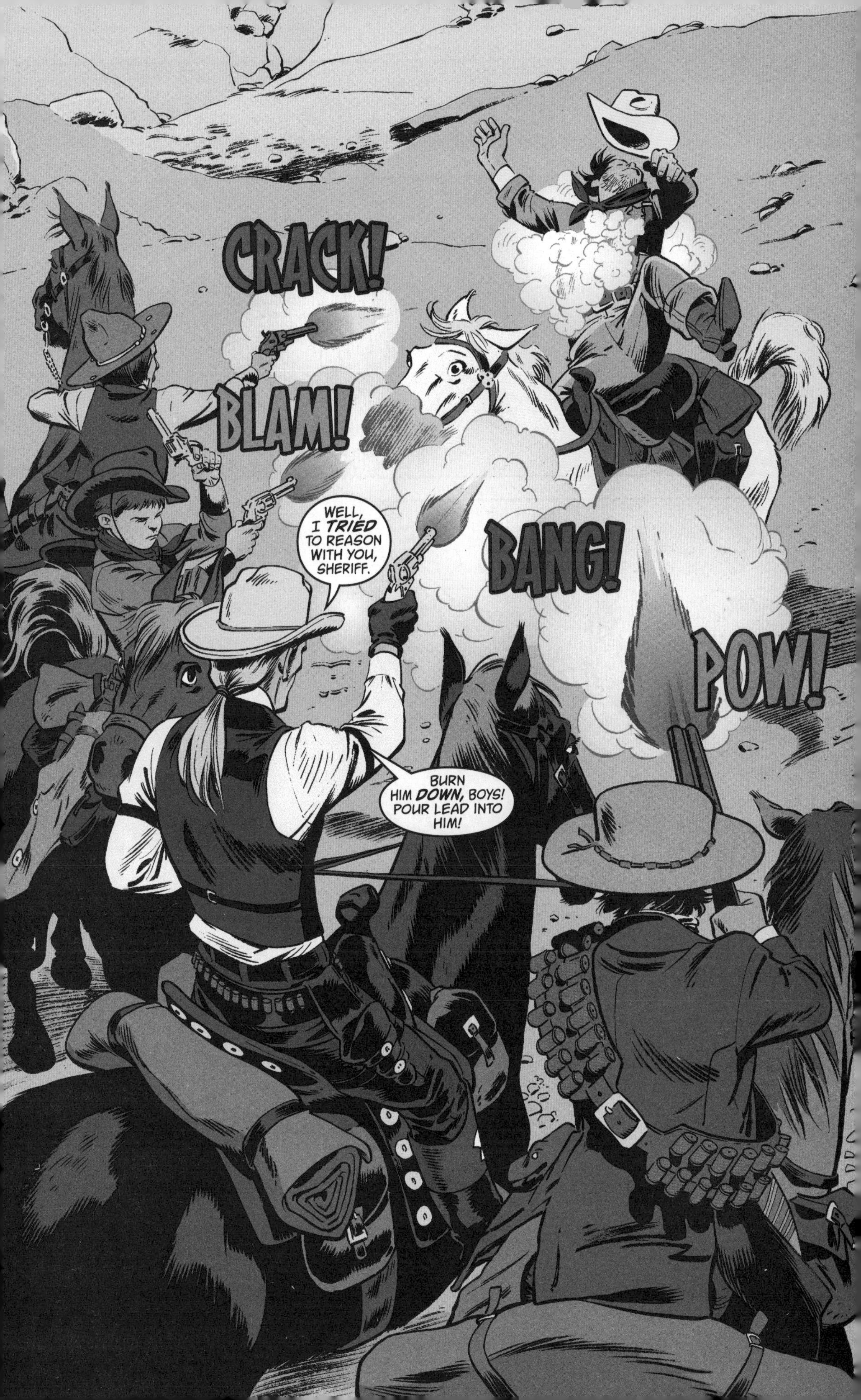
CRACK!
BLAM!
WELL, I TRIED TO REASON WITH YOU, SHERIFF.
BANG!
POW!
BURN HIM DOWN, BOYS! POUR LEAD INTO HIM!

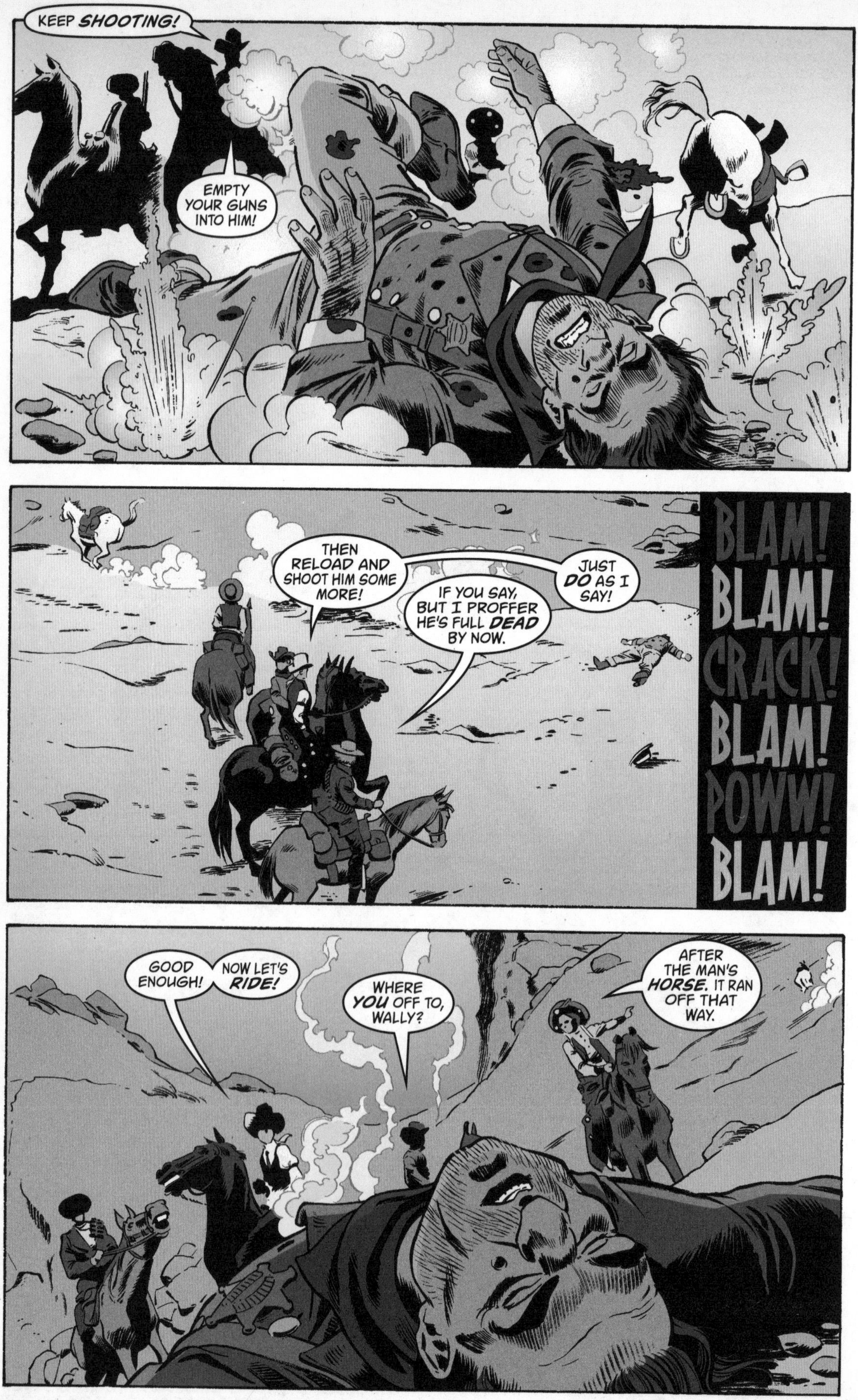
KEEP SHOOTING!
EMPTY YOUR GUNS INTO HIM!
THEN RELOAD AND SHOOT HIM SOME MORE!
IF YOU SAY, BUT I PROFFER HE'S FULL DEAD BY NOW.
JUST DO AS I SAY!
BLAM! BLAM! CRACK! BLAM! POWW! BLAM!
GOOD ENOUGH!
NOW LET'S RIDE!
WHERE YOU OFF TO, WALLY?
AFTER THE MAN'S HORSE. IT RAN OFF THAT WAY.

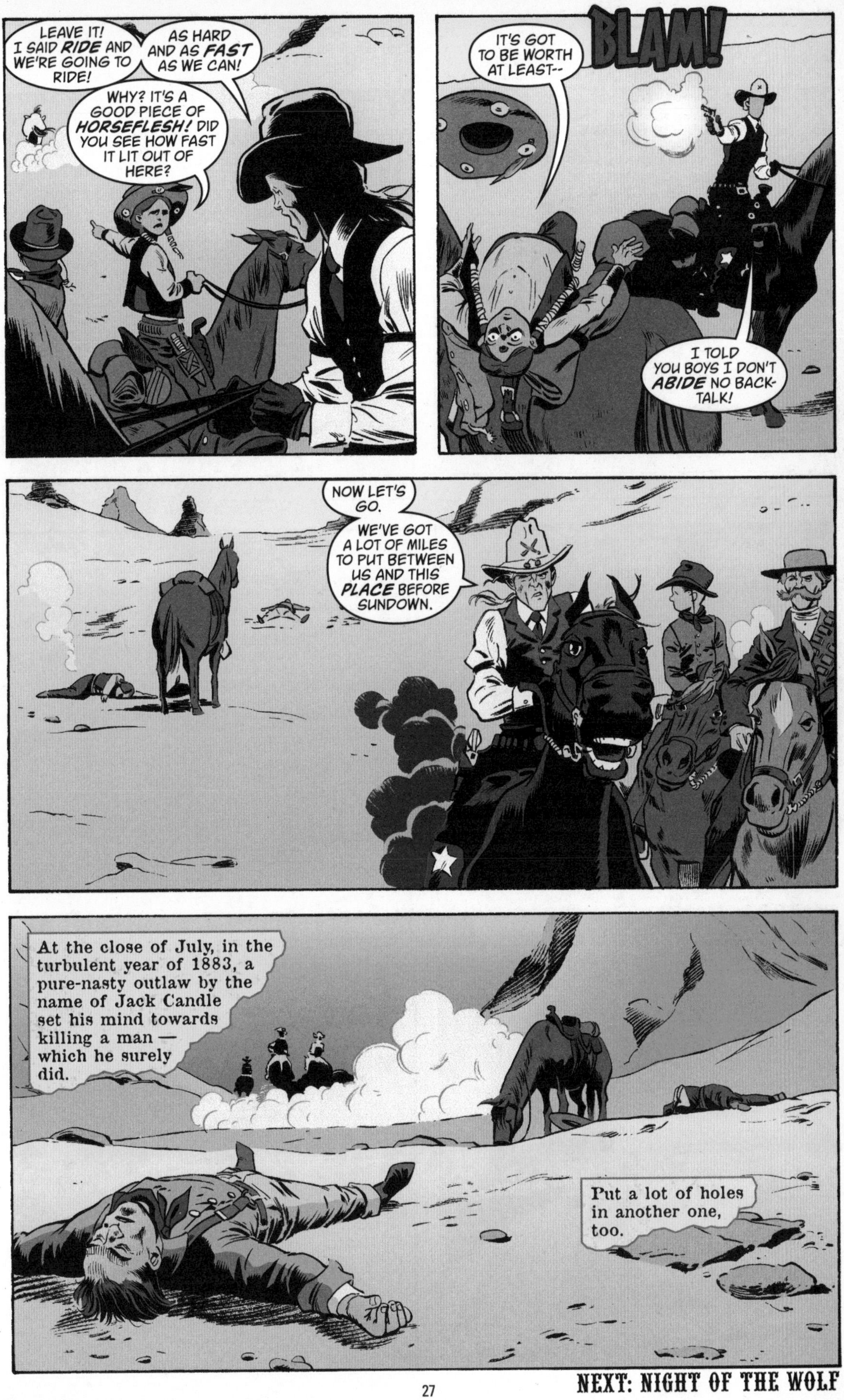
LEAVE IT! I SAID RIDE AND WE'RE GOING TO RIDE!
AS HARD AND AS FAST AS WE CAN!
WHY? IT'S A GOOD PIECE OF HORSEFLESH! DID YOU SEE HOW FAST IT LIT OUT OF HERE?
IT'S GOT TO BE WORTH AT LEAST--
BLAM!
I TOLD YOU BOYS I DON'T ABIDE NO BACK-TALK!
NOW LET'S GO.
WE'VE GOT A LOT OF MILES TO PUT BETWEEN US AND THIS PLACE BEFORE SUNDOWN.
At the close of July, in the turbulent year of 1883, a pure-nasty outlaw by the name of Jack Candle set his mind towards killing a man — which he surely did.
Put a lot of holes in another one, too.

NEXT: NIGHT OF THE WOLF

WE HERE AT FABLES CENTRAL REALIZE YOU'VE JUST ENDURED THE FIRST ISSUE OF JACK OF FABLES WITHOUT A SINGLE INTENTIONAL FUNNY BIT. IN ORDER TO INCLUDE THE MINIMUM RECOMMENDED DAILY ALLOWANCE OF ***HOO-HAH,*** AND TO KEEP YOUR FUNNYBONE ***PROPERLY*** TICKLED UNTIL THIS SERIES GETS SILLY AGAIN, WE OFFER YOU THIS MODERN-DAY INTERLUDE WITH OUR FAVORITE MINIATURE BLUE OX:

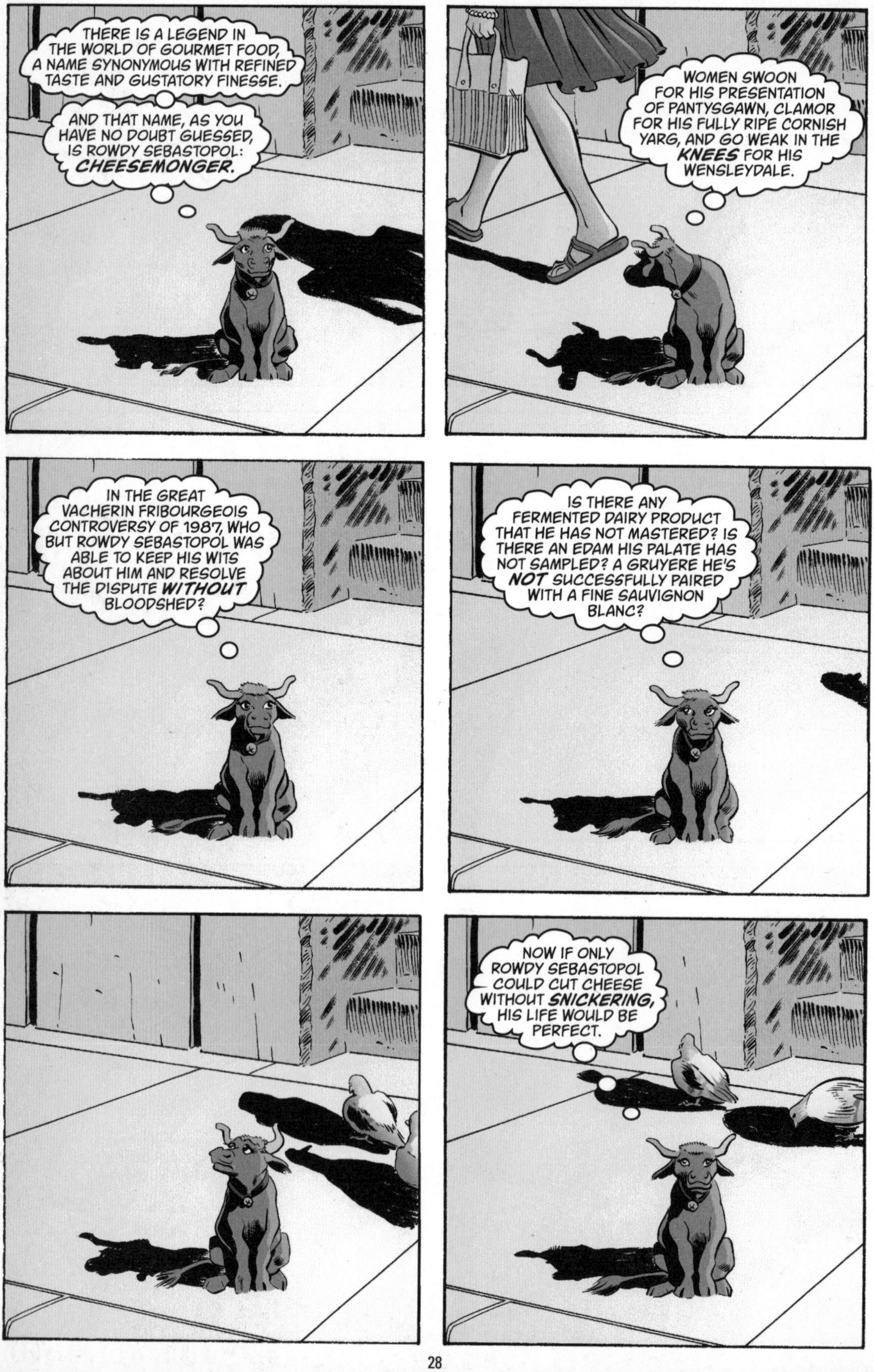
THERE IS A LEGEND IN THE WORLD OF GOURMET FOOD, A NAME SYNONYMOUS WITH REFINED TASTE AND GUSTATORY FINESSE.
AND THAT NAME, AS YOU HAVE NO DOUBT GUESSED, IS ROWDY SEBASTOPOL: CHEESEMONGER.
WOMEN SWOON FOR HIS PRESENTATION OF PANTYSGAWN, CLAMOR FOR HIS FULLY RIPE CORNISH YARG, AND GO WEAK IN THE KNEES FOR HIS WENSLEYDALE.
IN THE GREAT VACHERIN FRIBOURGEOIS CONTROVERSY OF 1987, WHO BUT ROWDY SEBASTOPOL WAS ABLE TO KEEP HIS WITS ABOUT HIM AND RESOLVE THE DISPUTE WITHOUT BLOODSHED?
IS THERE ANY FERMENTED DAIRY PRODUCT THAT HE HAS NOT MASTERED? IS THERE AN EDAM HIS PALATE HAS NOT SAMPLED? A GRUYERE HE'S NOT SUCCESSFULLY PAIRED WITH A FINE SAUVIGNON BLANC?
NOW IF ONLY ROWDY SEBASTOPOL COULD CUT CHEESE WITHOUT SNICKERING, HIS LIFE WOULD BE PERFECT.

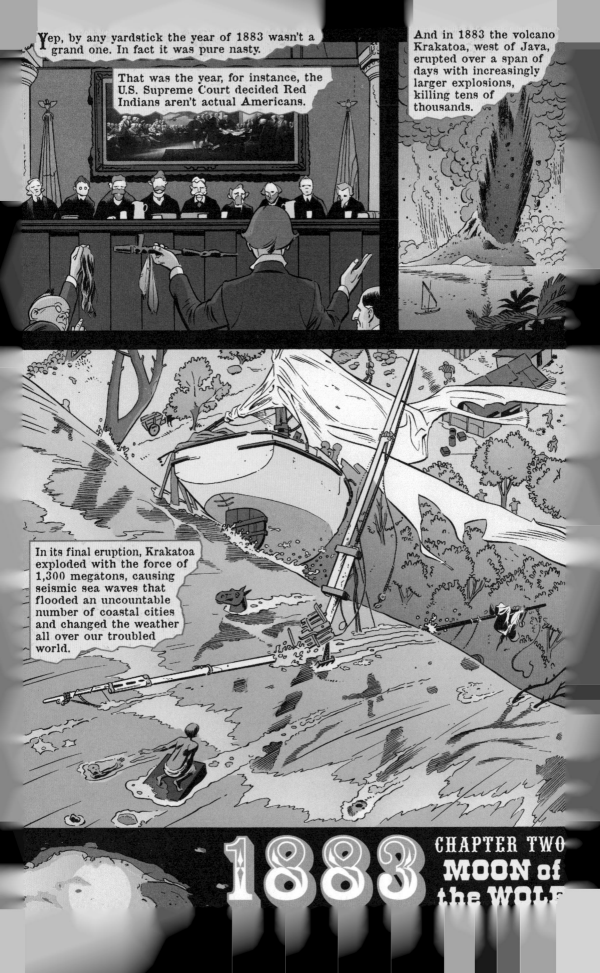

Yep, by any yardstick the year of 1883 wasn't a grand one. In fact it was pure nasty.

That was the year, for instance, the U.S. Supreme Court decided Red Indians aren't actual Americans.

And in 1883 the volcano Krakatoa, west of Java, erupted over a span of days with increasingly larger explosions, killing tens of thousands.

In its final eruption, Krakatoa exploded with the force of 1,300 megatons, causing seismic sea waves that flooded an uncountable number of coastal cities and changed the weather all over our troubled world.

1883

CHAPTER TWO
MOON of the WOLF

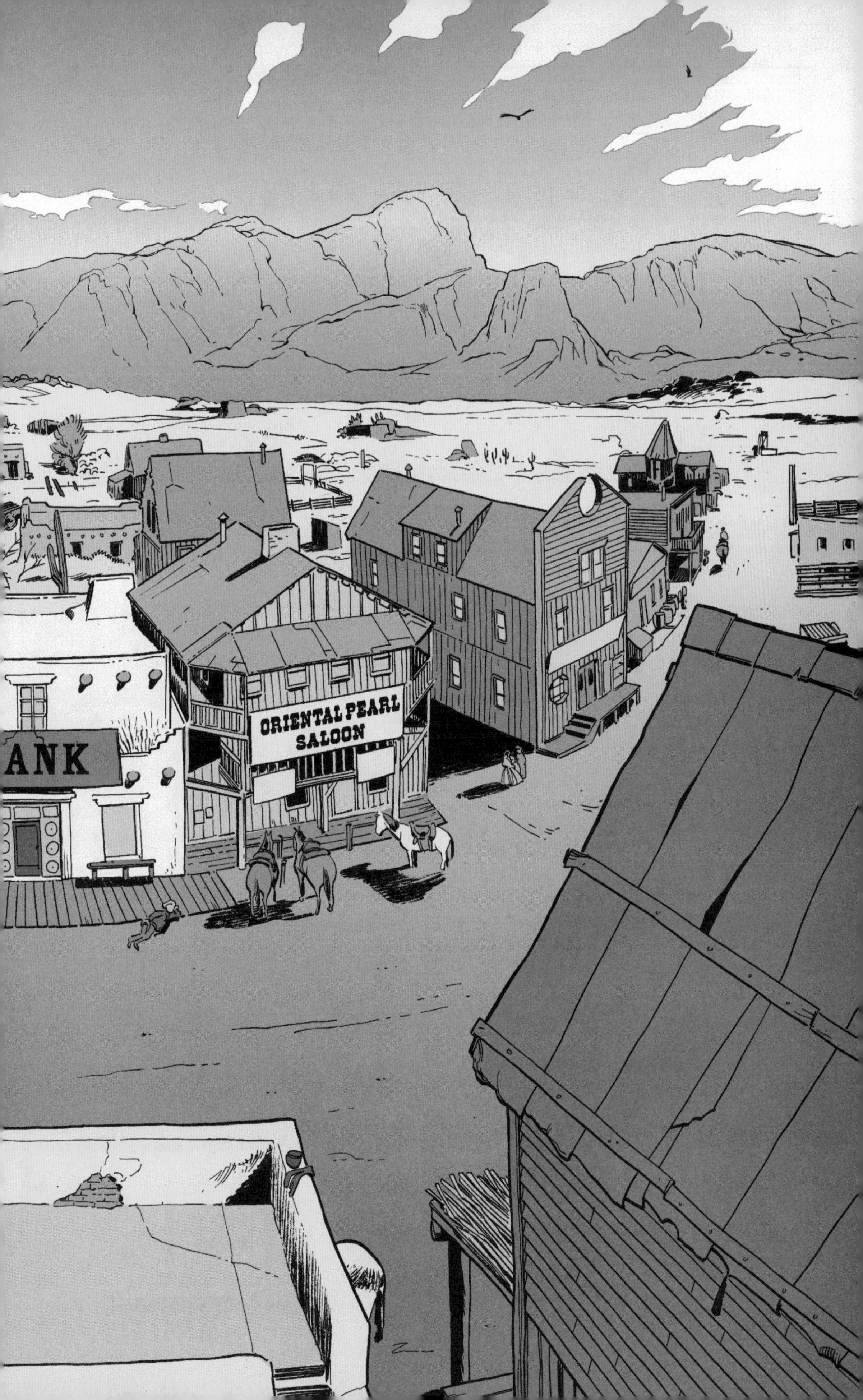
ORIENTAL PEARL
SALOON
ANK

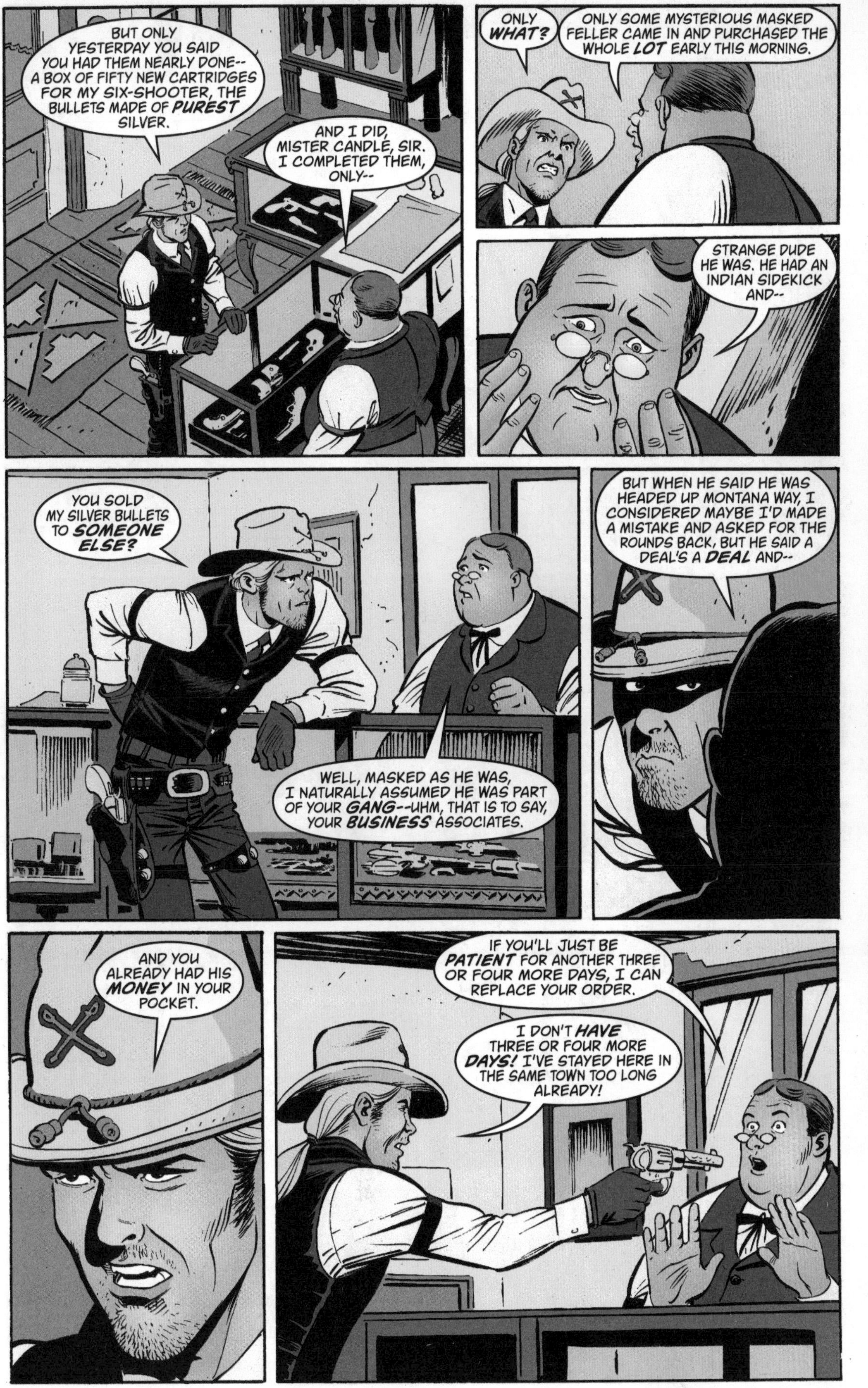
BUT ONLY YESTERDAY YOU SAID YOU HAD THEM NEARLY DONE-- A BOX OF FIFTY NEW CARTRIDGES FOR MY SIX-SHOOTER, THE BULLETS MADE OF *PUREST* SILVER.
AND I DID, MISTER CANDLE, SIR. I COMPLETED THEM, ONLY--
ONLY *WHAT?*
ONLY SOME MYSTERIOUS MASKED FELLER CAME IN AND PURCHASED THE WHOLE *LOT* EARLY THIS MORNING.
STRANGE DUDE HE WAS. HE HAD AN INDIAN SIDEKICK AND--
YOU SOLD MY SILVER BULLETS TO *SOMEONE ELSE?*
WELL, MASKED AS HE WAS, I NATURALLY ASSUMED HE WAS PART OF YOUR *GANG*--UHM, THAT IS TO SAY, YOUR *BUSINESS* ASSOCIATES.
BUT WHEN HE SAID HE WAS HEADED UP MONTANA WAY, I CONSIDERED MAYBE I'D MADE A MISTAKE AND ASKED FOR THE ROUNDS BACK, BUT HE SAID A DEAL'S A *DEAL* AND--
AND YOU ALREADY HAD HIS *MONEY* IN YOUR POCKET.
IF YOU'LL JUST BE *PATIENT* FOR ANOTHER THREE OR FOUR MORE DAYS, I CAN REPLACE YOUR ORDER.
I DON'T *HAVE* THREE OR FOUR MORE *DAYS!* I'VE STAYED HERE IN THE SAME TOWN TOO LONG ALREADY!

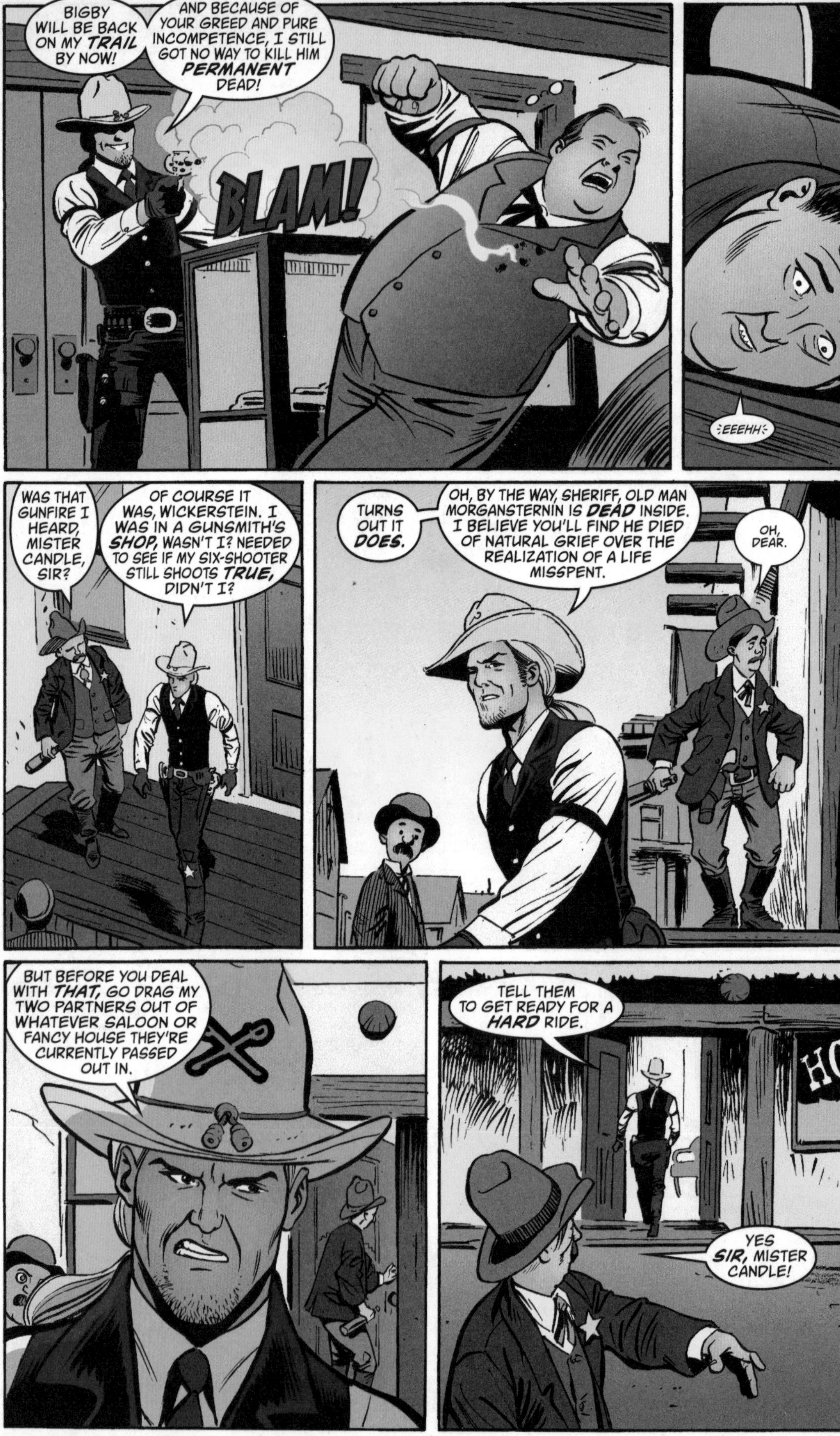
BIGBY WILL BE BACK ON MY TRAIL BY NOW!
AND BECAUSE OF YOUR GREED AND PURE INCOMPETENCE, I STILL GOT NO WAY TO KILL HIM PERMANENT DEAD!
BLAM!
EEEHH
WAS THAT GUNFIRE I HEARD, MISTER CANDLE, SIR?
OF COURSE IT WAS, WICKERSTEIN. I WAS IN A GUNSMITH'S SHOP, WASN'T I? NEEDED TO SEE IF MY SIX-SHOOTER STILL SHOOTS TRUE, DIDN'T I?
TURNS OUT IT DOES.
OH, BY THE WAY, SHERIFF, OLD MAN MORGANSTERNIN IS DEAD INSIDE. I BELIEVE YOU'LL FIND HE DIED OF NATURAL GRIEF OVER THE REALIZATION OF A LIFE MISSPENT.
OH, DEAR.
BUT BEFORE YOU DEAL WITH THAT, GO DRAG MY TWO PARTNERS OUT OF WHATEVER SALOON OR FANCY HOUSE THEY'RE CURRENTLY PASSED OUT IN.
TELL THEM TO GET READY FOR A HARD RIDE.
YES SIR, MISTER CANDLE!

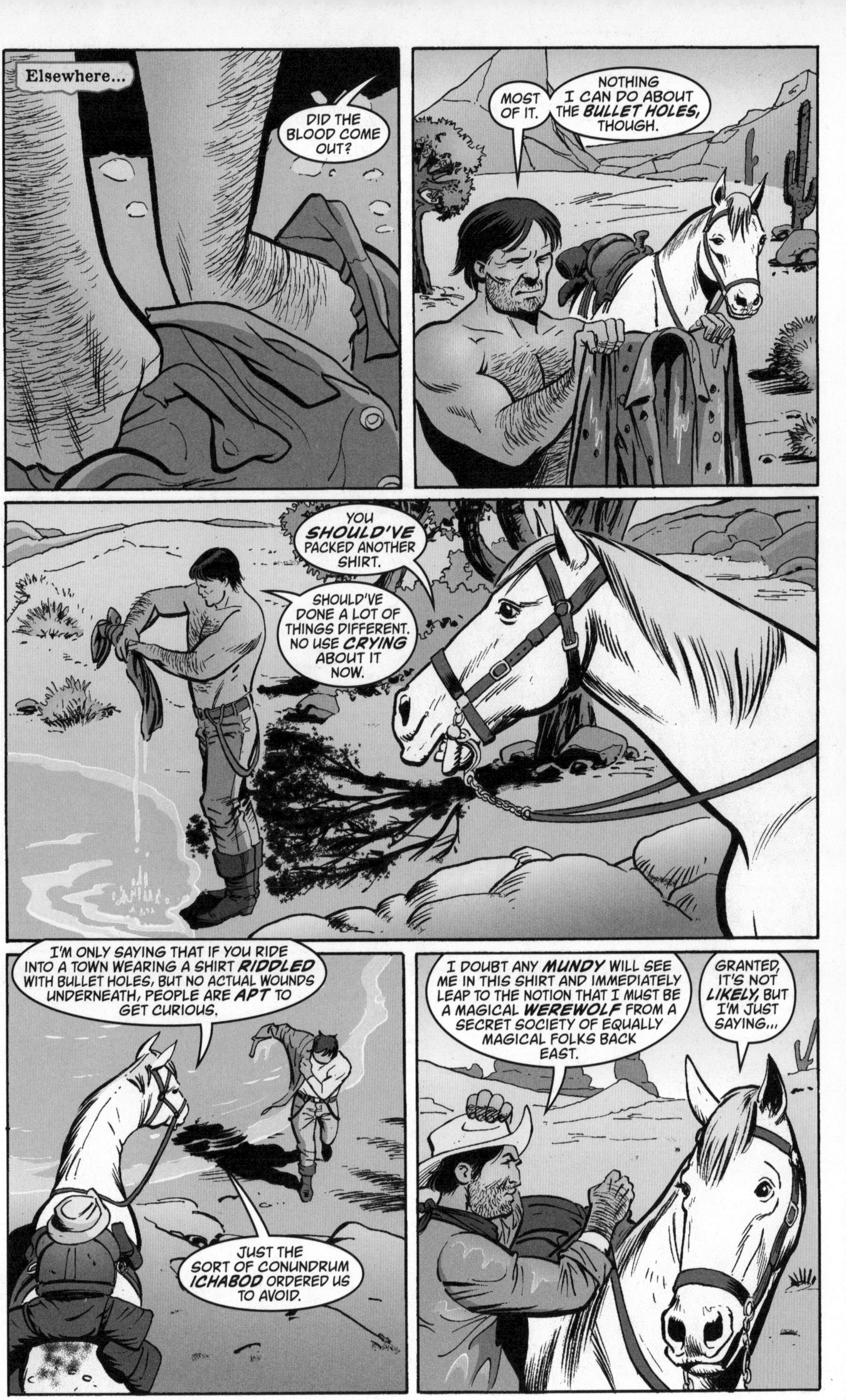
Elsewhere...
DID THE BLOOD COME OUT?
MOST OF IT.
NOTHING I CAN DO ABOUT THE BULLET HOLES, THOUGH.
YOU SHOULD'VE PACKED ANOTHER SHIRT.
SHOULD'VE DONE A LOT OF THINGS DIFFERENT. NO USE CRYING ABOUT IT NOW.
I'M ONLY SAYING THAT IF YOU RIDE INTO A TOWN WEARING A SHIRT RIDDLED WITH BULLET HOLES, BUT NO ACTUAL WOUNDS UNDERNEATH, PEOPLE ARE APT TO GET CURIOUS.
JUST THE SORT OF CONUNDRUM ICHABOD ORDERED US TO AVOID.
I DOUBT ANY MUNDY WILL SEE ME IN THIS SHIRT AND IMMEDIATELY LEAP TO THE NOTION THAT I MUST BE A MAGICAL WEREWOLF FROM A SECRET SOCIETY OF EQUALLY MAGICAL FOLKS BACK EAST.
GRANTED, IT'S NOT LIKELY, BUT I'M JUST SAYING...

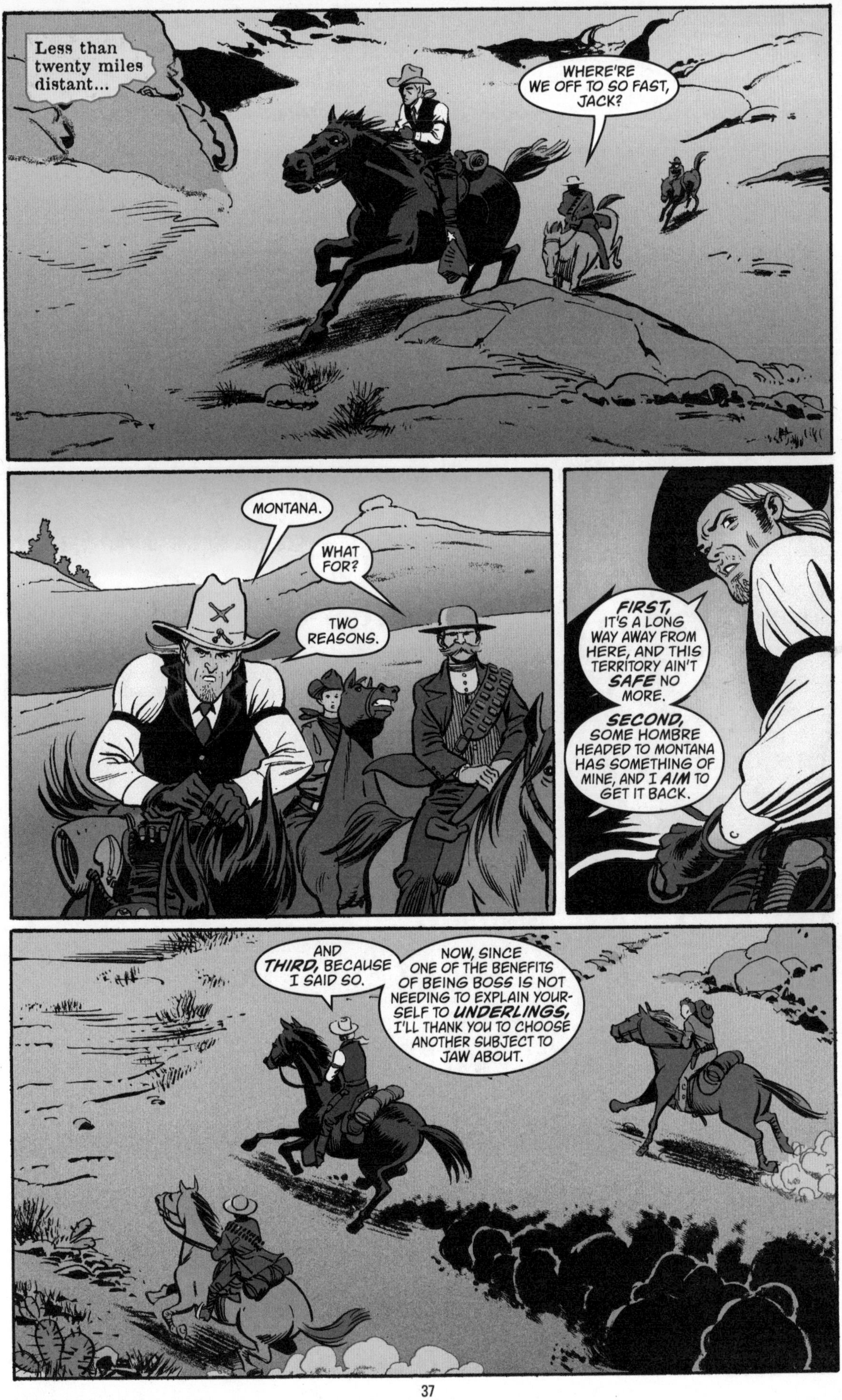
Less than twenty miles distant...
WHERE'RE WE OFF TO SO FAST, JACK?
MONTANA.
WHAT FOR?
TWO REASONS.
FIRST, IT'S A LONG WAY AWAY FROM HERE, AND THIS TERRITORY AIN'T SAFE NO MORE.
SECOND, SOME HOMBRE HEADED TO MONTANA HAS SOMETHING OF MINE, AND I AIM TO GET IT BACK.
AND THIRD, BECAUSE I SAID SO.
NOW, SINCE ONE OF THE BENEFITS OF BEING BOSS IS NOT NEEDING TO EXPLAIN YOURSELF TO UNDERLINGS, I'LL THANK YOU TO CHOOSE ANOTHER SUBJECT TO JAW ABOUT.

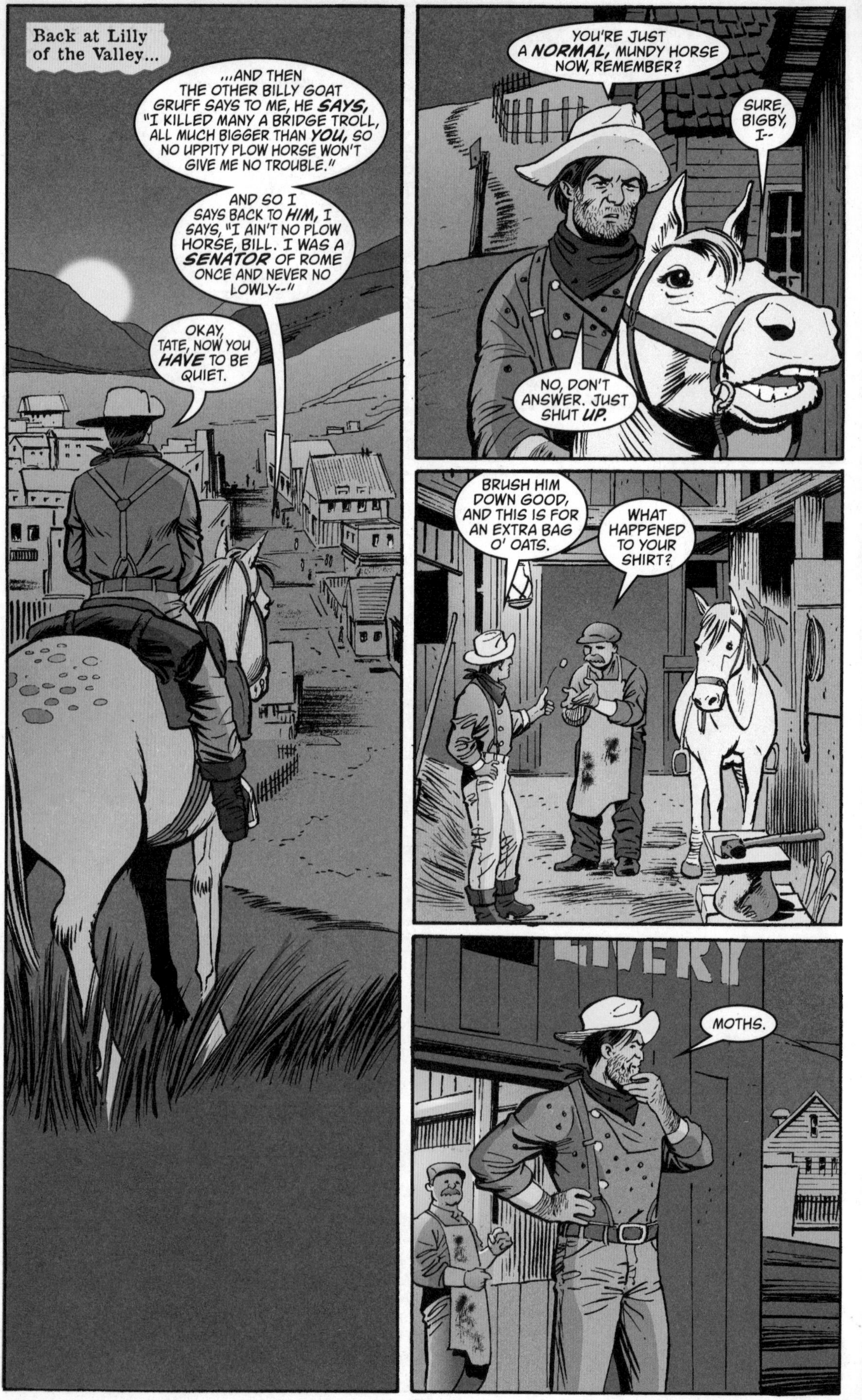
Back at Lilly of the Valley...
...AND THEN THE OTHER BILLY GOAT GRUFF SAYS TO ME, HE SAYS, "I KILLED MANY A BRIDGE TROLL, ALL MUCH BIGGER THAN YOU, SO NO UPPITY PLOW HORSE WON'T GIVE ME NO TROUBLE."
AND SO I SAYS BACK TO HIM, I SAYS, "I AIN'T NO PLOW HORSE, BILL. I WAS A SENATOR OF ROME ONCE AND NEVER NO LOWLY--"
OKAY, TATE, NOW YOU HAVE TO BE QUIET.
YOU'RE JUST A NORMAL, MUNDY HORSE NOW, REMEMBER?
SURE, BIGBY, I--
NO, DON'T ANSWER. JUST SHUT UP.
BRUSH HIM DOWN GOOD, AND THIS IS FOR AN EXTRA BAG O' OATS.
WHAT HAPPENED TO YOUR SHIRT?
LIVERY
MOTHS.

39

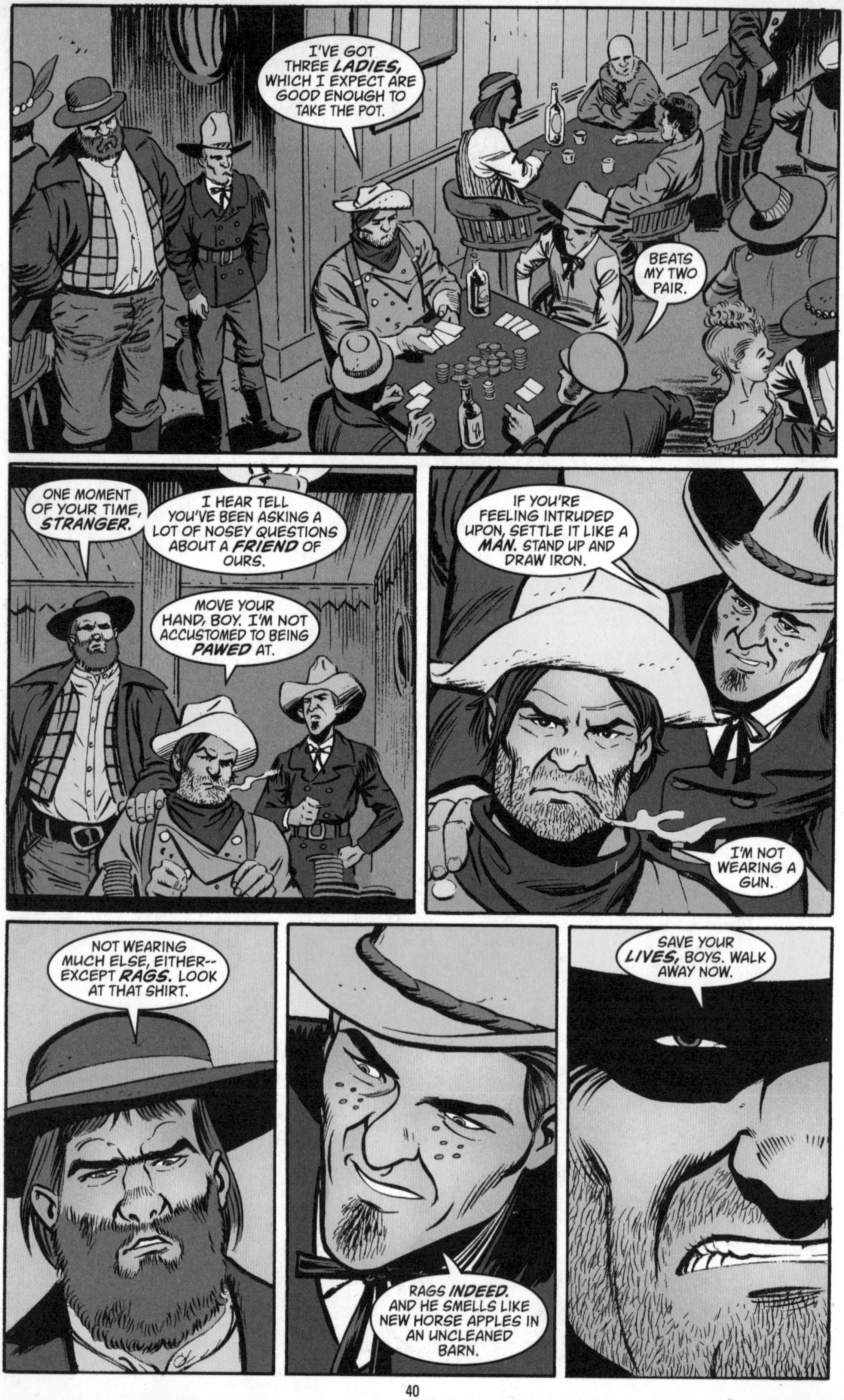
I'VE GOT THREE LADIES, WHICH I EXPECT ARE GOOD ENOUGH TO TAKE THE POT.
BEATS MY TWO PAIR.
ONE MOMENT OF YOUR TIME, STRANGER.
I HEAR TELL YOU'VE BEEN ASKING A LOT OF NOSEY QUESTIONS ABOUT A FRIEND OF OURS.
MOVE YOUR HAND, BOY. I'M NOT ACCUSTOMED TO BEING PAWED AT.
IF YOU'RE FEELING INTRUDED UPON, SETTLE IT LIKE A MAN. STAND UP AND DRAW IRON.
I'M NOT WEARING A GUN.
NOT WEARING MUCH ELSE, EITHER-- EXCEPT RAGS. LOOK AT THAT SHIRT.
RAGS INDEED. AND HE SMELLS LIKE NEW HORSE APPLES IN AN UNCLEANED BARN.
SAVE YOUR LIVES, BOYS. WALK AWAY NOW.

41

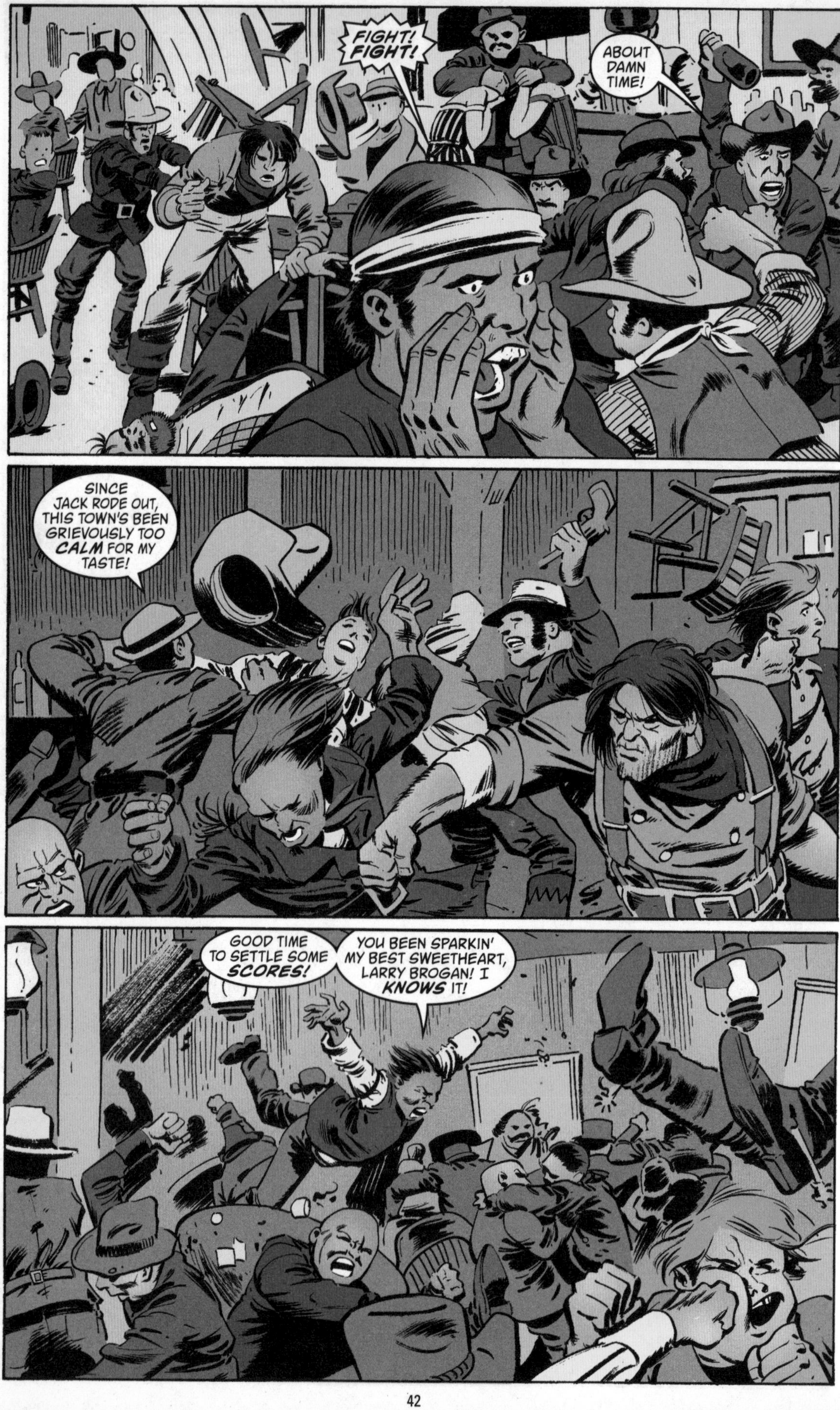
FIGHT! FIGHT!
ABOUT DAMN TIME!
SINCE JACK RODE OUT, THIS TOWN'S BEEN GRIEVOUSLY TOO CALM FOR MY TASTE!
GOOD TIME TO SETTLE SOME SCORES!
YOU BEEN SPARKIN' MY BEST SWEETHEART, LARRY BROGAN! I KNOWS IT!

On the fifth of August, in 1883, such a brawl broke out in the town of Lilly of the Valley, New Mexico, that it made most of the territory's papers.

Two men were killed outright. Three more later died of their injuries, and half a dozen others were maimed for life.

MY HAND'S GONE!

At the same time Smilin' Jack and his two surviving cohorts were nearly three hundred miles to the north and hadn't so much as cleared leather in four days.

MY POOR HAND!

SOMEONE RIPPED IT CLEAN OFF!

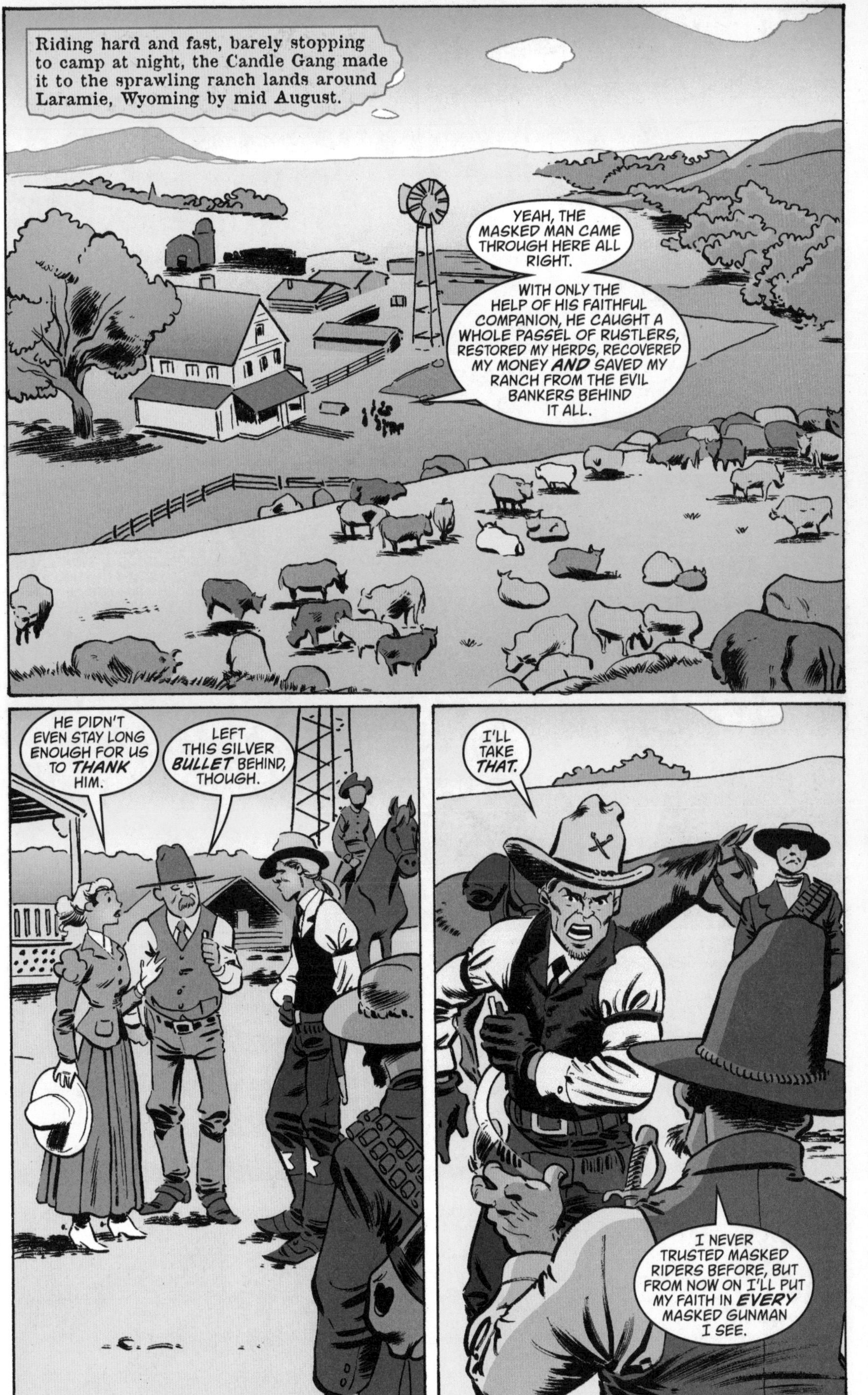
Riding hard and fast, barely stopping to camp at night, the Candle Gang made it to the sprawling ranch lands around Laramie, Wyoming by mid August.
YEAH, THE MASKED MAN CAME THROUGH HERE ALL RIGHT.
WITH ONLY THE HELP OF HIS FAITHFUL COMPANION, HE CAUGHT A WHOLE PASSEL OF RUSTLERS, RESTORED MY HERDS, RECOVERED MY MONEY AND SAVED MY RANCH FROM THE EVIL BANKERS BEHIND IT ALL.
HE DIDN'T EVEN STAY LONG ENOUGH FOR US TO THANK HIM.
LEFT THIS SILVER BULLET BEHIND, THOUGH.
I'LL TAKE THAT.
I NEVER TRUSTED MASKED RIDERS BEFORE, BUT FROM NOW ON I'LL PUT MY FAITH IN EVERY MASKED GUNMAN I SEE.

46

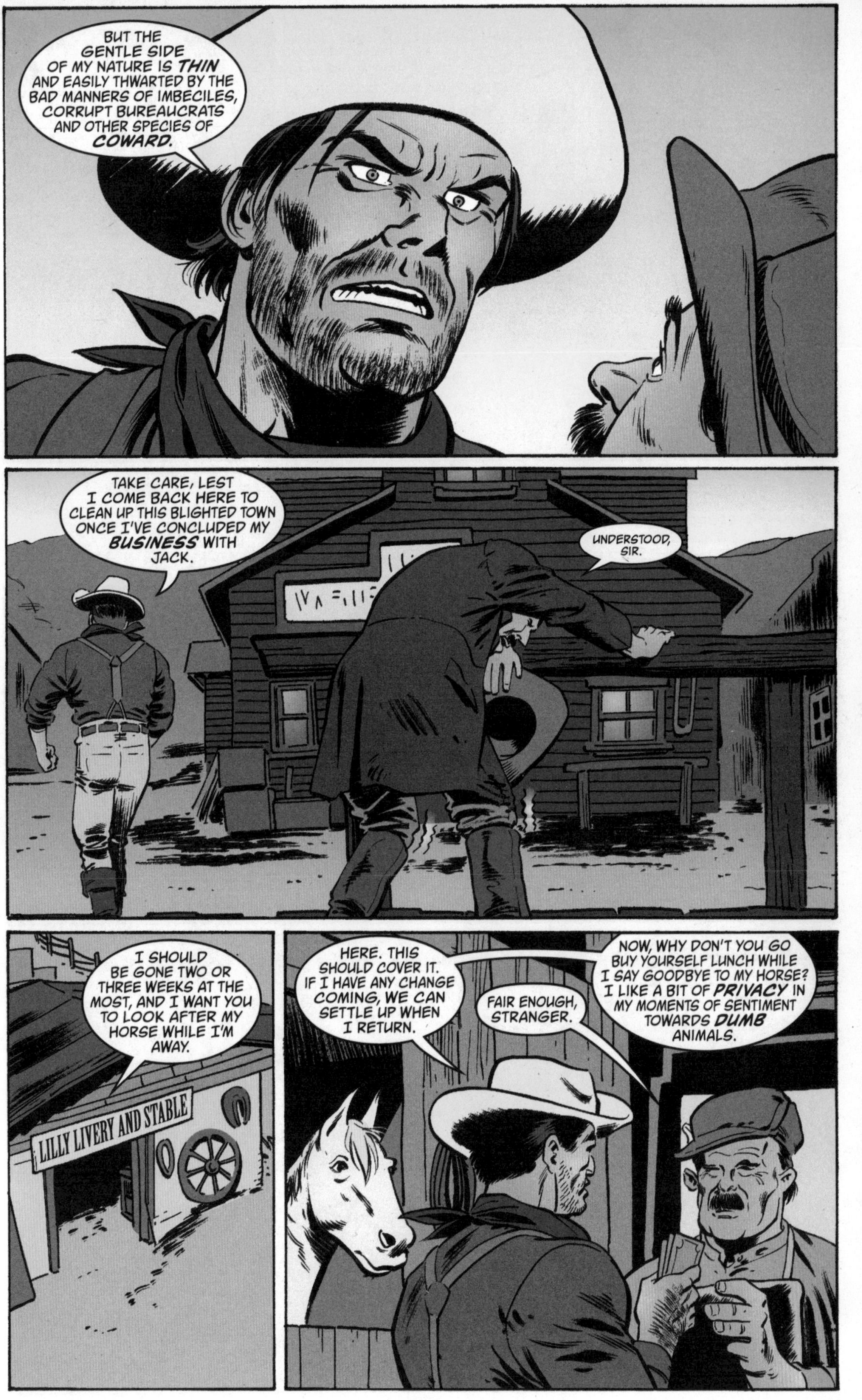
BUT THE GENTLE SIDE OF MY NATURE IS THIN AND EASILY THWARTED BY THE BAD MANNERS OF IMBECILES, CORRUPT BUREAUCRATS AND OTHER SPECIES OF COWARD.
TAKE CARE, LEST I COME BACK HERE TO CLEAN UP THIS BLIGHTED TOWN ONCE I'VE CONCLUDED MY BUSINESS WITH JACK.
UNDERSTOOD, SIR.
I SHOULD BE GONE TWO OR THREE WEEKS AT THE MOST, AND I WANT YOU TO LOOK AFTER MY HORSE WHILE I'M AWAY.
LILLY LIVERY AND STABLE
HERE. THIS SHOULD COVER IT. IF I HAVE ANY CHANGE COMING, WE CAN SETTLE UP WHEN I RETURN.
FAIR ENOUGH, STRANGER.
NOW, WHY DON'T YOU GO BUY YOURSELF LUNCH WHILE I SAY GOODBYE TO MY HORSE? I LIKE A BIT OF PRIVACY IN MY MOMENTS OF SENTIMENT TOWARDS DUMB ANIMALS.

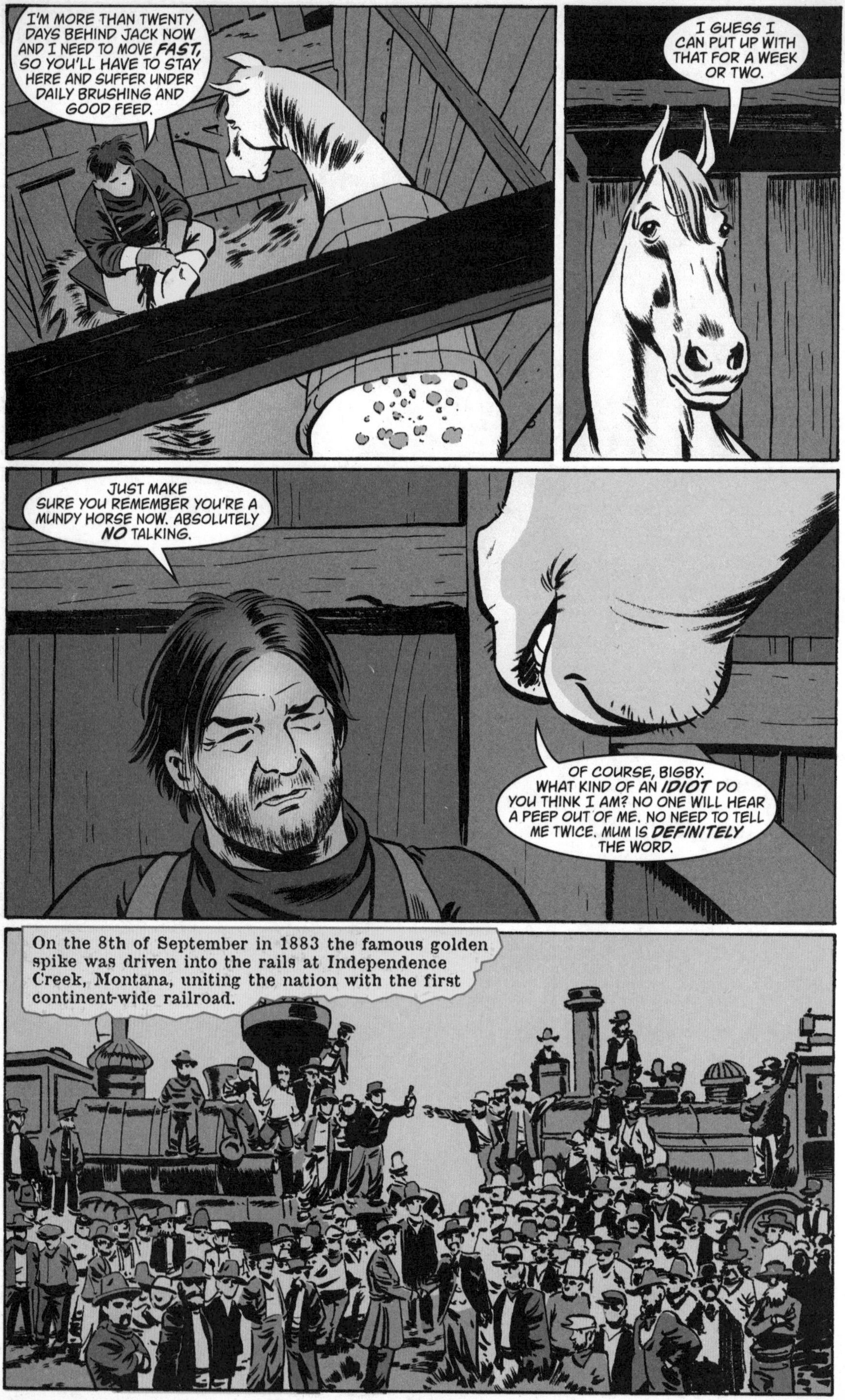
I'M MORE THAN TWENTY DAYS BEHIND JACK NOW AND I NEED TO MOVE FAST, SO YOU'LL HAVE TO STAY HERE AND SUFFER UNDER DAILY BRUSHING AND GOOD FEED.
I GUESS I CAN PUT UP WITH THAT FOR A WEEK OR TWO.
JUST MAKE SURE YOU REMEMBER YOU'RE A MUNDY HORSE NOW. ABSOLUTELY NO TALKING.
OF COURSE, BIGBY. WHAT KIND OF AN IDIOT DO YOU THINK I AM? NO ONE WILL HEAR A PEEP OUT OF ME. NO NEED TO TELL ME TWICE. MUM IS DEFINITELY THE WORD.
On the 8th of September in 1883 the famous golden spike was driven into the rails at Independence Creek, Montana, uniting the nation with the first continent-wide railroad.

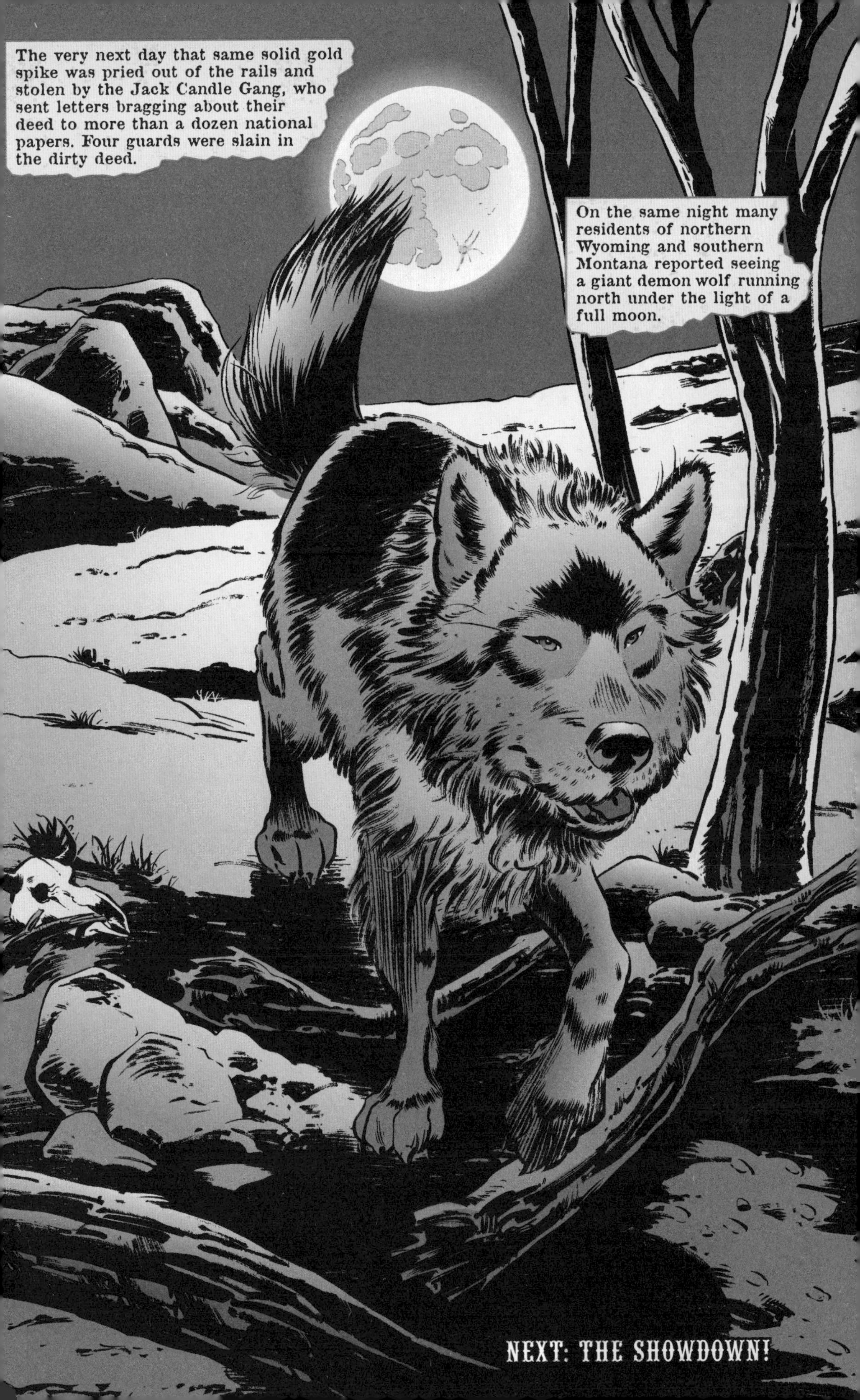
The very next day that same solid gold spike was pried out of the rails and stolen by the Jack Candle Gang, who sent letters bragging about their deed to more than a dozen national papers. Four guards were slain in the dirty deed.
On the same night many residents of northern Wyoming and southern Montana reported seeing a giant demon wolf running north under the light of a full moon.
NEXT: THE SHOWDOWN!

A SECOND ISSUE OF JACK OF FABLES HAS NOW COME AND GONE WITHOUT A SINGLE INTENTIONALLY FUNNY MOMENT? ARE WE GETTING TIRESOME AND SERIOUS IN OUR OLD AGE? ARE WE "MELLOWING OUT," AS THEY SAY? NOPE--AND HERE'S A RIDICULOUS BABE PAGE TO PROVE IT...

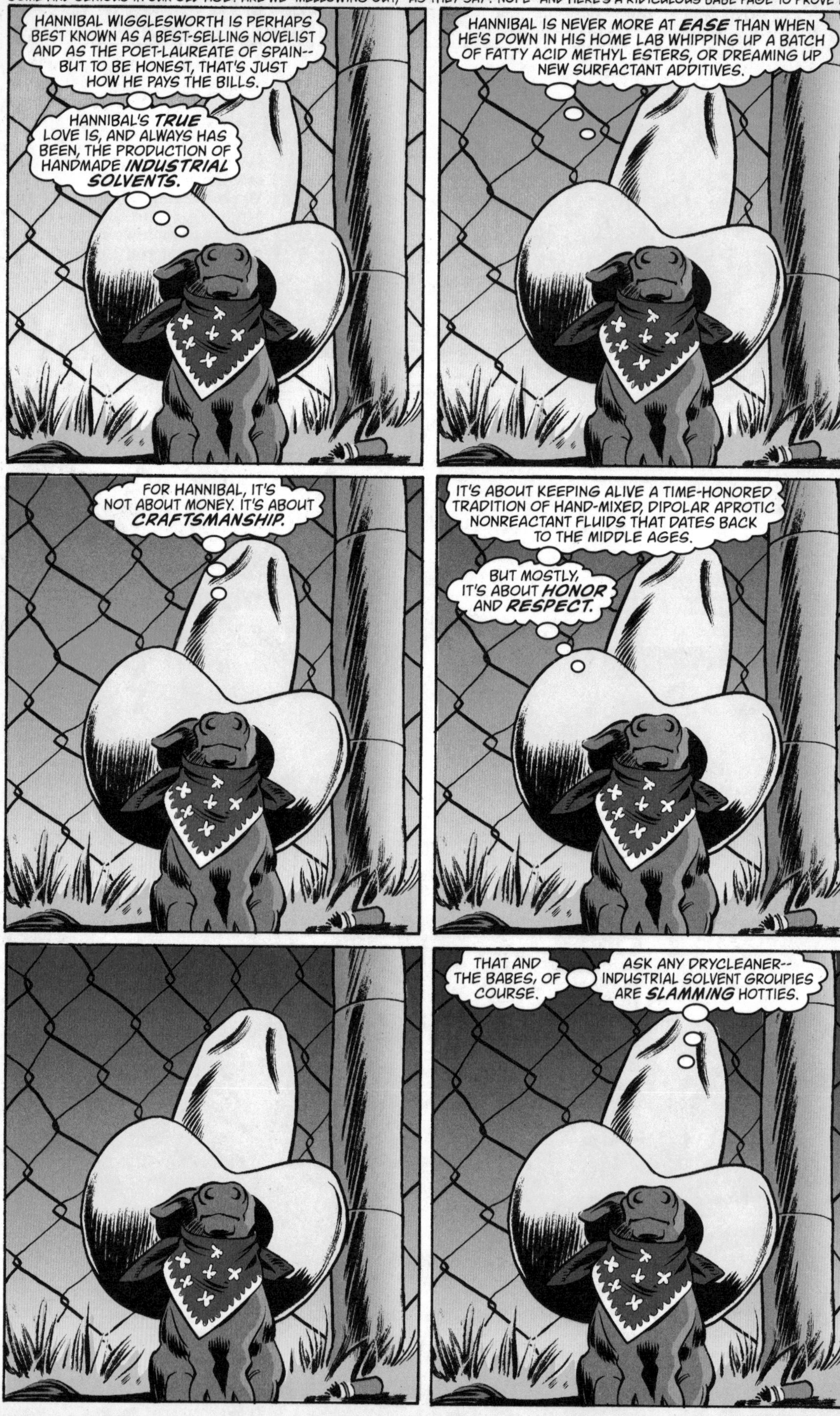
HANNIBAL WIGGLESWORTH IS PERHAPS BEST KNOWN AS A BEST-SELLING NOVELIST AND AS THE POET-LAUREATE OF SPAIN--BUT TO BE HONEST, THAT'S JUST HOW HE PAYS THE BILLS.
HANNIBAL'S TRUE LOVE IS, AND ALWAYS HAS BEEN, THE PRODUCTION OF HANDMADE INDUSTRIAL SOLVENTS.
HANNIBAL IS NEVER MORE AT EASE THAN WHEN HE'S DOWN IN HIS HOME LAB WHIPPING UP A BATCH OF FATTY ACID METHYL ESTERS, OR DREAMING UP NEW SURFACTANT ADDITIVES.
FOR HANNIBAL, IT'S NOT ABOUT MONEY. IT'S ABOUT CRAFTSMANSHIP.
IT'S ABOUT KEEPING ALIVE A TIME-HONORED TRADITION OF HAND-MIXED, DIPOLAR APROTIC NONREACTANT FLUIDS THAT DATES BACK TO THE MIDDLE AGES.
BUT MOSTLY, IT'S ABOUT HONOR AND RESPECT.
THAT AND THE BABES, OF COURSE.
ASK ANY DRYCLEANER--INDUSTRIAL SOLVENT GROUPIES ARE SLAMMING HOTTIES.

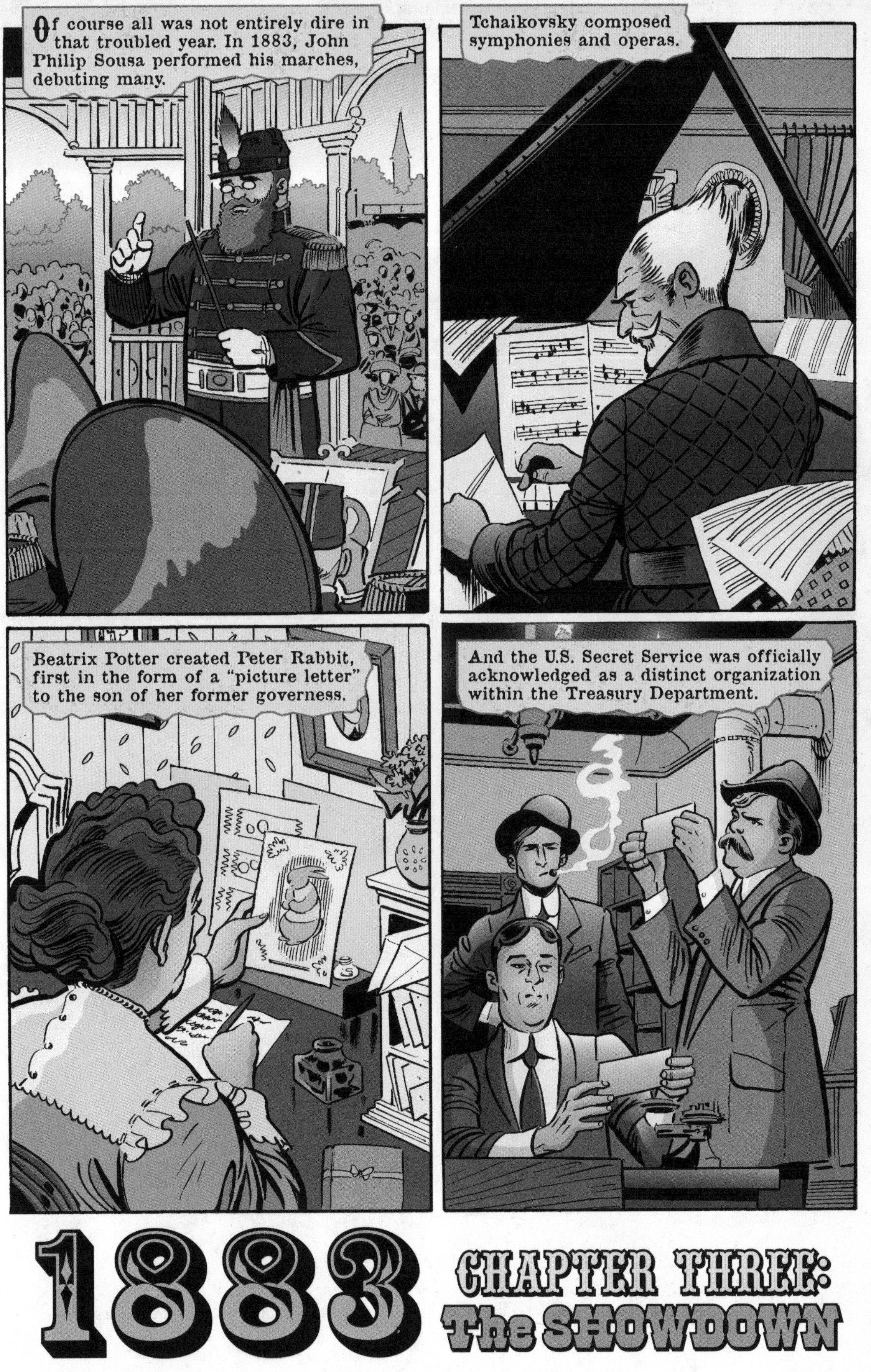
Of course all was not entirely dire in that troubled year. In 1883, John Philip Sousa performed his marches, debuting many.
Tchaikovsky composed symphonies and operas.
Beatrix Potter created Peter Rabbit, first in the form of a "picture letter" to the son of her former governess.
And the U.S. Secret Service was officially acknowledged as a distinct organization within the Treasury Department.

1883 CHAPTER THREE: The SHOWDOWN

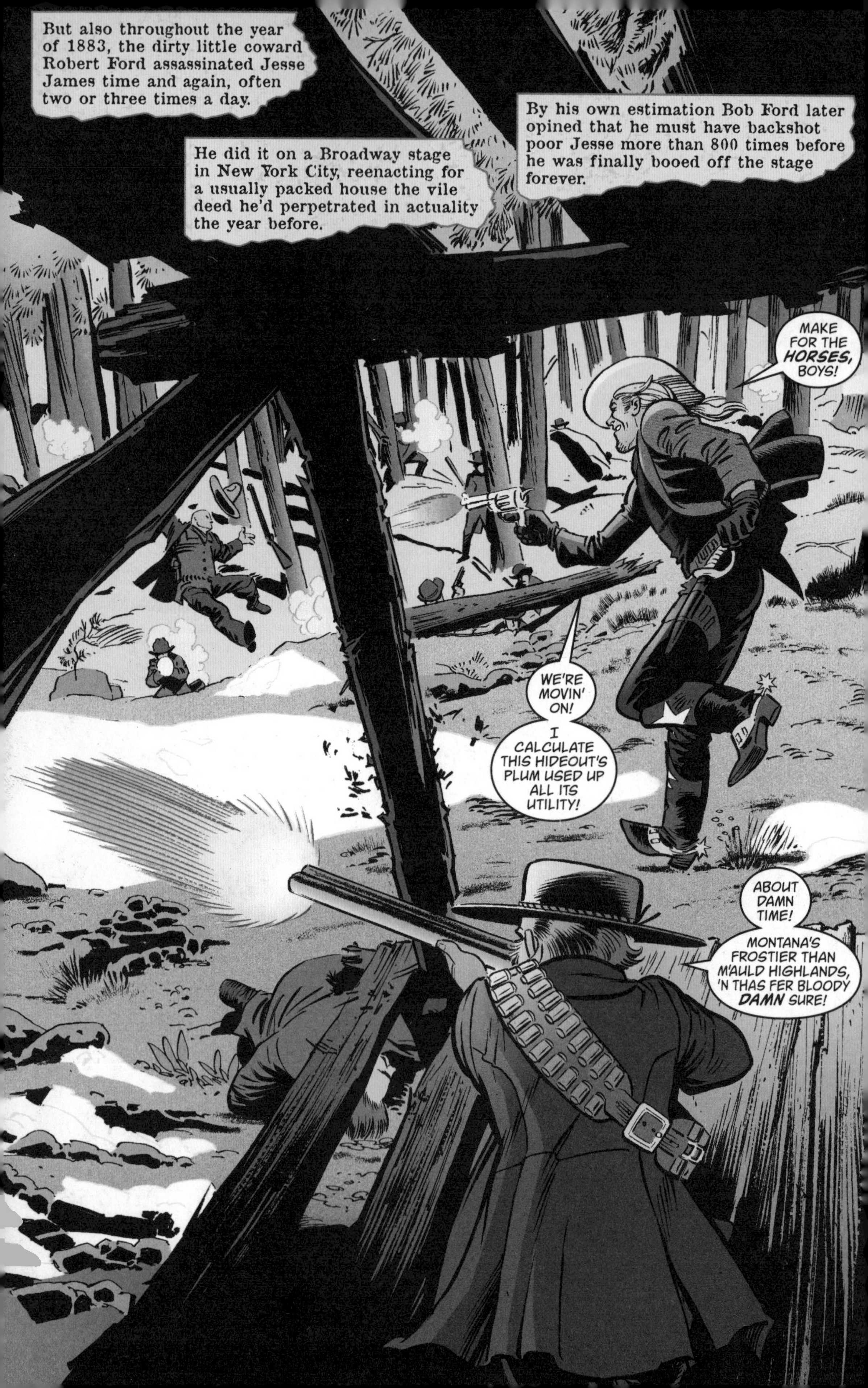

But also throughout the year of 1883, the dirty little coward Robert Ford assassinated Jesse James time and again, often two or three times a day.
He did it on a Broadway stage in New York City, reenacting for a usually packed house the vile deed he'd perpetrated in actuality the year before.
By his own estimation Bob Ford later opined that he must have backshot poor Jesse more than 800 times before he was finally booed off the stage forever.
MAKE FOR THE HORSES, BOYS!
WE'RE MOVIN' ON!
I CALCULATE THIS HIDEOUT'S PLUM USED UP ALL ITS UTILITY!
ABOUT DAMN TIME!
MONTANA'S FROSTIER THAN M'AULD HIGHLANDS, 'N THAS FER BLOODY DAMN SURE!

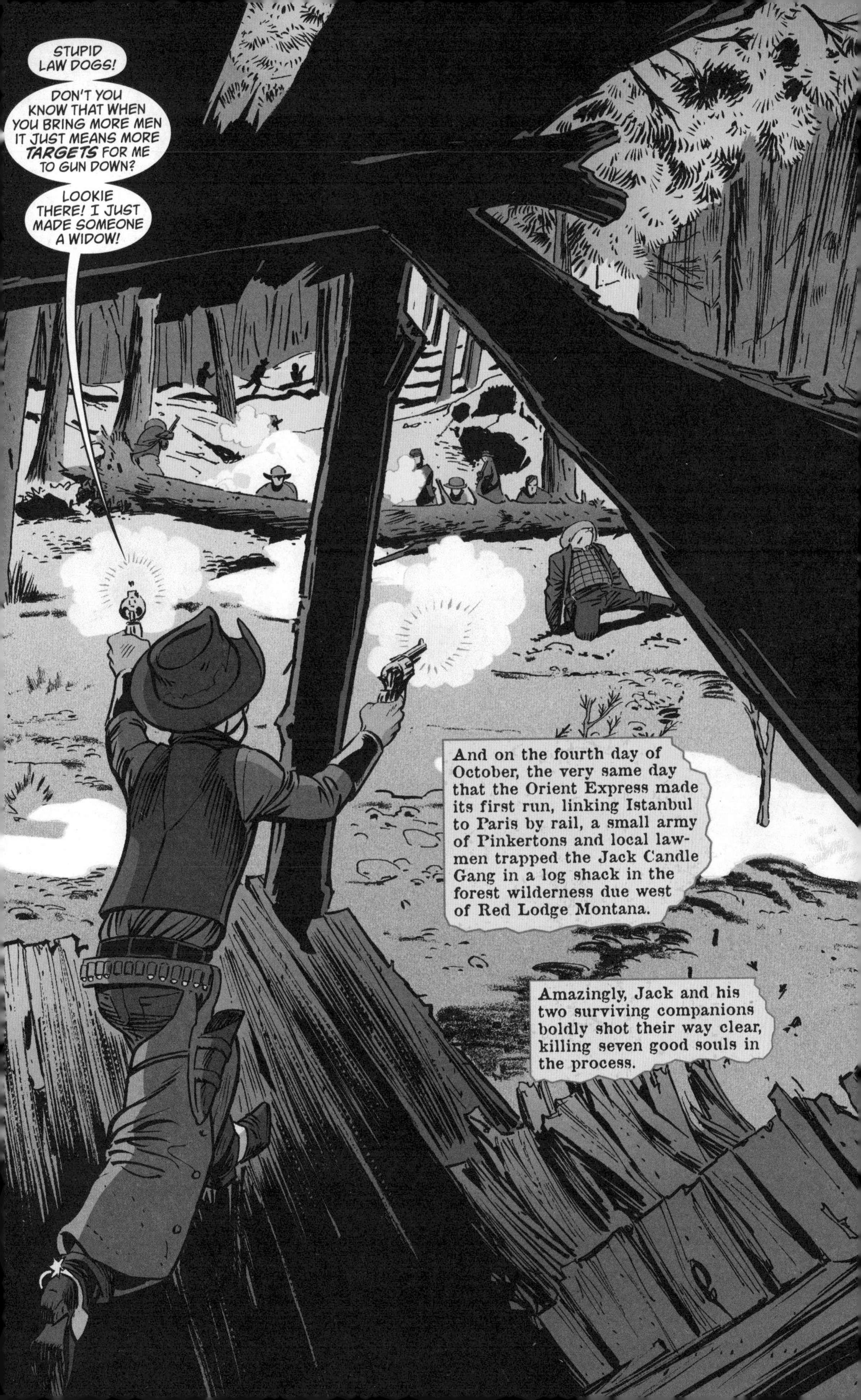
STUPID LAW DOGS!
DON'T YOU KNOW THAT WHEN YOU BRING MORE MEN IT JUST MEANS MORE *TARGETS* FOR ME TO GUN DOWN?
LOOKIE THERE! I JUST MADE SOMEONE A WIDOW!
And on the fourth day of October, the very same day that the Orient Express made its first run, linking Istanbul to Paris by rail, a small army of Pinkertons and local lawmen trapped the Jack Candle Gang in a log shack in the forest wilderness due west of Red Lodge Montana.
Amazingly, Jack and his two surviving companions boldly shot their way clear, killing seven good souls in the process.

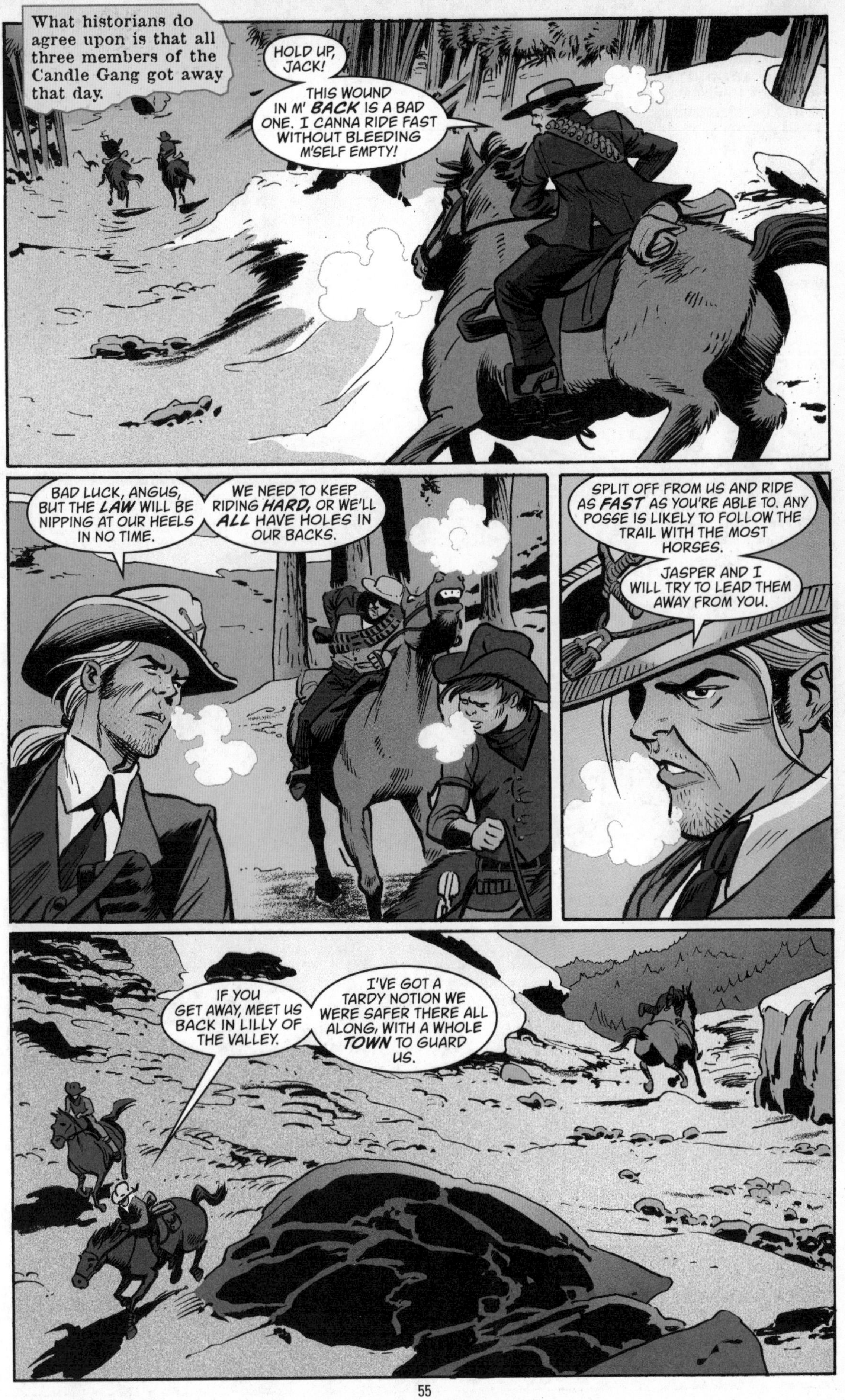
What historians do agree upon is that all three members of the Candle Gang got away that day.
HOLD UP, JACK!
THIS WOUND IN M' BACK IS A BAD ONE. I CANNA RIDE FAST WITHOUT BLEEDING M'SELF EMPTY!
BAD LUCK, ANGUS, BUT THE LAW WILL BE NIPPING AT OUR HEELS IN NO TIME.
WE NEED TO KEEP RIDING HARD, OR WE'LL ALL HAVE HOLES IN OUR BACKS.
SPLIT OFF FROM US AND RIDE AS FAST AS YOU'RE ABLE TO. ANY POSSE IS LIKELY TO FOLLOW THE TRAIL WITH THE MOST HORSES.
JASPER AND I WILL TRY TO LEAD THEM AWAY FROM YOU.
IF YOU GET AWAY, MEET US BACK IN LILLY OF THE VALLEY.
I'VE GOT A TARDY NOTION WE WERE SAFER THERE ALL ALONG, WITH A WHOLE TOWN TO GUARD US.

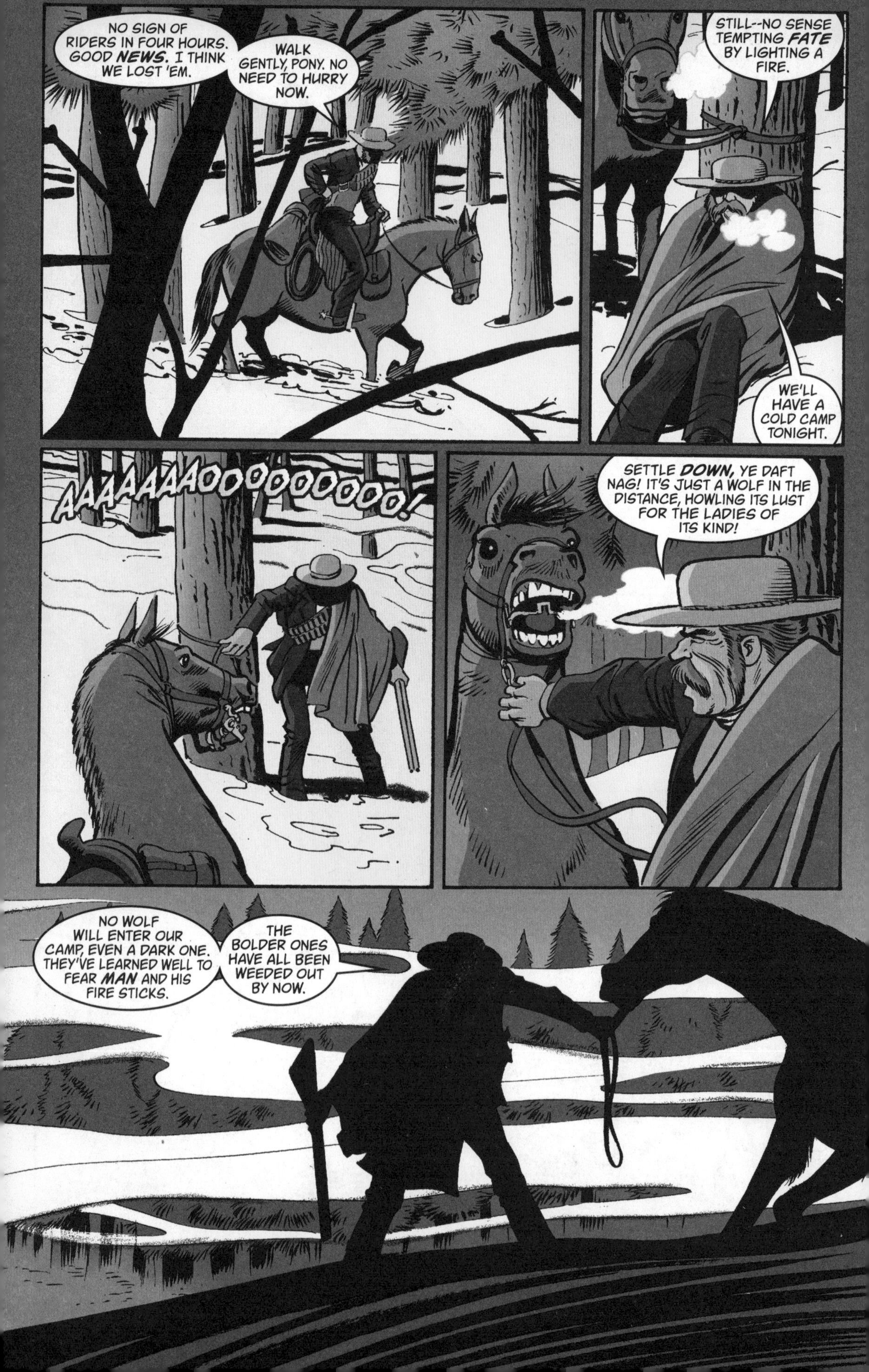
NO SIGN OF RIDERS IN FOUR HOURS. GOOD NEWS. I THINK WE LOST 'EM.
WALK GENTLY, PONY. NO NEED TO HURRY NOW.
STILL--NO SENSE TEMPTING FATE BY LIGHTING A FIRE.
WE'LL HAVE A COLD CAMP TONIGHT.
AAAAAAAOOOOOOOOOOO!
SETTLE DOWN, YE DAFT NAG! IT'S JUST A WOLF IN THE DISTANCE, HOWLING ITS LUST FOR THE LADIES OF ITS KIND!
NO WOLF WILL ENTER OUR CAMP, EVEN A DARK ONE. THEY'VE LEARNED WELL TO FEAR MAN AND HIS FIRE STICKS.
THE BOLDER ONES HAVE ALL BEEN WEEDED OUT BY NOW.

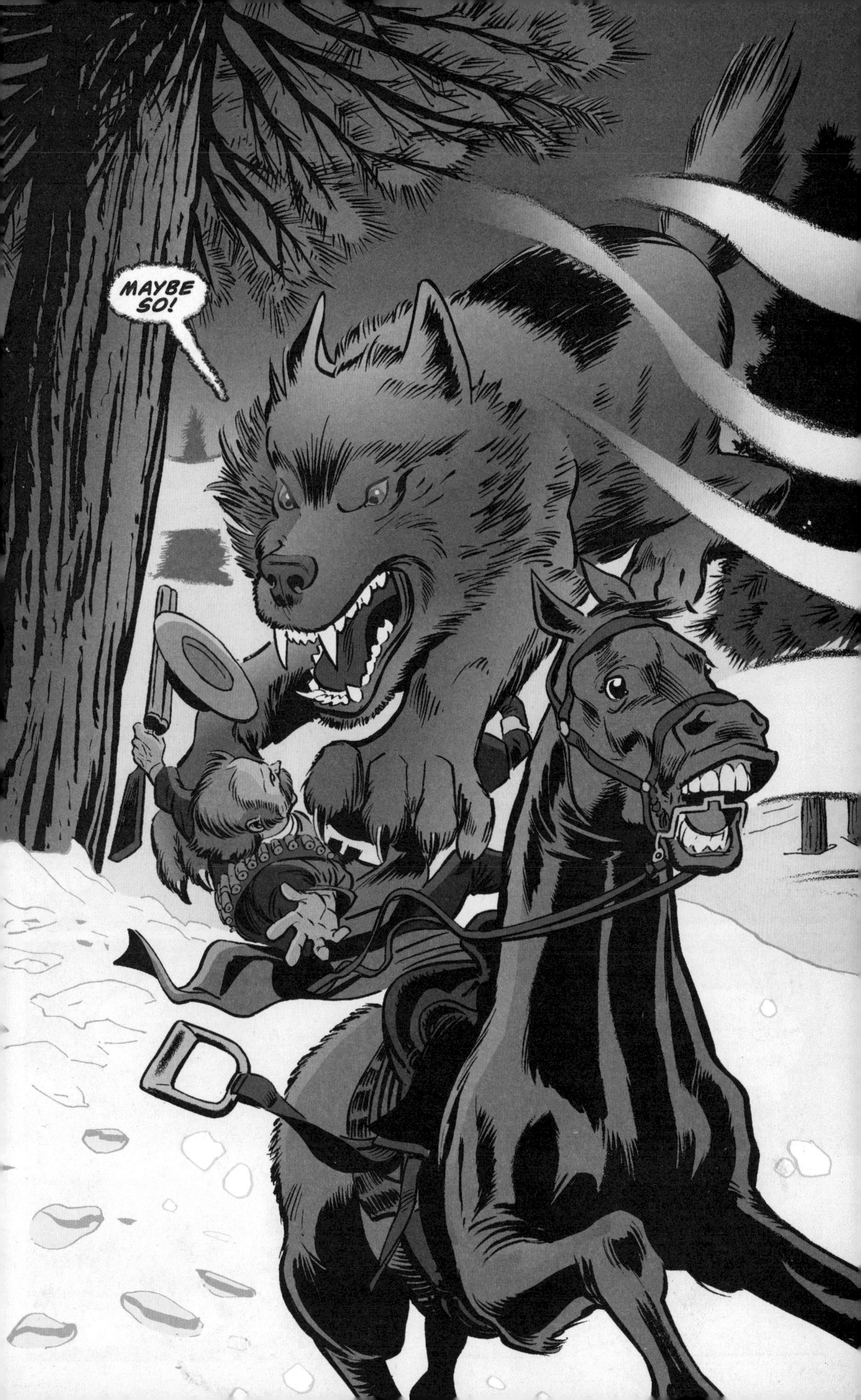
MAYBE SO!

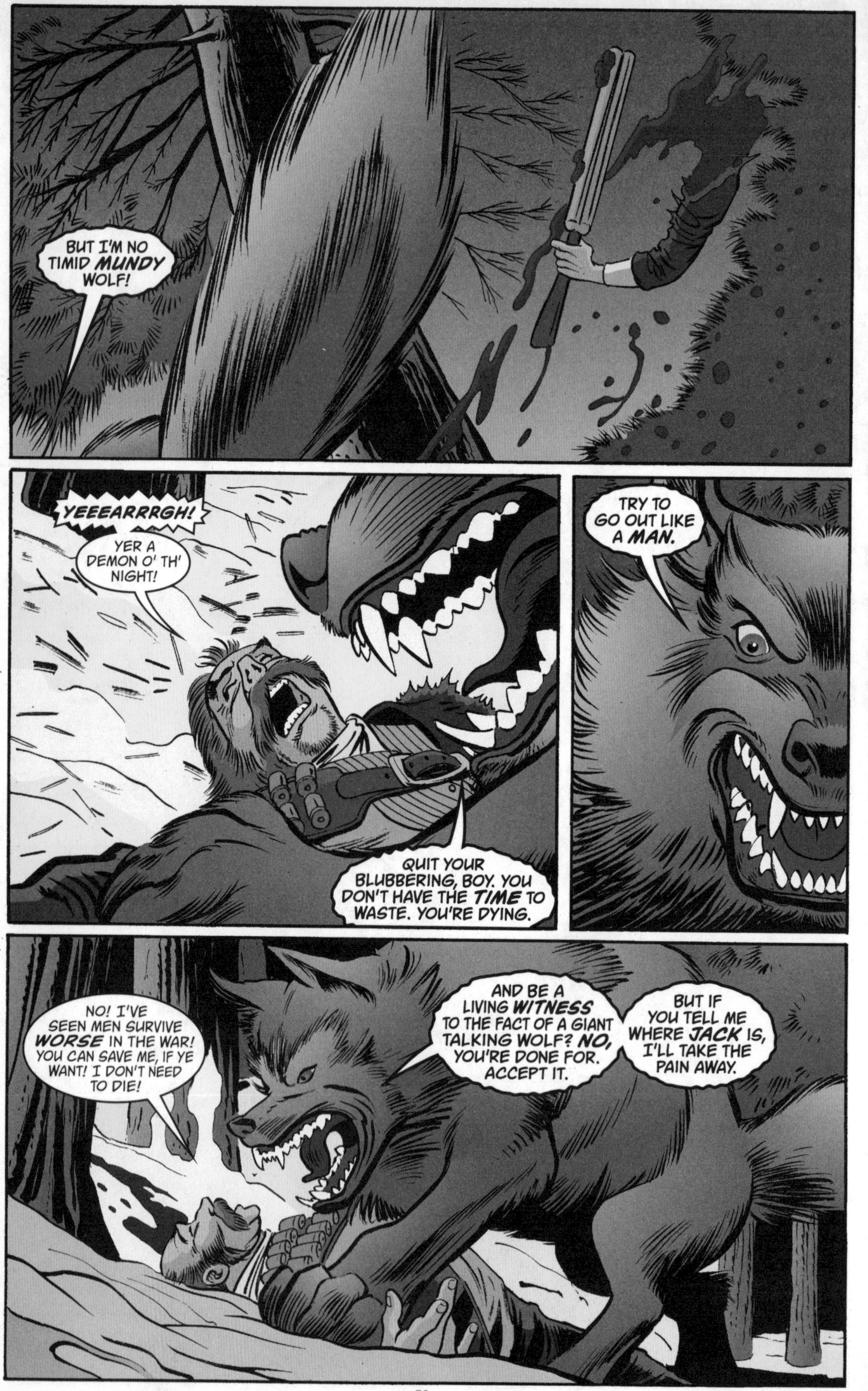
BUT I'M NO TIMID MUNDY WOLF!
YEEEARRRGH!
YER A DEMON O' TH' NIGHT!
QUIT YOUR BLUBBERING, BOY. YOU DON'T HAVE THE TIME TO WASTE. YOU'RE DYING.
TRY TO GO OUT LIKE A MAN.
NO! I'VE SEEN MEN SURVIVE WORSE IN THE WAR! YOU CAN SAVE ME, IF YE WANT! I DON'T NEED TO DIE!
AND BE A LIVING WITNESS TO THE FACT OF A GIANT TALKING WOLF? NO, YOU'RE DONE FOR. ACCEPT IT.
BUT IF YOU TELL ME WHERE JACK IS, I'LL TAKE THE PAIN AWAY.

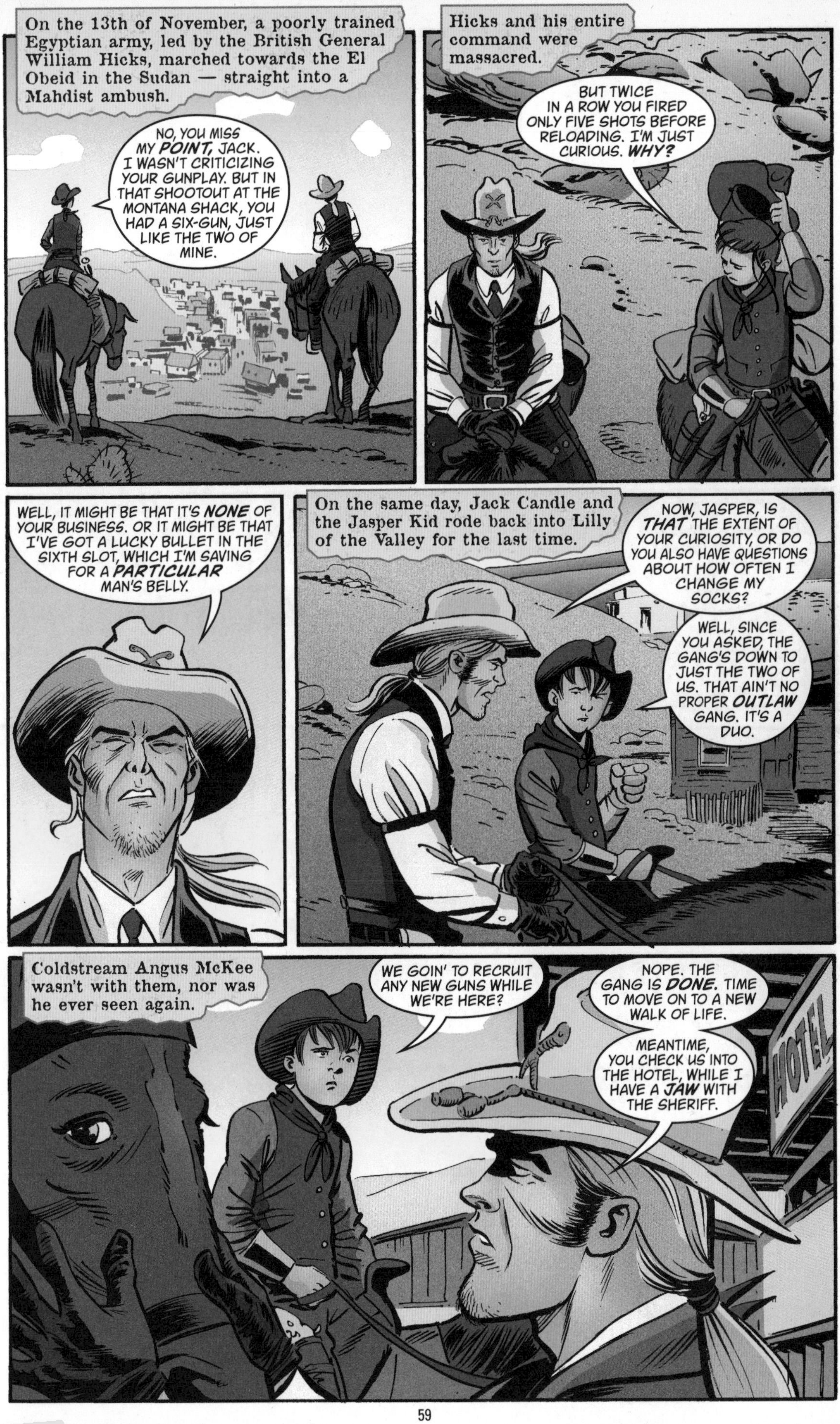
On the 13th of November, a poorly trained Egyptian army, led by the British General William Hicks, marched towards the El Obeid in the Sudan — straight into a Mahdist ambush.
NO, YOU MISS MY POINT, JACK. I WASN'T CRITICIZING YOUR GUNPLAY. BUT IN THAT SHOOTOUT AT THE MONTANA SHACK, YOU HAD A SIX-GUN, JUST LIKE THE TWO OF MINE.
Hicks and his entire command were massacred.
BUT TWICE IN A ROW YOU FIRED ONLY FIVE SHOTS BEFORE RELOADING. I'M JUST CURIOUS. WHY?
WELL, IT MIGHT BE THAT IT'S NONE OF YOUR BUSINESS. OR IT MIGHT BE THAT I'VE GOT A LUCKY BULLET IN THE SIXTH SLOT, WHICH I'M SAVING FOR A PARTICULAR MAN'S BELLY.
On the same day, Jack Candle and the Jasper Kid rode back into Lilly of the Valley for the last time.
NOW, JASPER, IS THAT THE EXTENT OF YOUR CURIOSITY, OR DO YOU ALSO HAVE QUESTIONS ABOUT HOW OFTEN I CHANGE MY SOCKS?
WELL, SINCE YOU ASKED, THE GANG'S DOWN TO JUST THE TWO OF US. THAT AIN'T NO PROPER OUTLAW GANG. IT'S A DUO.
Coldstream Angus McKee wasn't with them, nor was he ever seen again.
WE GOIN' TO RECRUIT ANY NEW GUNS WHILE WE'RE HERE?
NOPE. THE GANG IS DONE. TIME TO MOVE ON TO A NEW WALK OF LIFE.
MEANTIME, YOU CHECK US INTO THE HOTEL, WHILE I HAVE A JAW WITH THE SHERIFF.
HOTEL

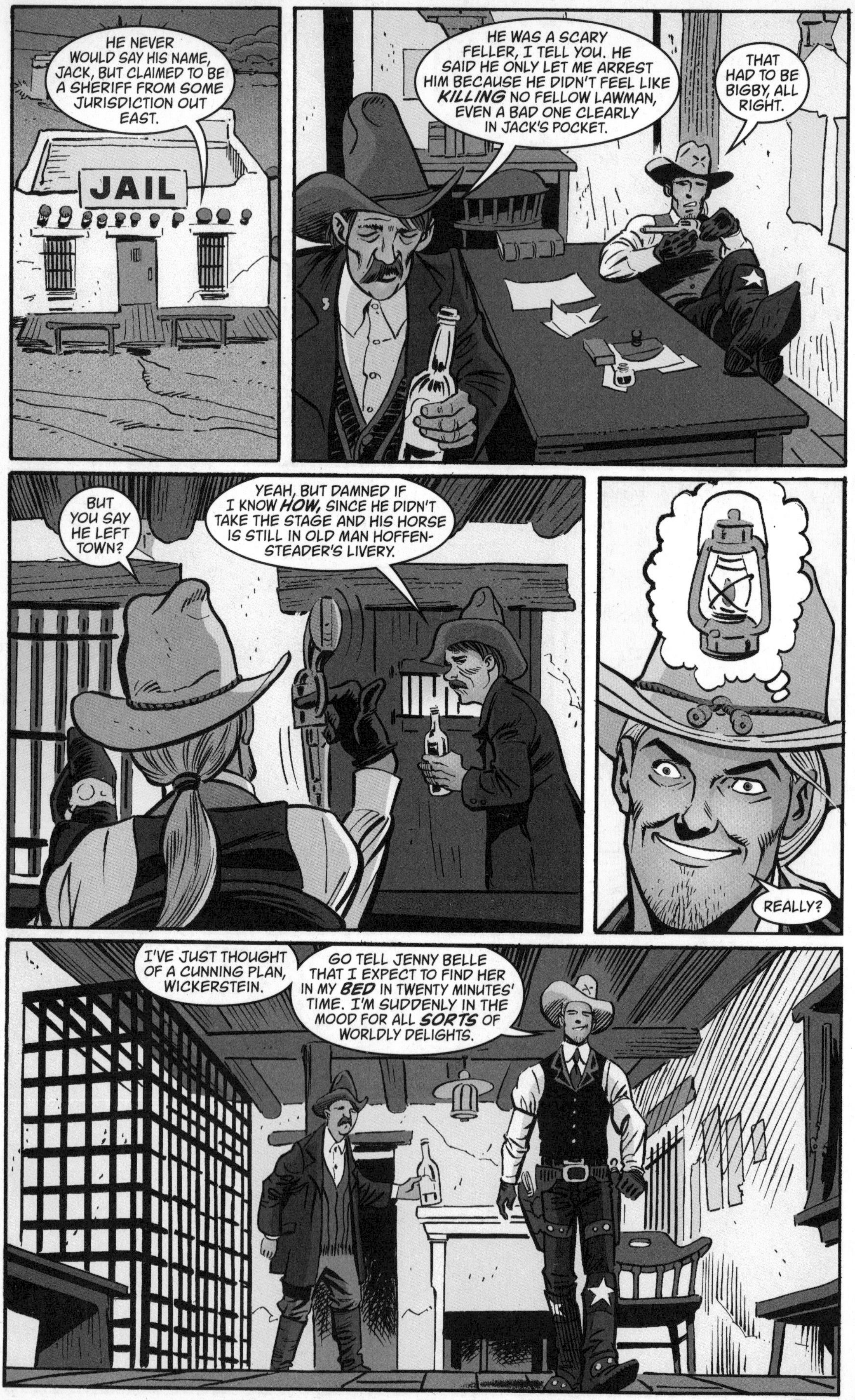
HE NEVER WOULD SAY HIS NAME, JACK, BUT CLAIMED TO BE A SHERIFF FROM SOME JURISDICTION OUT EAST.
JAIL
HE WAS A SCARY FELLER, I TELL YOU. HE SAID HE ONLY LET ME ARREST HIM BECAUSE HE DIDN'T FEEL LIKE KILLING NO FELLOW LAWMAN, EVEN A BAD ONE CLEARLY IN JACK'S POCKET.
THAT HAD TO BE BIGBY, ALL RIGHT.
BUT YOU SAY HE LEFT TOWN?
YEAH, BUT DAMNED IF I KNOW HOW, SINCE HE DIDN'T TAKE THE STAGE AND HIS HORSE IS STILL IN OLD MAN HOFFEN-STEADER'S LIVERY.
REALLY?
I'VE JUST THOUGHT OF A CUNNING PLAN, WICKERSTEIN.
GO TELL JENNY BELLE THAT I EXPECT TO FIND HER IN MY BED IN TWENTY MINUTES' TIME. I'M SUDDENLY IN THE MOOD FOR ALL SORTS OF WORLDLY DELIGHTS.

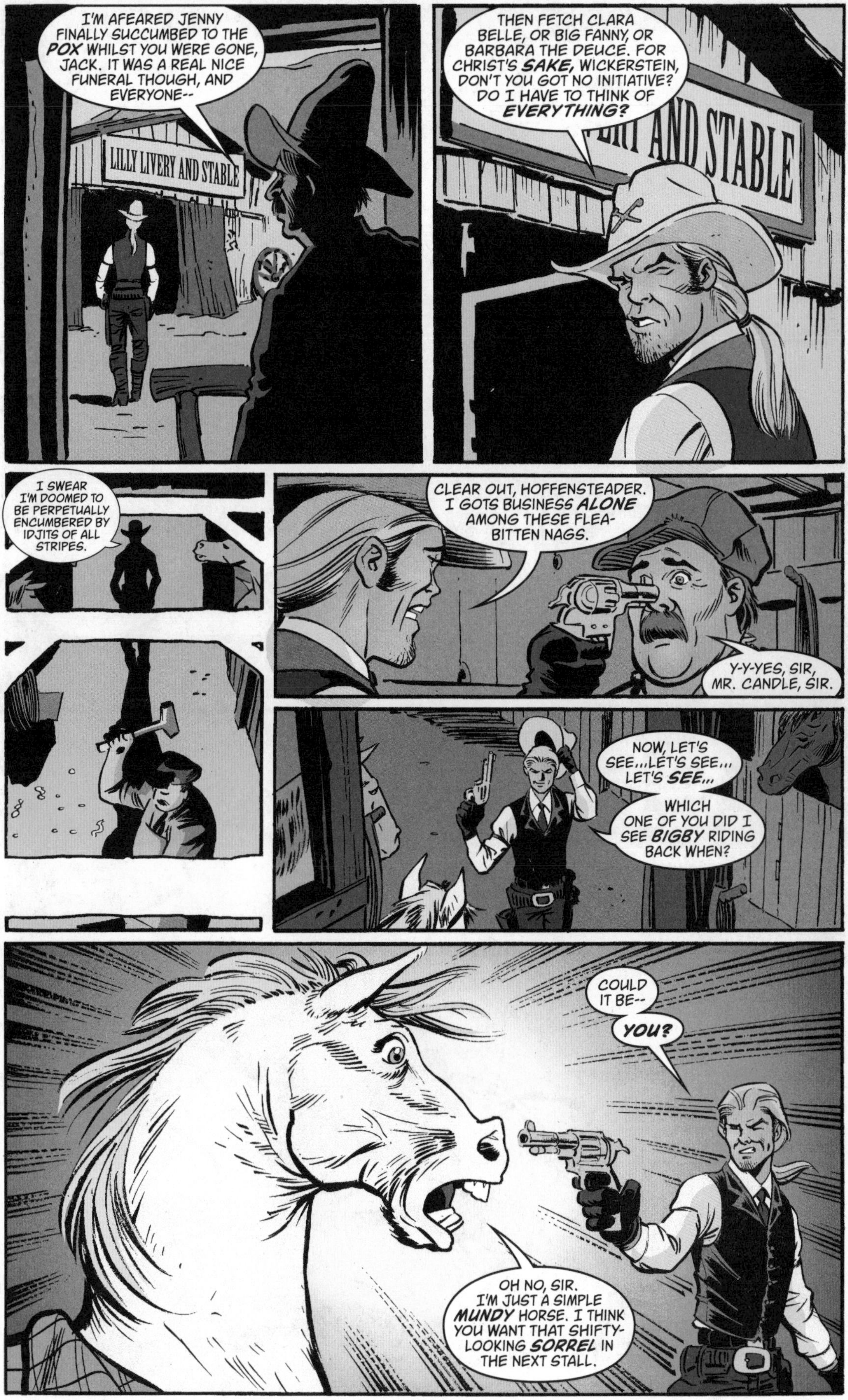
I'M AFEARED JENNY FINALLY SUCCUMBED TO THE POX WHILST YOU WERE GONE, JACK. IT WAS A REAL NICE FUNERAL THOUGH, AND EVERYONE--
LILLY LIVERY AND STABLE
THEN FETCH CLARA BELLE, OR BIG FANNY, OR BARBARA THE DEUCE. FOR CHRIST'S SAKE, WICKERSTEIN, DON'T YOU GOT NO INITIATIVE? DO I HAVE TO THINK OF EVERYTHING?
I SWEAR I'M DOOMED TO BE PERPETUALLY ENCUMBERED BY IDJITS OF ALL STRIPES.
CLEAR OUT, HOFFENSTEADER. I GOTS BUSINESS ALONE AMONG THESE FLEA-BITTEN NAGS.
Y-Y-YES, SIR, MR. CANDLE, SIR.
NOW, LET'S SEE...LET'S SEE... LET'S SEE...
WHICH ONE OF YOU DID I SEE BIGBY RIDING BACK WHEN?
COULD IT BE--
YOU?
OH NO, SIR. I'M JUST A SIMPLE MUNDY HORSE. I THINK YOU WANT THAT SHIFTY-LOOKING SORREL IN THE NEXT STALL.

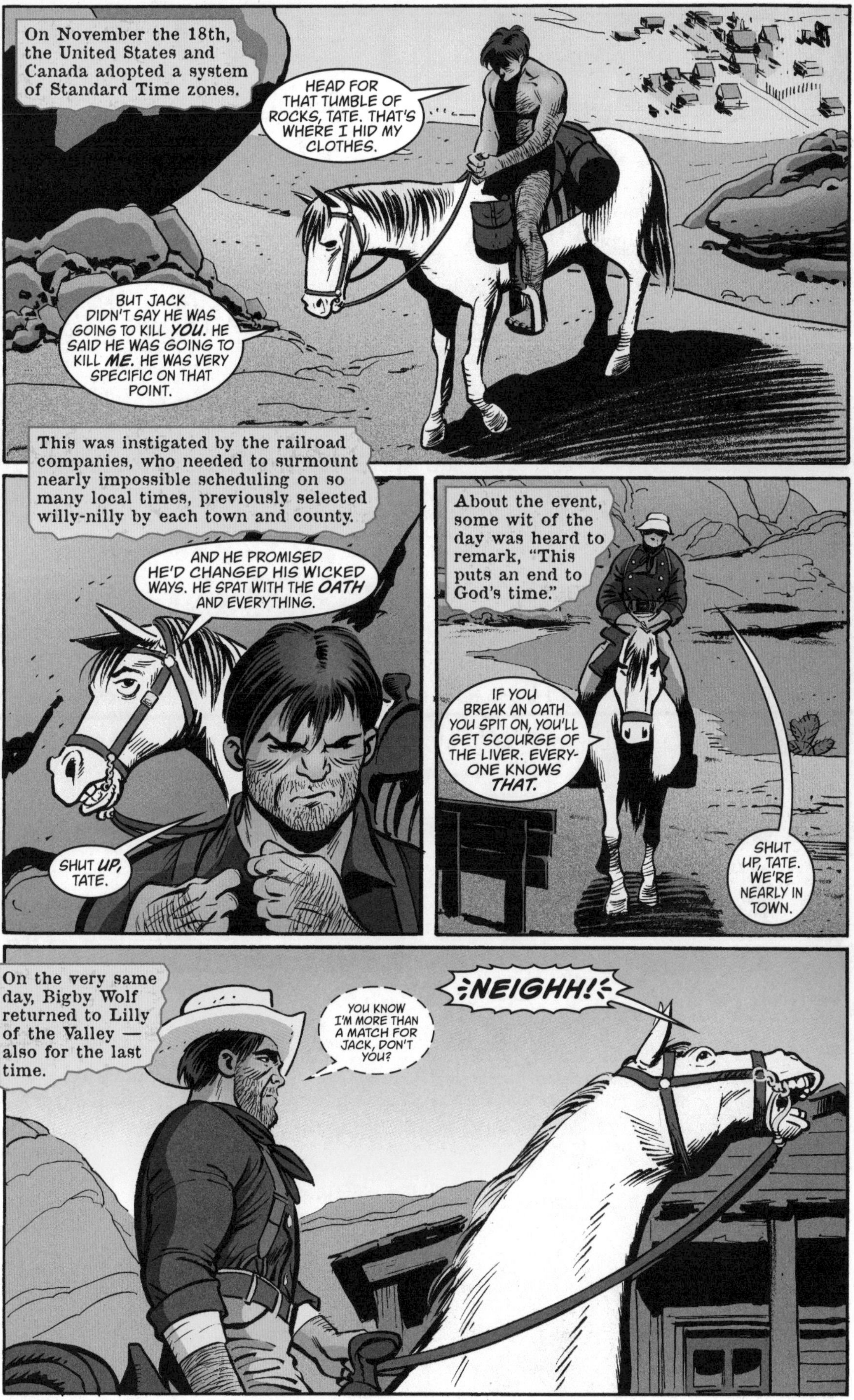

On November the 18th, the United States and Canada adopted a system of Standard Time zones.
HEAD FOR THAT TUMBLE OF ROCKS, TATE. THAT'S WHERE I HID MY CLOTHES.
BUT JACK DIDN'T SAY HE WAS GOING TO KILL YOU. HE SAID HE WAS GOING TO KILL ME. HE WAS VERY SPECIFIC ON THAT POINT.
This was instigated by the railroad companies, who needed to surmount nearly impossible scheduling on so many local times, previously selected willy-nilly by each town and county.
AND HE PROMISED HE'D CHANGED HIS WICKED WAYS. HE SPAT WITH THE OATH AND EVERYTHING.
SHUT UP, TATE.
About the event, some wit of the day was heard to remark, "This puts an end to God's time."
IF YOU BREAK AN OATH YOU SPIT ON, YOU'LL GET SCOURGE OF THE LIVER. EVERYONE KNOWS THAT.
SHUT UP, TATE. WE'RE NEARLY IN TOWN.
On the very same day, Bigby Wolf returned to Lilly of the Valley — also for the last time.
YOU KNOW I'M MORE THAN A MATCH FOR JACK, DON'T YOU?
NEIGHH!

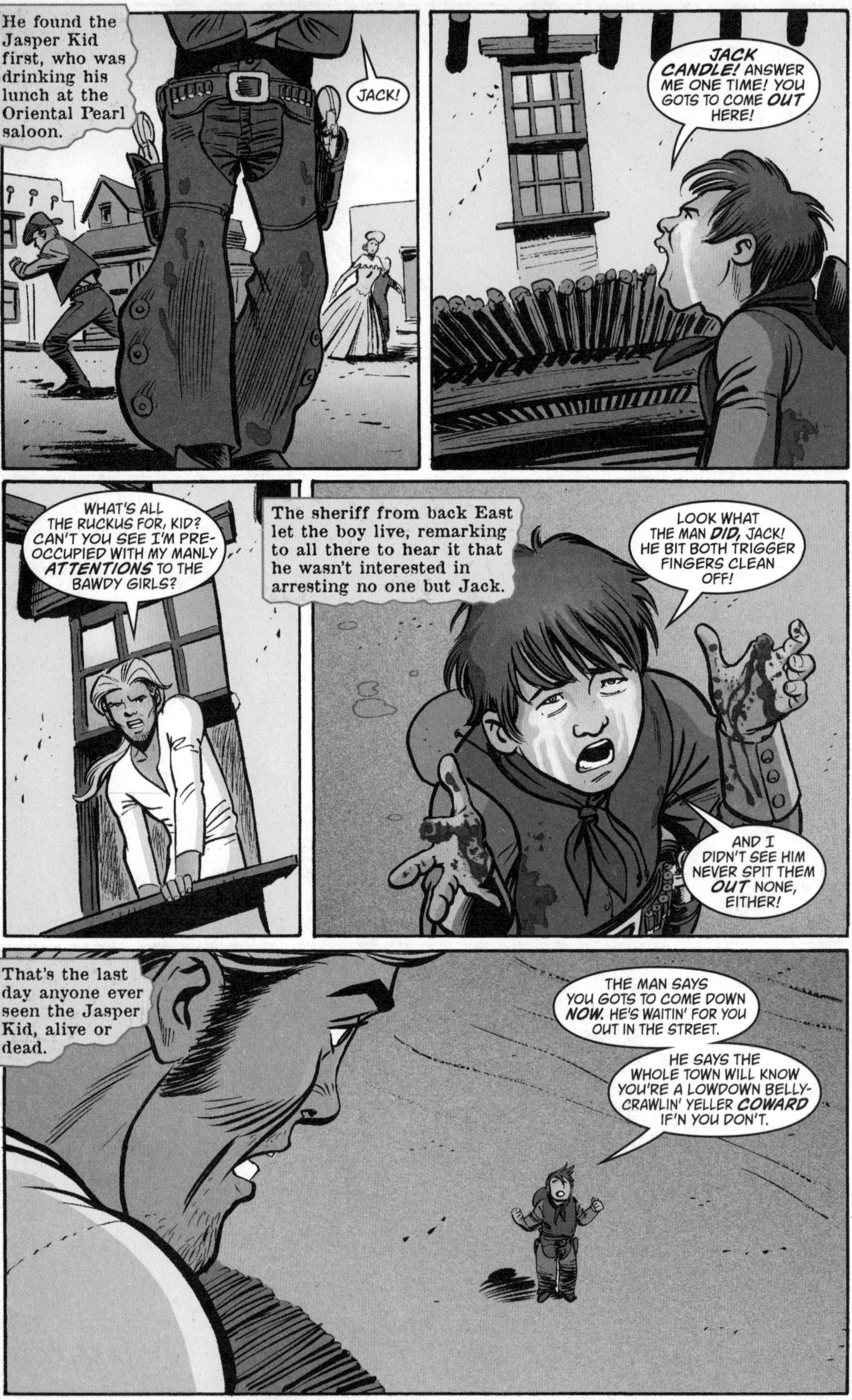
He found the Jasper Kid first, who was drinking his lunch at the Oriental Pearl saloon.
JACK!
JACK CANDLE! ANSWER ME ONE TIME! YOU GOTS TO COME OUT HERE!
WHAT'S ALL THE RUCKUS FOR, KID? CAN'T YOU SEE I'M PRE-OCCUPIED WITH MY MANLY ATTENTIONS TO THE BAWDY GIRLS?
The sheriff from back East let the boy live, remarking to all there to hear it that he wasn't interested in arresting no one but Jack.
LOOK WHAT THE MAN DID, JACK! HE BIT BOTH TRIGGER FINGERS CLEAN OFF!
AND I DIDN'T SEE HIM NEVER SPIT THEM OUT NONE, EITHER!
That's the last day anyone ever seen the Jasper Kid, alive or dead.
THE MAN SAYS YOU GOTS TO COME DOWN NOW. HE'S WAITIN' FOR YOU OUT IN THE STREET.
HE SAYS THE WHOLE TOWN WILL KNOW YOU'RE A LOWDOWN BELLY-CRAWLIN' YELLER COWARD IF'N YOU DON'T.

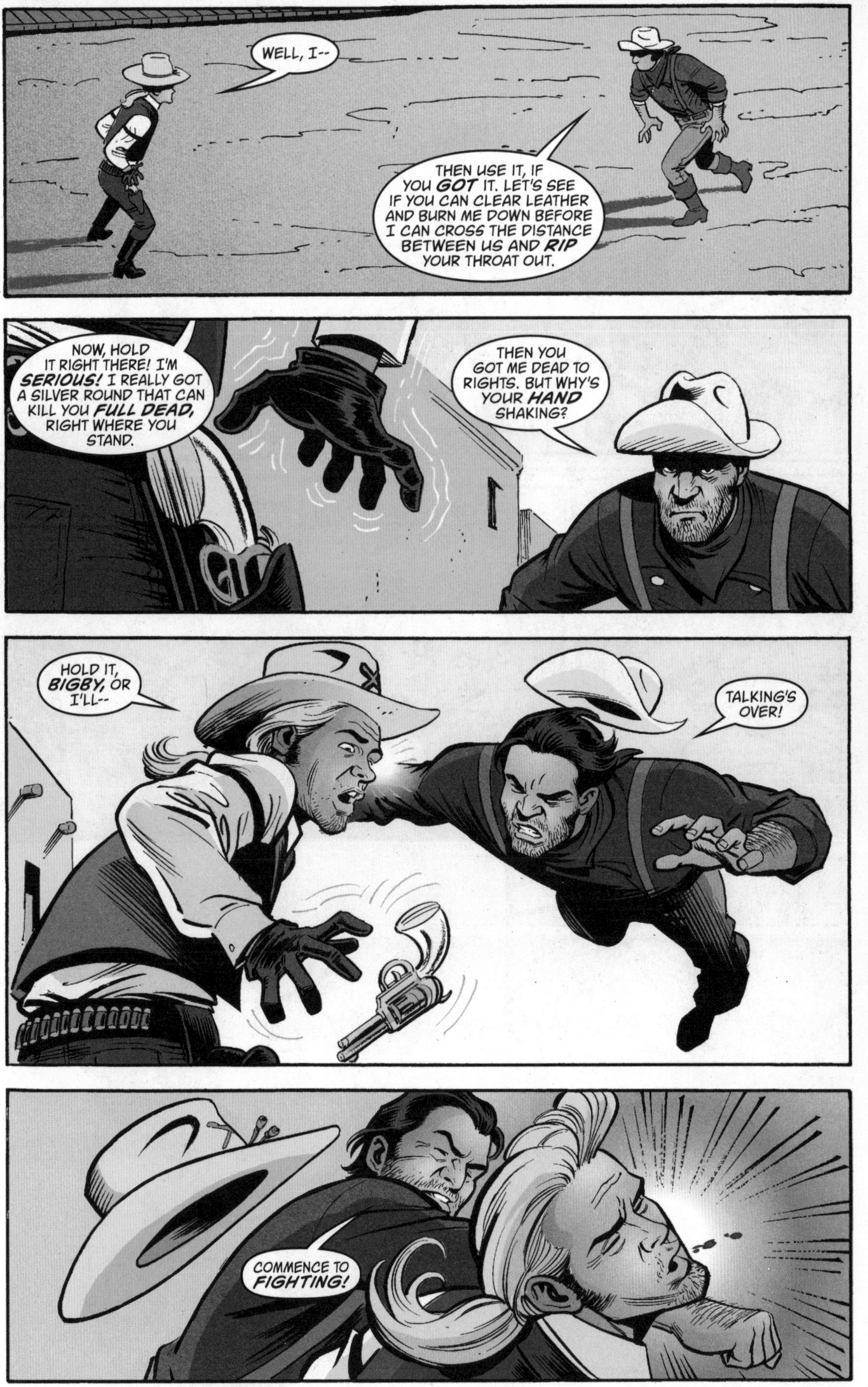
WELL, I--
THEN USE IT, IF YOU GOT IT. LET'S SEE IF YOU CAN CLEAR LEATHER AND BURN ME DOWN BEFORE I CAN CROSS THE DISTANCE BETWEEN US AND RIP YOUR THROAT OUT.
NOW, HOLD IT RIGHT THERE! I'M SERIOUS! I REALLY GOT A SILVER ROUND THAT CAN KILL YOU FULL DEAD, RIGHT WHERE YOU STAND.
THEN YOU GOT ME DEAD TO RIGHTS. BUT WHY'S YOUR HAND SHAKING?
HOLD IT, BIGBY, OR I'LL--
TALKING'S OVER!
COMMENCE TO FIGHTING!

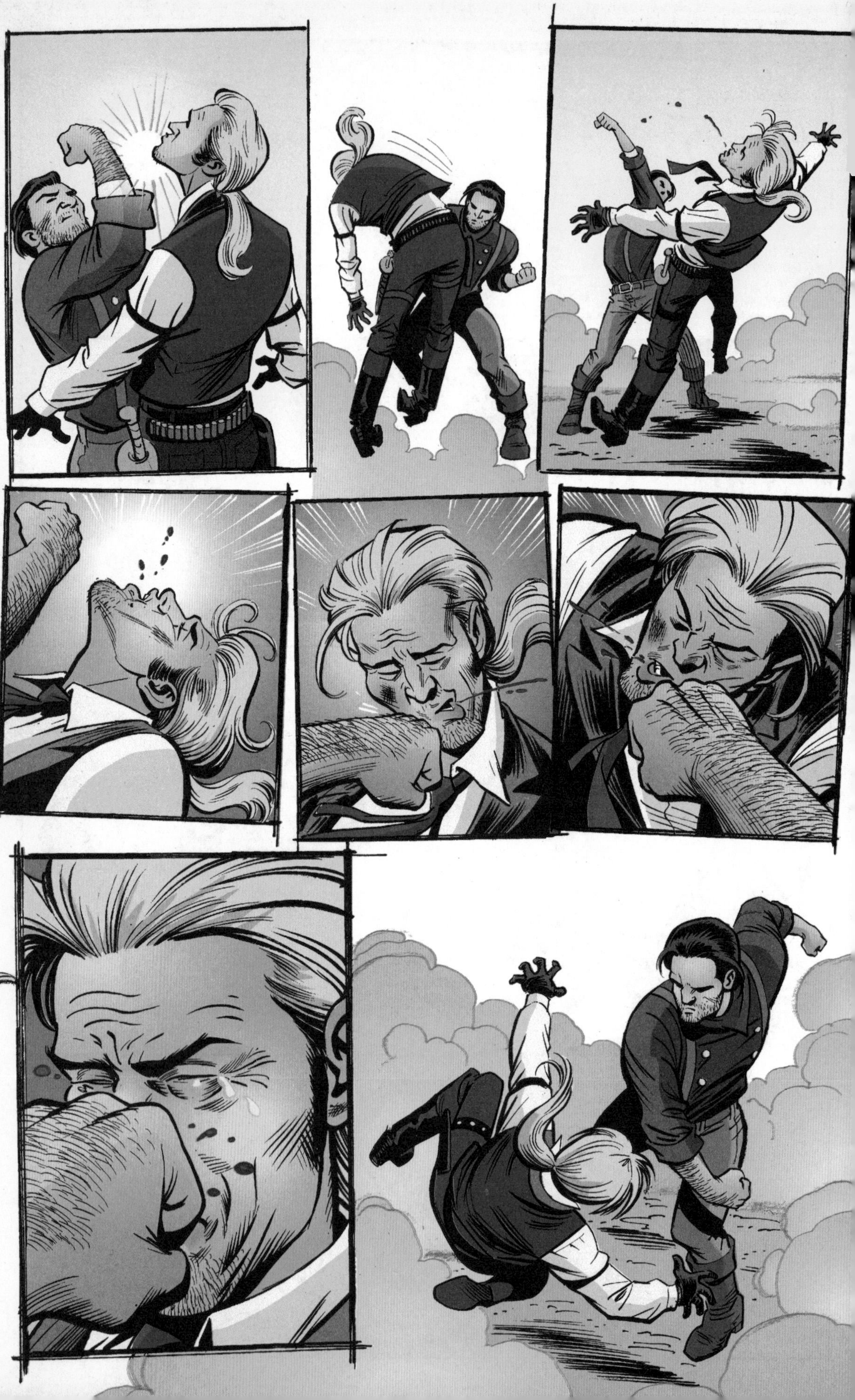

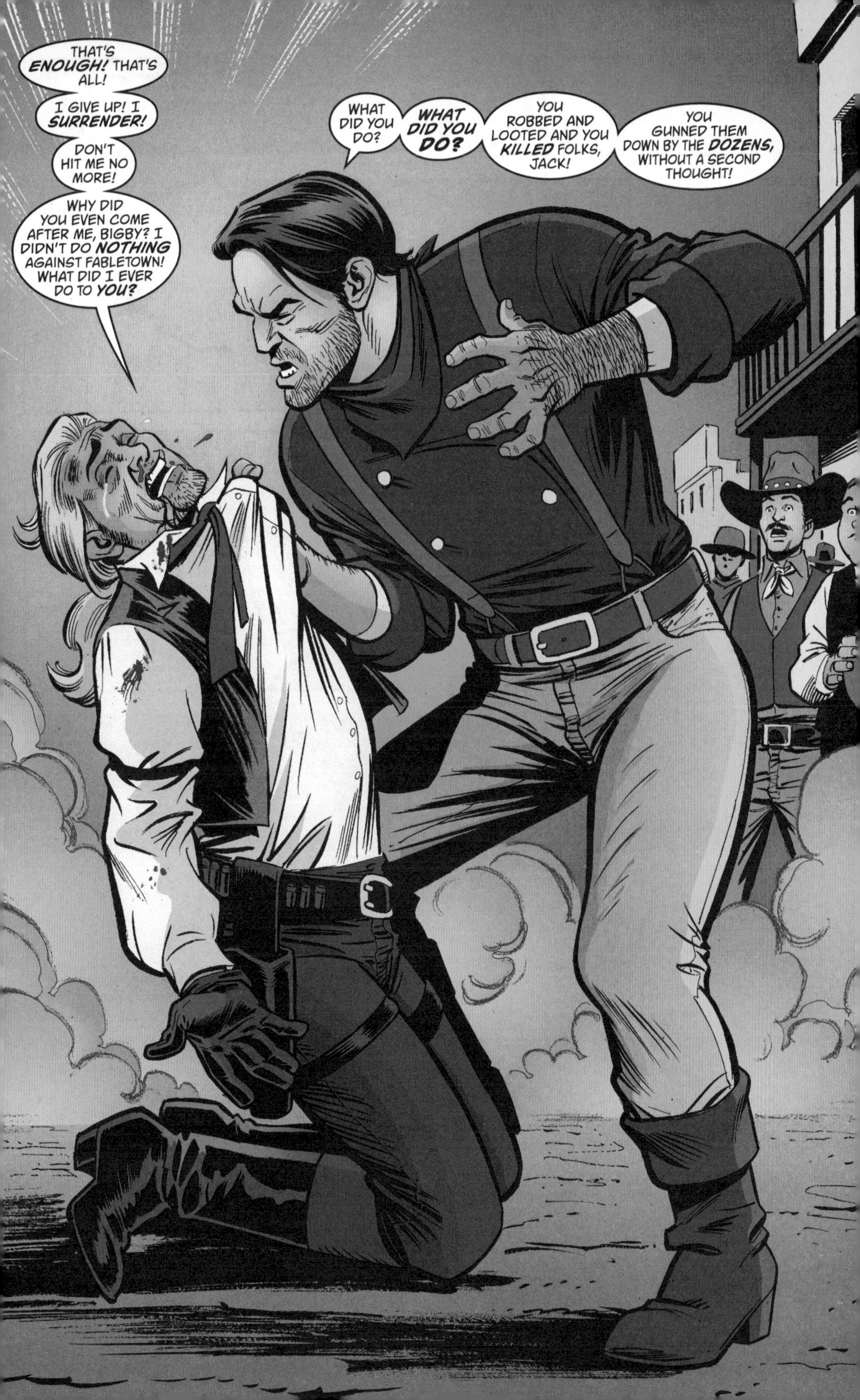
THAT'S ENOUGH! THAT'S ALL!
I GIVE UP! I SURRENDER!
DON'T HIT ME NO MORE!
WHY DID YOU EVEN COME AFTER ME, BIGBY? I DIDN'T DO NOTHING AGAINST FABLETOWN! WHAT DID I EVER DO TO YOU?
WHAT DID YOU DO?
WHAT DID YOU DO?
YOU ROBBED AND LOOTED AND YOU KILLED FOLKS, JACK!
YOU GUNNED THEM DOWN BY THE DOZENS, WITHOUT A SECOND THOUGHT!

70

In the winter of 1883, Teddy Roosevelt killed his first buffalo, Johannes Brahms premiered his Third Symphony in F, and two German fellows, Gottlieb Daimler and Wilhelm Maybach, developed a self-propelled bicycle — the world's first motorcycle.

And an unnamed sheriff from the East forever put an end to Jack Candle and his depredations across the Wild West.

--FIND YOU *GUILTY* OF ALL CHARGES AND SENTENCE YOU TO *FIFTY YEARS* OF HARD LABOR UP AT--

By Christmas Day, Jack Horner — he'd never again use the Candle name — was serving hard time as a plow horse in some unnamed location.

Jack didn't serve his full sentence. He escaped in little more than a year.

One traveling Fable claimed to have spotted him shortly thereafter in Morocco, a trading port in the north of Africa.

It's been remarked that Jack Horner and Bigby Wolf have been sore unpleased with each other ever since that tumultuous year of 1883.

NEXT: WE RETURN TO THE PRESENT DAY WITH A WHOLE NEW STORYLINE--"TURNING PAGES." IT GETS A LITTLE GIRLY IN PLACES, BUT THERE ARE ALSO SOME HALF-NAKED BROADS IN IT, SO THERE'S SOMETHING FOR EVERY-ONE. PLUS: WICKED JOHN IS TRANSPORTED TO MARS, WHERE HE MARRIES A GIANT GREEN HAMSTER-CREATURE.

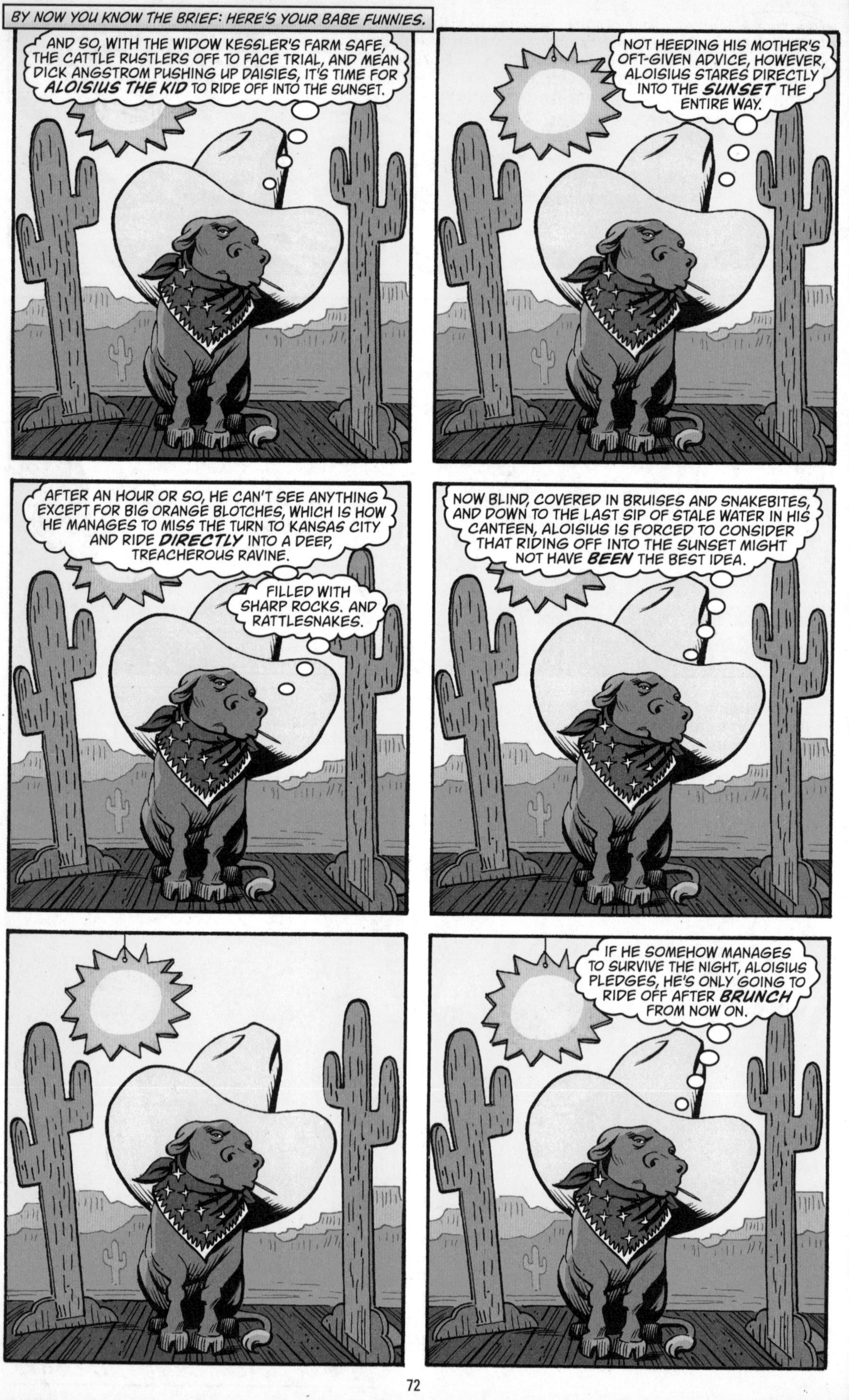
BY NOW YOU KNOW THE BRIEF: HERE'S YOUR BABE FUNNIES.
AND SO, WITH THE WIDOW KESSLER'S FARM SAFE, THE CATTLE RUSTLERS OFF TO FACE TRIAL, AND MEAN DICK ANGSTROM PUSHING UP DAISIES, IT'S TIME FOR ALOISIUS THE KID TO RIDE OFF INTO THE SUNSET.
NOT HEEDING HIS MOTHER'S OFT-GIVEN ADVICE, HOWEVER, ALOISIUS STARES DIRECTLY INTO THE SUNSET THE ENTIRE WAY.
AFTER AN HOUR OR SO, HE CAN'T SEE ANYTHING EXCEPT FOR BIG ORANGE BLOTCHES, WHICH IS HOW HE MANAGES TO MISS THE TURN TO KANSAS CITY AND RIDE DIRECTLY INTO A DEEP, TREACHEROUS RAVINE.
FILLED WITH SHARP ROCKS. AND RATTLESNAKES.
NOW BLIND, COVERED IN BRUISES AND SNAKEBITES, AND DOWN TO THE LAST SIP OF STALE WATER IN HIS CANTEEN, ALOISIUS IS FORCED TO CONSIDER THAT RIDING OFF INTO THE SUNSET MIGHT NOT HAVE BEEN THE BEST IDEA.
IF HE SOMEHOW MANAGES TO SURVIVE THE NIGHT, ALOISIUS PLEDGES, HE'S ONLY GOING TO RIDE OFF AFTER BRUNCH FROM NOW ON.

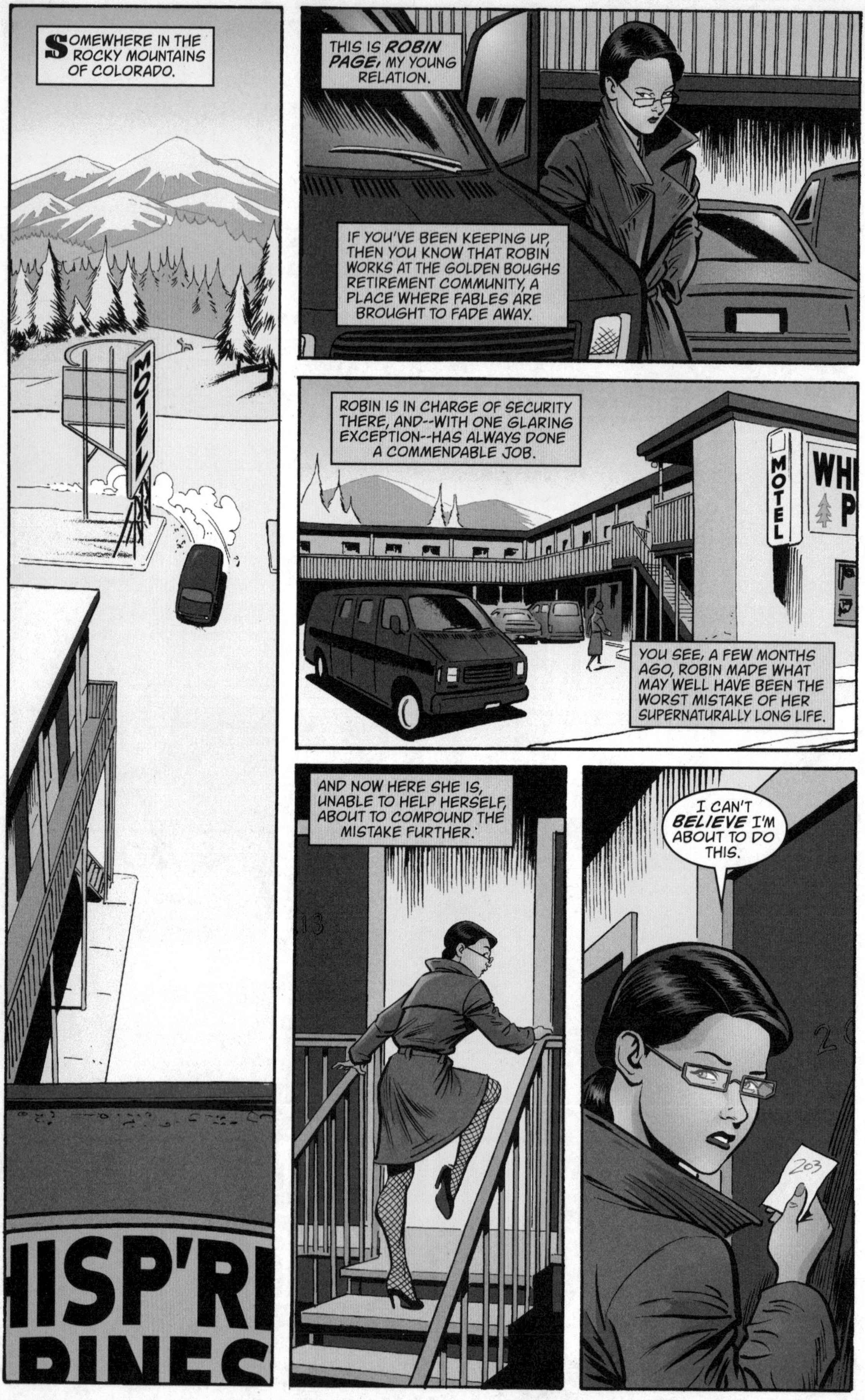
SOMEWHERE IN THE ROCKY MOUNTAINS OF COLORADO.
MOTEL
HISP'RI
PINES
THIS IS ROBIN PAGE, MY YOUNG RELATION.
IF YOU'VE BEEN KEEPING UP, THEN YOU KNOW THAT ROBIN WORKS AT THE GOLDEN BOUGHS RETIREMENT COMMUNITY, A PLACE WHERE FABLES ARE BROUGHT TO FADE AWAY.
ROBIN IS IN CHARGE OF SECURITY THERE, AND--WITH ONE GLARING EXCEPTION--HAS ALWAYS DONE A COMMENDABLE JOB.
MOTEL
YOU SEE, A FEW MONTHS AGO, ROBIN MADE WHAT MAY WELL HAVE BEEN THE WORST MISTAKE OF HER SUPERNATURALLY LONG LIFE.
AND NOW HERE SHE IS, UNABLE TO HELP HERSELF, ABOUT TO COMPOUND THE MISTAKE FURTHER.
I CAN'T BELIEVE I'M ABOUT TO DO THIS.
203

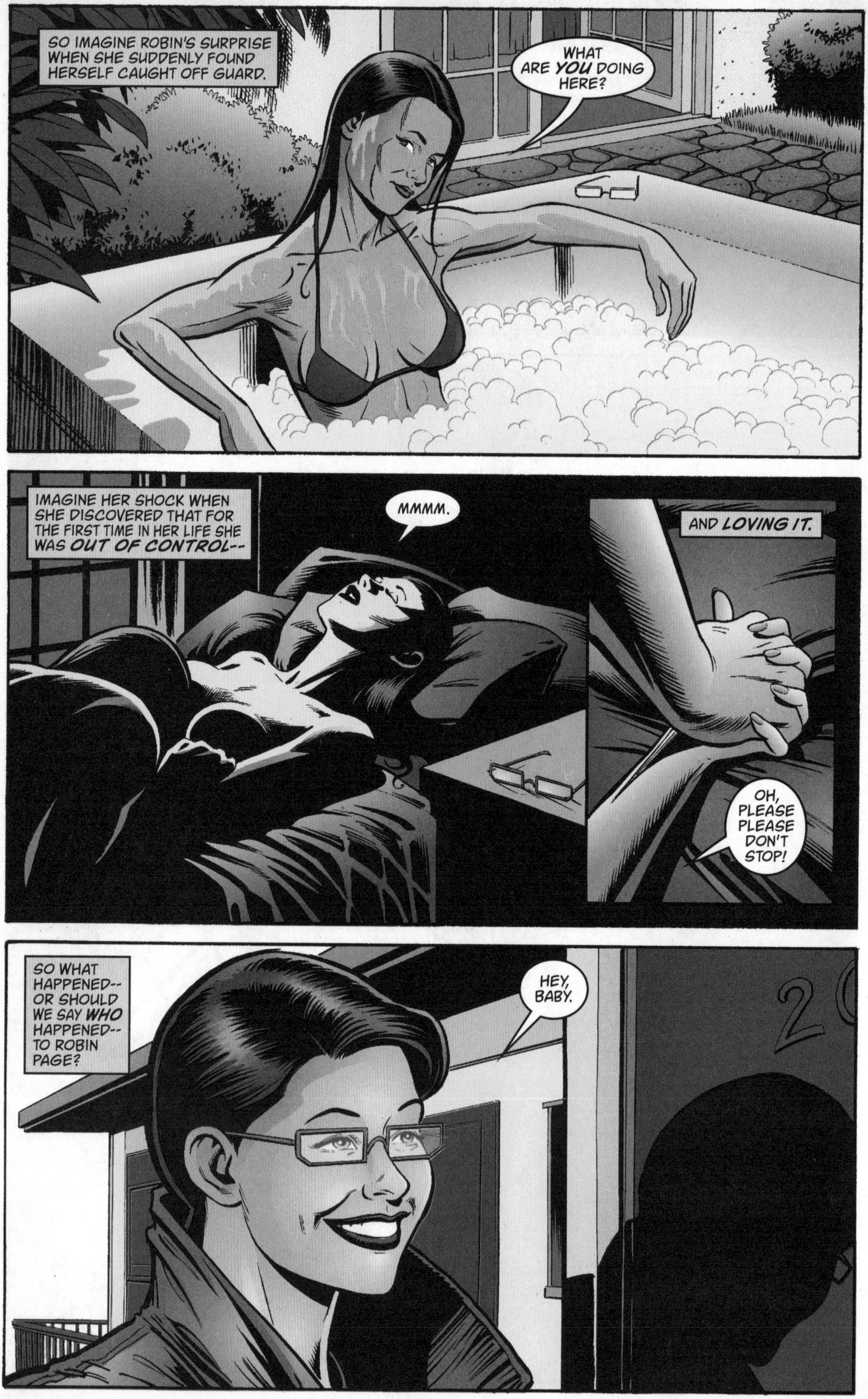

SO IMAGINE ROBIN'S SURPRISE WHEN SHE SUDDENLY FOUND HERSELF CAUGHT OFF GUARD.
WHAT ARE *YOU* DOING HERE?
IMAGINE HER SHOCK WHEN SHE DISCOVERED THAT FOR THE FIRST TIME IN HER LIFE SHE WAS ***OUT OF CONTROL***--
MMMM.
AND ***LOVING IT.***
OH, PLEASE PLEASE DON'T STOP!
SO WHAT HAPPENED-- OR SHOULD WE SAY ***WHO*** HAPPENED-- TO ROBIN PAGE?
HEY, BABY.

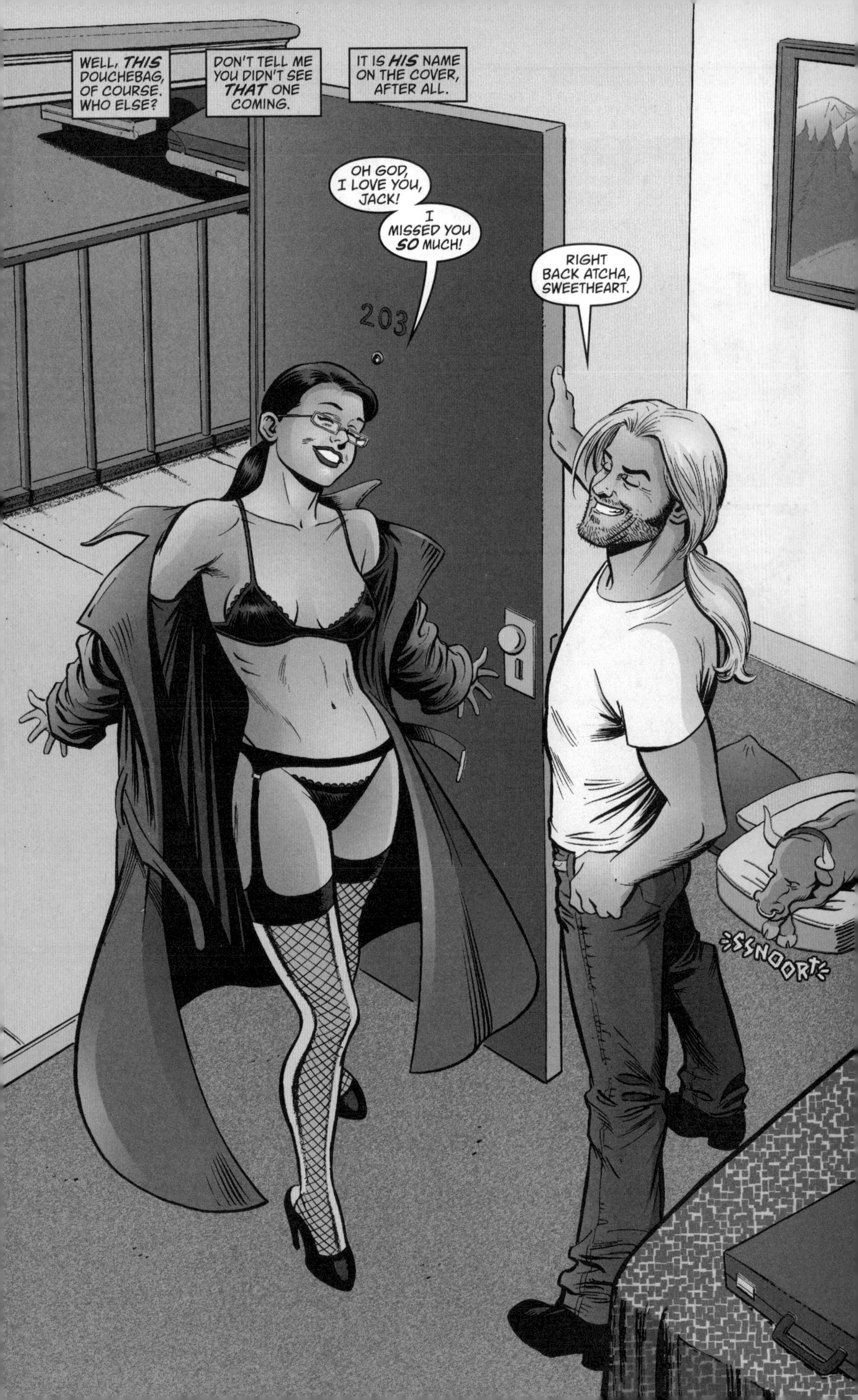
WELL, THIS DOUCHEBAG, OF COURSE. WHO ELSE?
DON'T TELL ME YOU DIDN'T SEE THAT ONE COMING.
IT IS HIS NAME ON THE COVER, AFTER ALL.
OH GOD, I LOVE YOU, JACK!
I MISSED YOU SO MUCH!
203
RIGHT BACK ATCHA, SWEETHEART.
SSNOORT

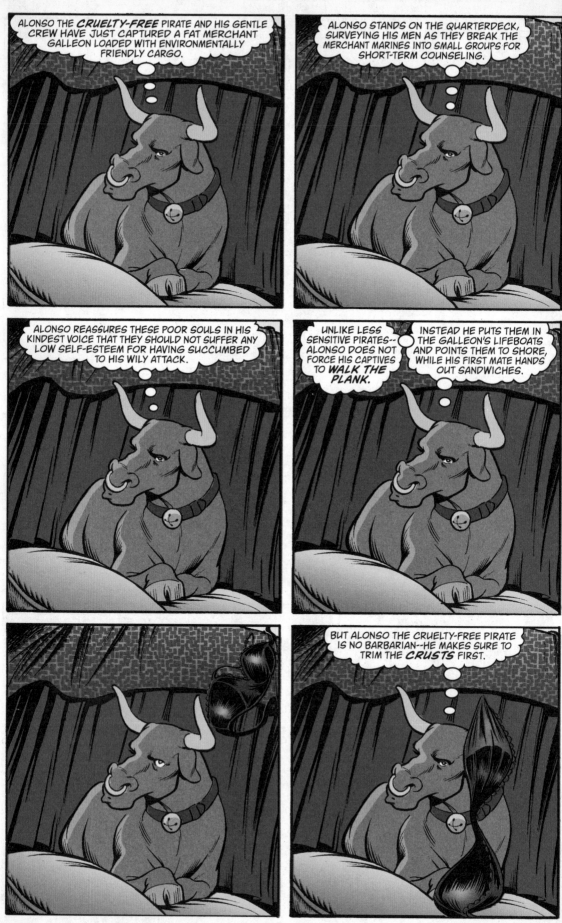

ALONSO THE *CRUELTY-FREE* PIRATE AND HIS GENTLE CREW HAVE JUST CAPTURED A FAT MERCHANT GALLEON LOADED WITH ENVIRONMENTALLY FRIENDLY CARGO.

ALONSO STANDS ON THE QUARTERDECK, SURVEYING HIS MEN AS THEY BREAK THE MERCHANT MARINES INTO SMALL GROUPS FOR SHORT-TERM COUNSELING.

ALONSO REASSURES THESE POOR SOULS IN HIS KINDEST VOICE THAT THEY SHOULD NOT SUFFER ANY LOW SELF-ESTEEM FOR HAVING SUCCUMBED TO HIS WILY ATTACK.

UNLIKE LESS SENSITIVE PIRATES-- ALONSO DOES NOT FORCE HIS CAPTIVES TO *WALK THE PLANK.*

INSTEAD HE PUTS THEM IN THE GALLEON'S LIFEBOATS AND POINTS THEM TO SHORE, WHILE HIS FIRST MATE HANDS OUT SANDWICHES.

BUT ALONSO THE CRUELTY-FREE PIRATE IS NO BARBARIAN--HE MAKES SURE TO TRIM THE *CRUSTS* FIRST.

AND MAKE SURE *ROBIN* IS NOTIFIED ABOUT THE NEW ARRIVAL.

...AND SHE WAS *REALLY* TRYING TO PUT ON A ONE-WOMAN SHOW ABOUT THE LIFE OF JUDY GARLAND?

YEP, AND THE *BEST* PART IS, SHE CAN'T EVEN SING.

ROBIN IS ON VACATION, MA'AM. IN THE MUNDY.

DON'T SUPPOSE YOU'VE HEARD FROM HILLARY?

HEAD LIBRARIAN

NOT A PEEP IN THREE MONTHS. AND DON'T SAY THAT *NAME* WITHIN A HUNDRED YARDS OF THIS OFFICE IF YOU LIKE YOUR JOB.

OKAY, LET'S SEE WHAT I'M GOING TO GET MY ASS RIPPED FOR *TODAY*.

PRISCILLA.

THE *SWEET* SMELL OF SUCCESS!

NOT BAD, EH?

MM.

HI, PRISCILLA.

HI, KEVIN.

80

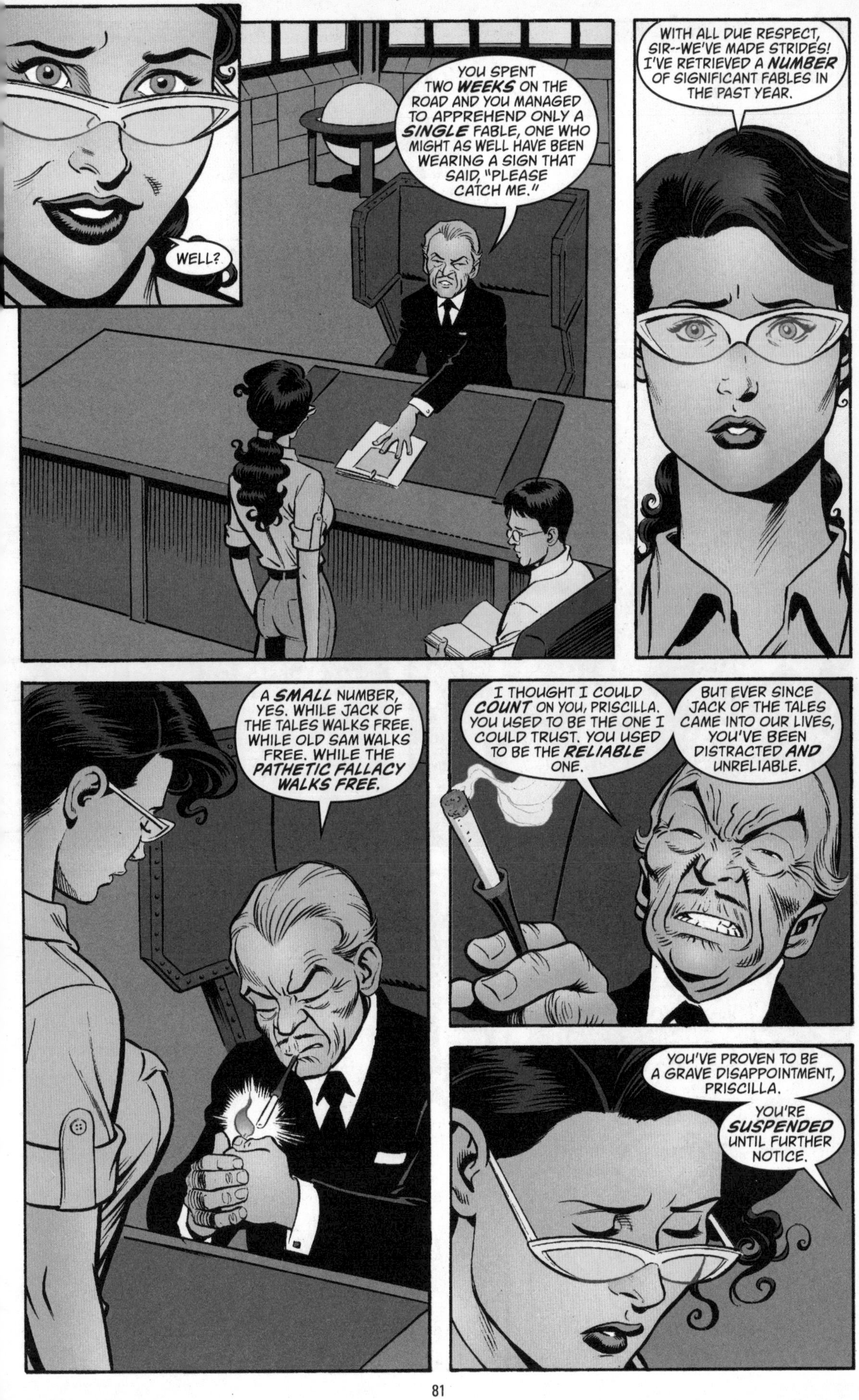

WELL?
YOU SPENT TWO WEEKS ON THE ROAD AND YOU MANAGED TO APPREHEND ONLY A SINGLE FABLE, ONE WHO MIGHT AS WELL HAVE BEEN WEARING A SIGN THAT SAID, "PLEASE CATCH ME."
WITH ALL DUE RESPECT, SIR--WE'VE MADE STRIDES! I'VE RETRIEVED A NUMBER OF SIGNIFICANT FABLES IN THE PAST YEAR.
A SMALL NUMBER, YES. WHILE JACK OF THE TALES WALKS FREE. WHILE OLD SAM WALKS FREE. WHILE THE PATHETIC FALLACY WALKS FREE.
I THOUGHT I COULD COUNT ON YOU, PRISCILLA. YOU USED TO BE THE ONE I COULD TRUST. YOU USED TO BE THE RELIABLE ONE.
BUT EVER SINCE JACK OF THE TALES CAME INTO OUR LIVES, YOU'VE BEEN DISTRACTED AND UNRELIABLE.
YOU'VE PROVEN TO BE A GRAVE DISAPPOINTMENT, PRISCILLA.
YOU'RE SUSPENDED UNTIL FURTHER NOTICE.

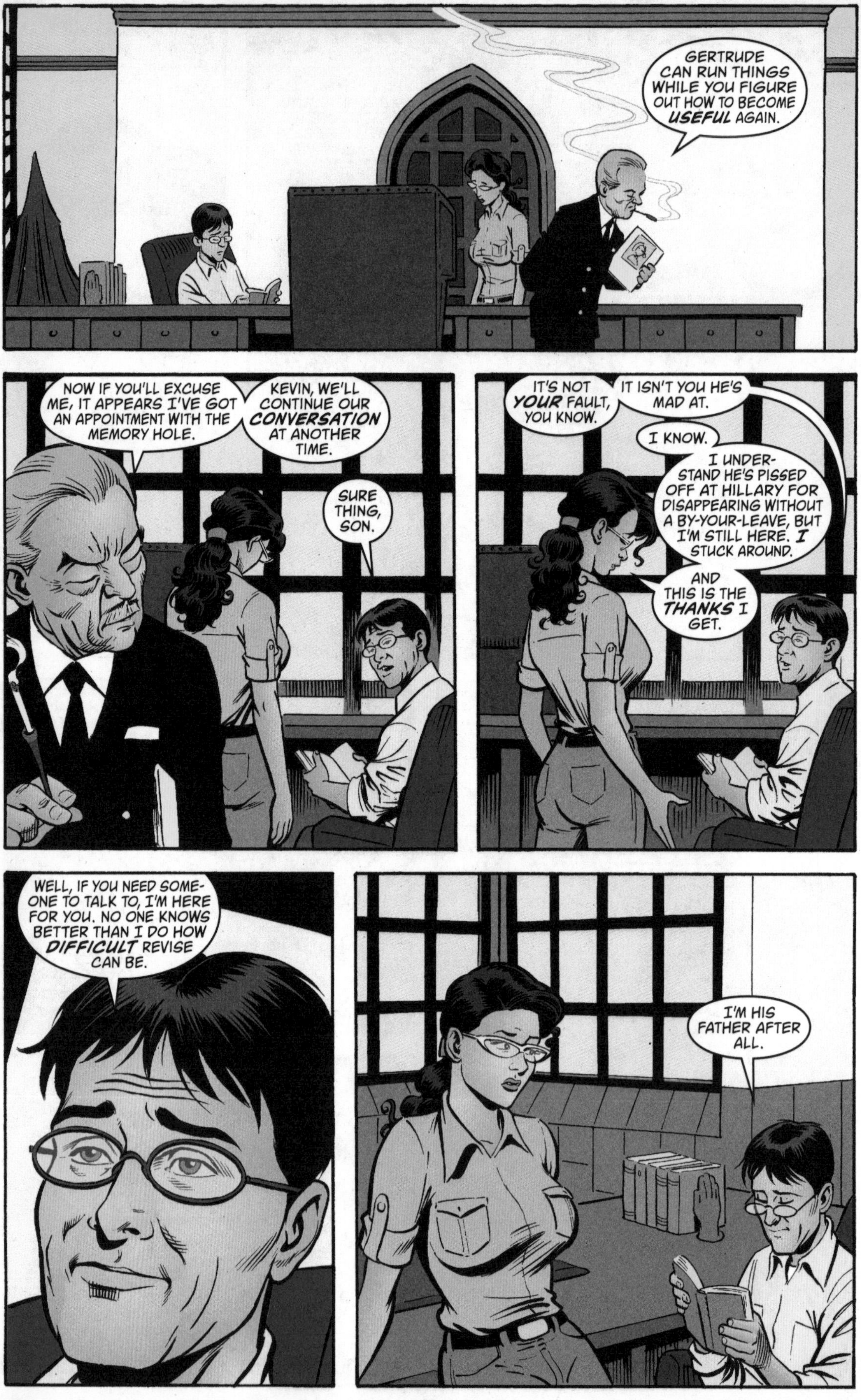
GERTRUDE CAN RUN THINGS WHILE YOU FIGURE OUT HOW TO BECOME USEFUL AGAIN.
NOW IF YOU'LL EXCUSE ME, IT APPEARS I'VE GOT AN APPOINTMENT WITH THE MEMORY HOLE.
KEVIN, WE'LL CONTINUE OUR CONVERSATION AT ANOTHER TIME.
SURE THING, SON.
IT'S NOT YOUR FAULT, YOU KNOW.
IT ISN'T YOU HE'S MAD AT.
I KNOW.
I UNDERSTAND HE'S PISSED OFF AT HILLARY FOR DISAPPEARING WITHOUT A BY-YOUR-LEAVE, BUT I'M STILL HERE. I STUCK AROUND.
AND THIS IS THE THANKS I GET.
WELL, IF YOU NEED SOMEONE TO TALK TO, I'M HERE FOR YOU. NO ONE KNOWS BETTER THAN I DO HOW DIFFICULT REVISE CAN BE.
I'M HIS FATHER AFTER ALL.

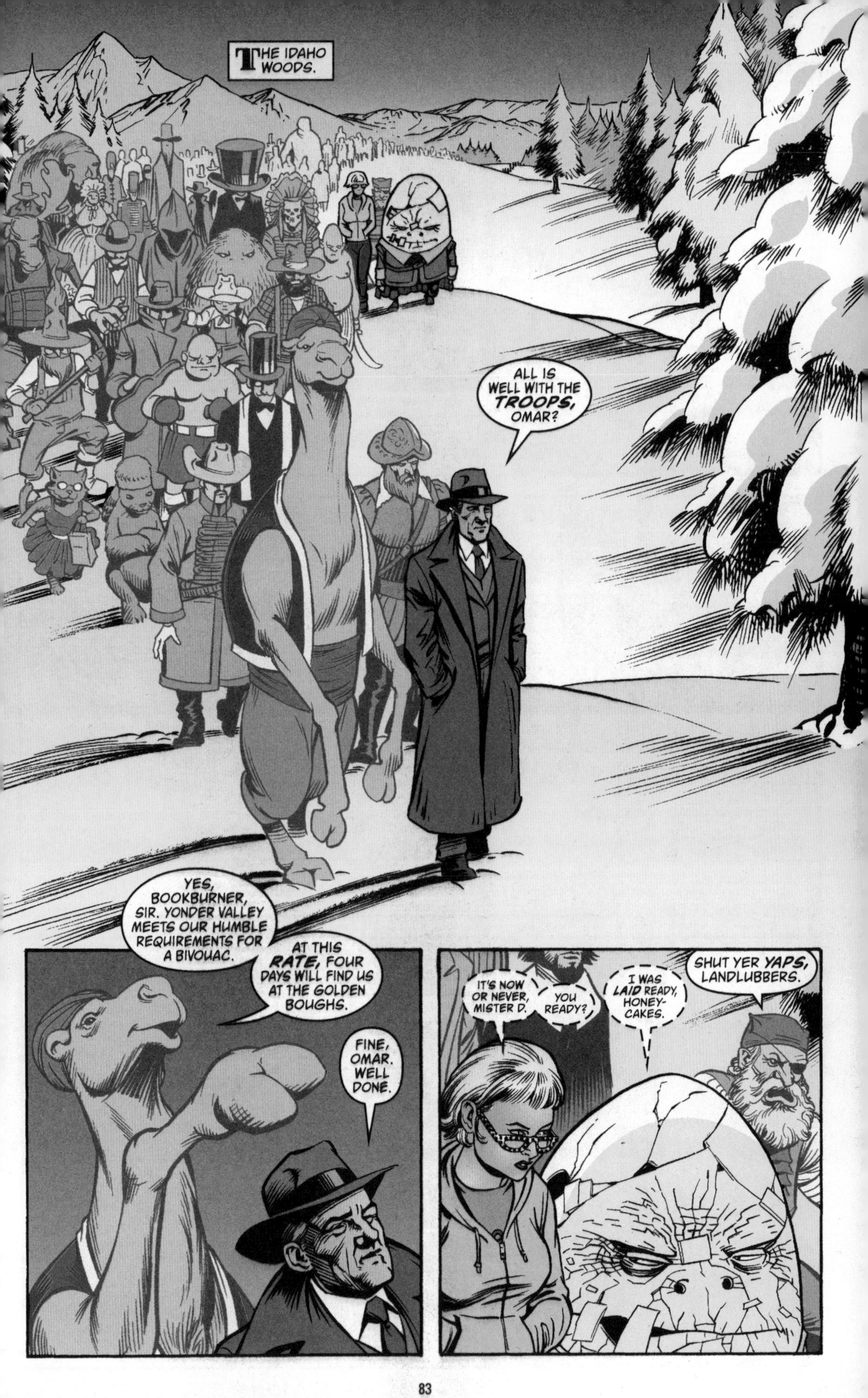
THE IDAHO WOODS.
ALL IS WELL WITH THE TROOPS, OMAR?
YES, BOOKBURNER, SIR. YONDER VALLEY MEETS OUR HUMBLE REQUIREMENTS FOR A BIVOUAC.
AT THIS RATE, FOUR DAYS WILL FIND US AT THE GOLDEN BOUGHS.
FINE, OMAR. WELL DONE.
IT'S NOW OR NEVER, MISTER D.
YOU READY?
I WAS LAID READY, HONEY-CAKES.
SHUT YER YAPS, LANDLUBBERS.

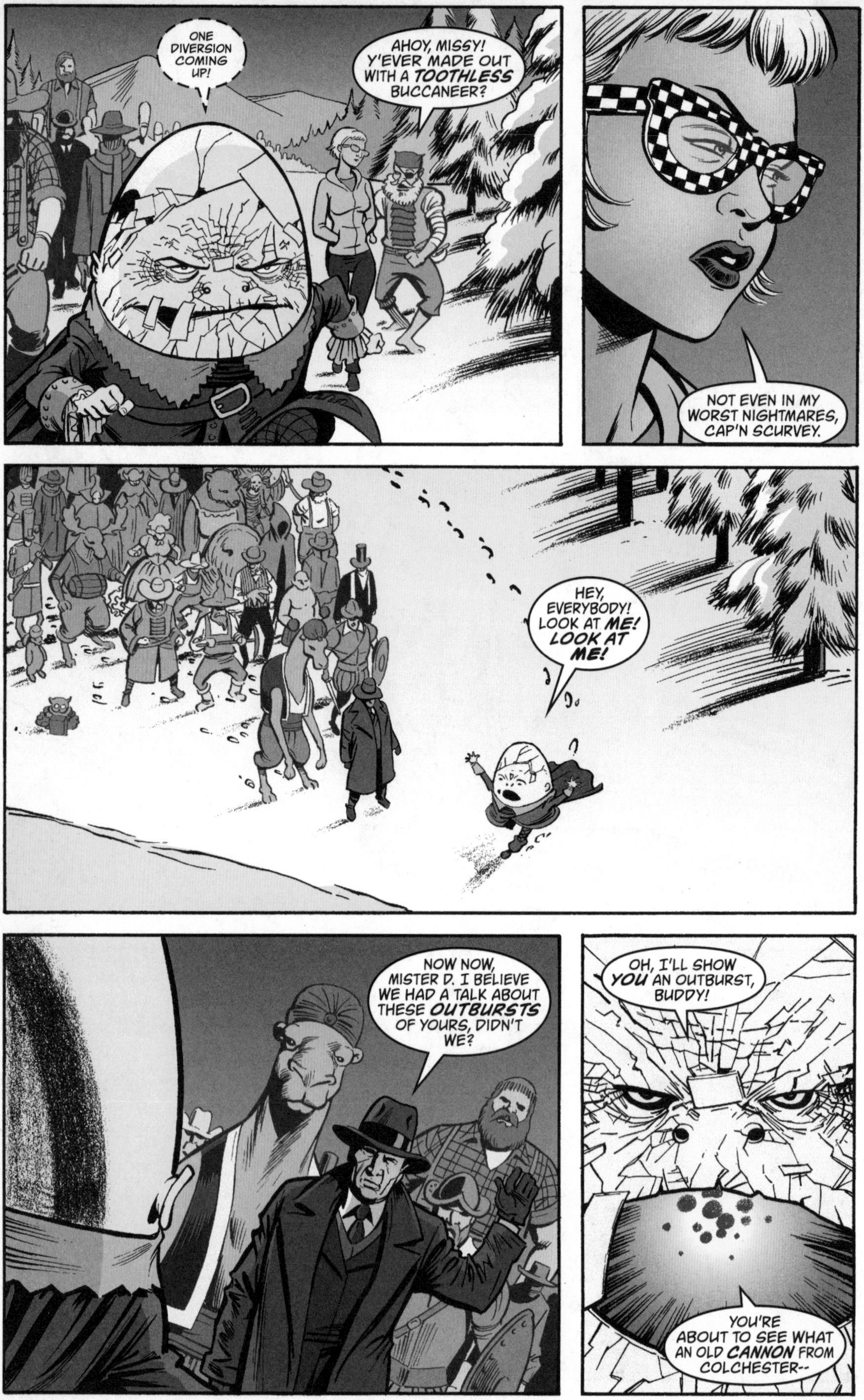
ONE DIVERSION COMING UP!
AHOY, MISSY! Y'EVER MADE OUT WITH A TOOTHLESS BUCCANEER?
NOT EVEN IN MY WORST NIGHTMARES, CAP'N SCURVEY.
HEY, EVERYBODY! LOOK AT ME! LOOK AT ME!
NOW NOW, MISTER D. I BELIEVE WE HAD A TALK ABOUT THESE OUTBURSTS OF YOURS, DIDN'T WE?
OH, I'LL SHOW YOU AN OUTBURST, BUDDY!
YOU'RE ABOUT TO SEE WHAT AN OLD CANNON FROM COLCHESTER--

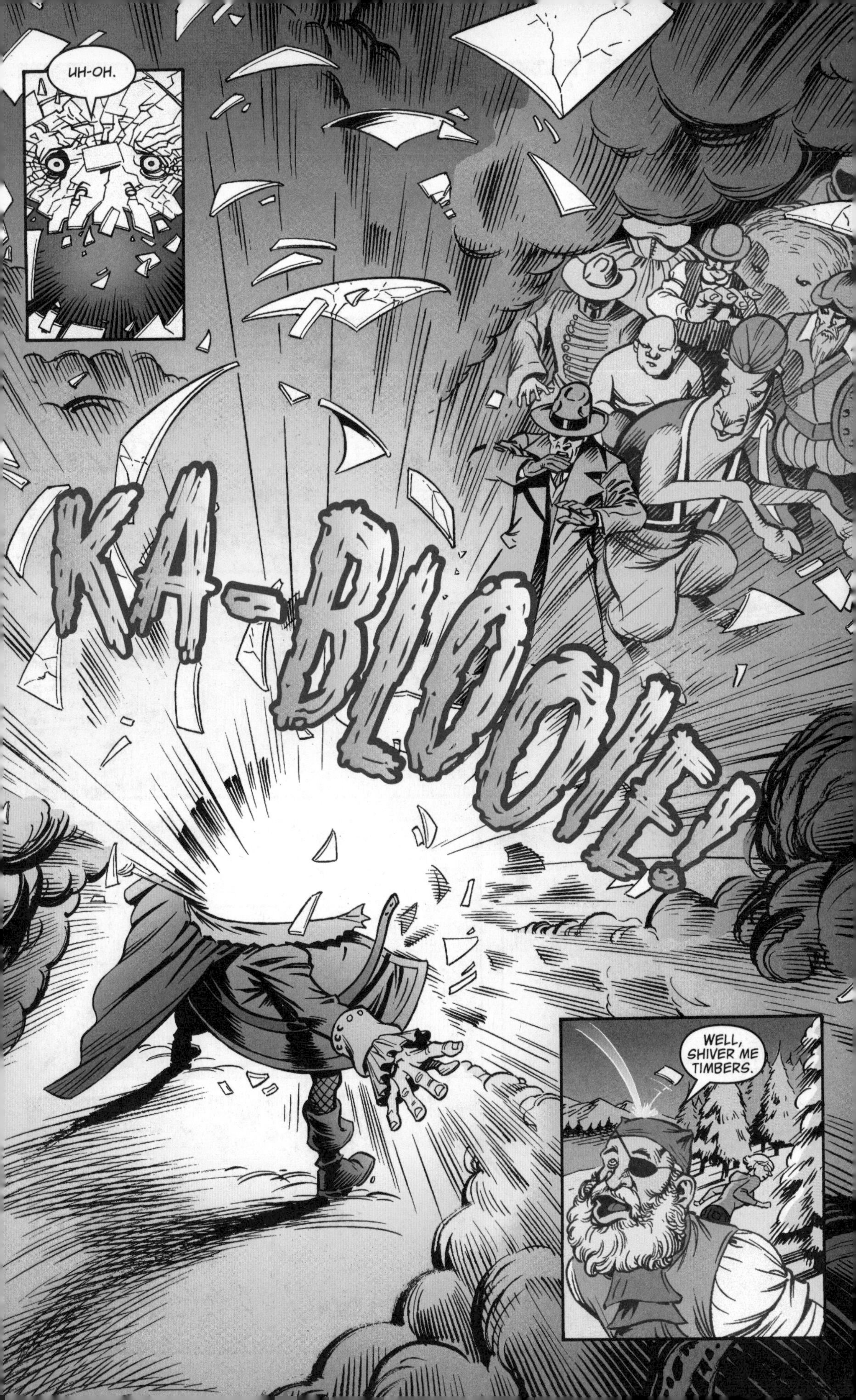
UH-OH.
KA-BLOOIE!!
WELL, SHIVER ME TIMBERS.

OH, NOW WHERE WAS I?

YOU'LL HAVE TO PARDON ME--I'M NOT MUCH OF A NARRATOR. LIKE I SAID, I'M USUALLY SOMEONE WHO TRIES TO GO UN-NOTICED AS MUCH AS POSSIBLE.

GASSUP GASSUP

AND AFTER ALL, WE'RE NOT HERE TO TALK ABOUT ME. WE'RE HERE TO TALK ABOUT ROBIN.

I NEED TO MAKE A COLLECT CALL, PLEASE!

HEH. GUESS I MISFIRED.

OMAR, I WANT EVERY LAST PIECE OF THIS DAMNED EGG PICKED UP IN TWENTY MINUTES, DO YOU HEAR ME?

I'LL PUT THE CROWS AND THE MICE ON IT, SIR.

UM, ER, EXCUSE ME, YER HONOR, BUT...

CAP'N SCURVEY!

WHERE IS HILLARY PAGE?!

AND JACK, OF COURSE. IF WE MUST.

86

JACK HORNER, AS YOU KNOW, IS SOMETHING OF A CAD.

AND THEN WITH *NO PROVOCATION WHATSOEVER*, HILLARY AND THE EGG TRIED TO ROB ME BLIND.

AND SHE TRIED TO *KILL* ME, TOO! FOR NO REASON!

A LIAR, TOO. BUT--AS IS OFTEN THE WAY WITH MEN LIKE HIM--INEXPLICABLY GOOD WITH WOMEN.

OH, THAT *LITTLE BRAT!*

HILLARY ALWAYS *WAS* A PROBLEM CHILD.

AND SO WHAT NOW, BABY? IS IT TIME TO RUN OFF TO THE BAHAMAS AND SPEND *ALL* THAT DIRTY MONEY?

JUST SOMETHING ABOUT BAD BOYS, I SUPPOSE.

WHA-- *SPEND?* OH, HELL *NO*, WOMAN!

OH, GREAT SPIRIT. HERE WE GO *AGAIN.*

LISTEN, SWEETHEART. EVERY SINGLE TIME I'VE COME INTO MONEY, SOMETHING'S ALWAYS GONE WRONG.

AND I'VE *FINALLY* FIGURED OUT WHAT IT IS.

89

YES, A GIRL IN LOVE WILL DO MANY THINGS SHE OUGHTN'T.

JACK, YOU DON'T UNDERSTAND. BOOKBURNER IS A *MONSTER!* REVISE USED TO TELL US STORIES ABOUT BOOKBURNER TO SCARE US AS KIDS.

NO, BABE-- *YOU* DON'T UNDERSTAND. THERE'S STILL SOME SANDWICH ON THAT PLATE!

SHE'LL PUT UP WITH ALL SORTS OF NONSENSE FROM HER *BELOVED.*

BY THE WAY, ROBIN, CAN YOU GET THIS ONE? I LEFT MY WALLET BACK AT THE MOTEL.

SHE'LL EVEN RUN AWAY FROM HOME TO BE WITH HIM.

LISTEN!

IF BOOK-BURNER GETS TO THE GOLDEN BOUGHS, HE WON'T JUST KILL REVISE AND ALL OF THE FABLES LIVING THERE.

BUT ROBIN PAGE HAS BEEN IN SECURITY A LOT LONGER THAN SHE'S BEEN IN LOVE.

IF HE GETS HOLD OF REVISE'S LIBRARY, HE'LL KILL *ALL* OF YOU. EVERY FABLE *EVERYWHERE.*

THAT'S WHAT HE WANTS. THAT'S *ALL* HE WANTS.

THIS COULD WORK OUT.

PRISCILLA AND ROBIN WERE BORN ON THE SAME DAY, ONLY *MINUTES* APART. GROWING UP, THEY WERE BOTH HEADSTRONG, CLEVER, AND RESOURCEFUL.

IT WAS *HER* IDEA!

UNFORTUNATELY FOR PRIS, THAT'S WHERE THE SIMILARITIES ENDED.

WHY, PRISCILLA! I'M *MOST* DISAPPOINTED!

HELLO...?

ME?

WHERE ROBIN WAS CONFIDENT AND POPULAR, PRIS NEVER *QUITE* FIT IN, AND FOR MOST OF HER YOUTH, THAT WAS FINE BY HER.

WHEN I GROW UP, I'M GOING TO BE THE *HEAD* OF SECURITY, AND I'M GOING TO HAVE A DOZEN TIGERS TO REND THE FABLES LIMB FROM *LIMB!* WHAT ABOUT YOU?

I WANT TO BE A MARINE BIOLOGIST AND STUDY NARWHALS. I MIGHT *MARRY* A NARWHAL.

ALL HER LIFE, SHE HAD BEEN TOLD THAT IF SHE WOULD JUST "BE HERSELF" THAT SHE'D DO JUST FINE IN LIFE.

HEY, RONNIE! YOU'RE SUPPOSED TO BE *MY* DATE, REMEMBER?

BUT AS THE YEARS WENT BY, PRISCILLA BEGAN TO SUSPECT THAT THIS ADVICE WAS BULLSHIT.

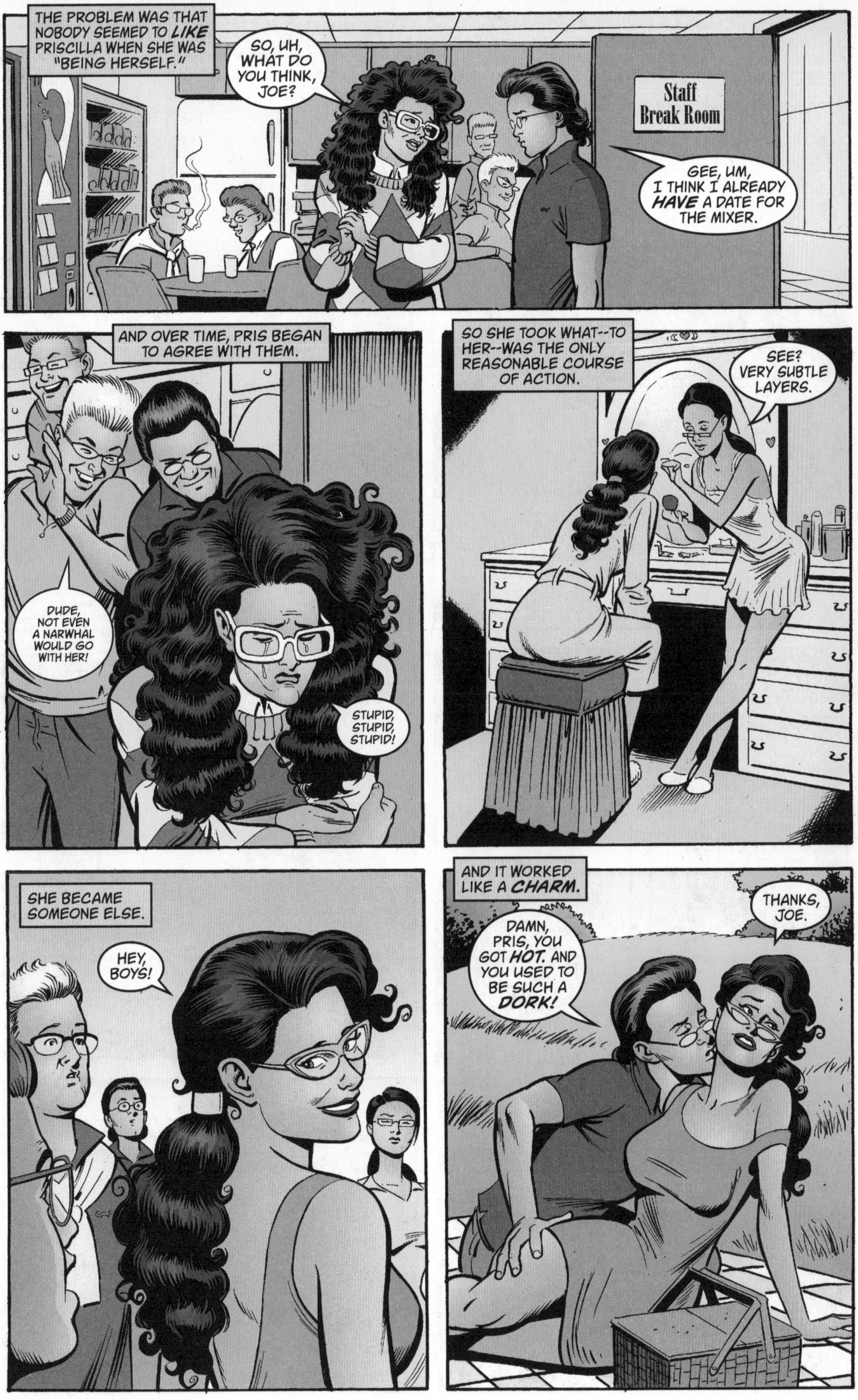
THE PROBLEM WAS THAT NOBODY SEEMED TO LIKE PRISCILLA WHEN SHE WAS "BEING HERSELF."
SO, UH, WHAT DO YOU THINK, JOE?
Staff Break Room
GEE, UM, I THINK I ALREADY HAVE A DATE FOR THE MIXER.
AND OVER TIME, PRIS BEGAN TO AGREE WITH THEM.
DUDE, NOT EVEN A NARWHAL WOULD GO WITH HER!
STUPID, STUPID, STUPID!
SO SHE TOOK WHAT--TO HER--WAS THE ONLY REASONABLE COURSE OF ACTION.
SEE? VERY SUBTLE LAYERS.
SHE BECAME SOMEONE ELSE.
HEY, BOYS!
AND IT WORKED LIKE A CHARM.
DAMN, PRIS, YOU GOT HOT. AND YOU USED TO BE SUCH A DORK!
THANKS, JOE.

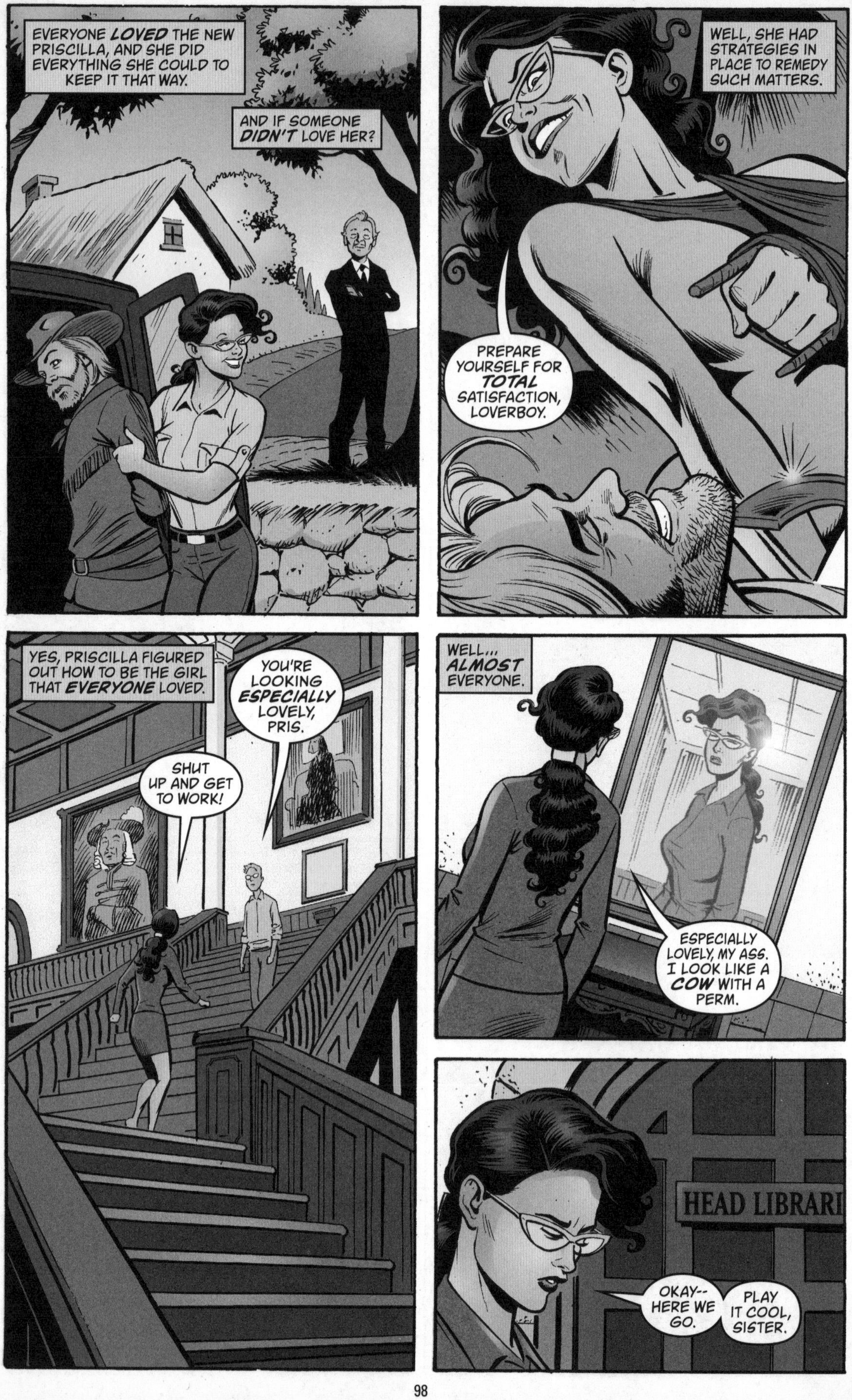

EVERYONE LOVED THE NEW PRISCILLA, AND SHE DID EVERYTHING SHE COULD TO KEEP IT THAT WAY.
AND IF SOMEONE DIDN'T LOVE HER?
WELL, SHE HAD STRATEGIES IN PLACE TO REMEDY SUCH MATTERS.
PREPARE YOURSELF FOR TOTAL SATISFACTION, LOVERBOY.
YES, PRISCILLA FIGURED OUT HOW TO BE THE GIRL THAT EVERYONE LOVED.
YOU'RE LOOKING ESPECIALLY LOVELY, PRIS.
SHUT UP AND GET TO WORK!
WELL... ALMOST EVERYONE.
ESPECIALLY LOVELY, MY ASS. I LOOK LIKE A COW WITH A PERM.
HEAD LIBRARI
OKAY-- HERE WE GO.
PLAY IT COOL, SISTER.

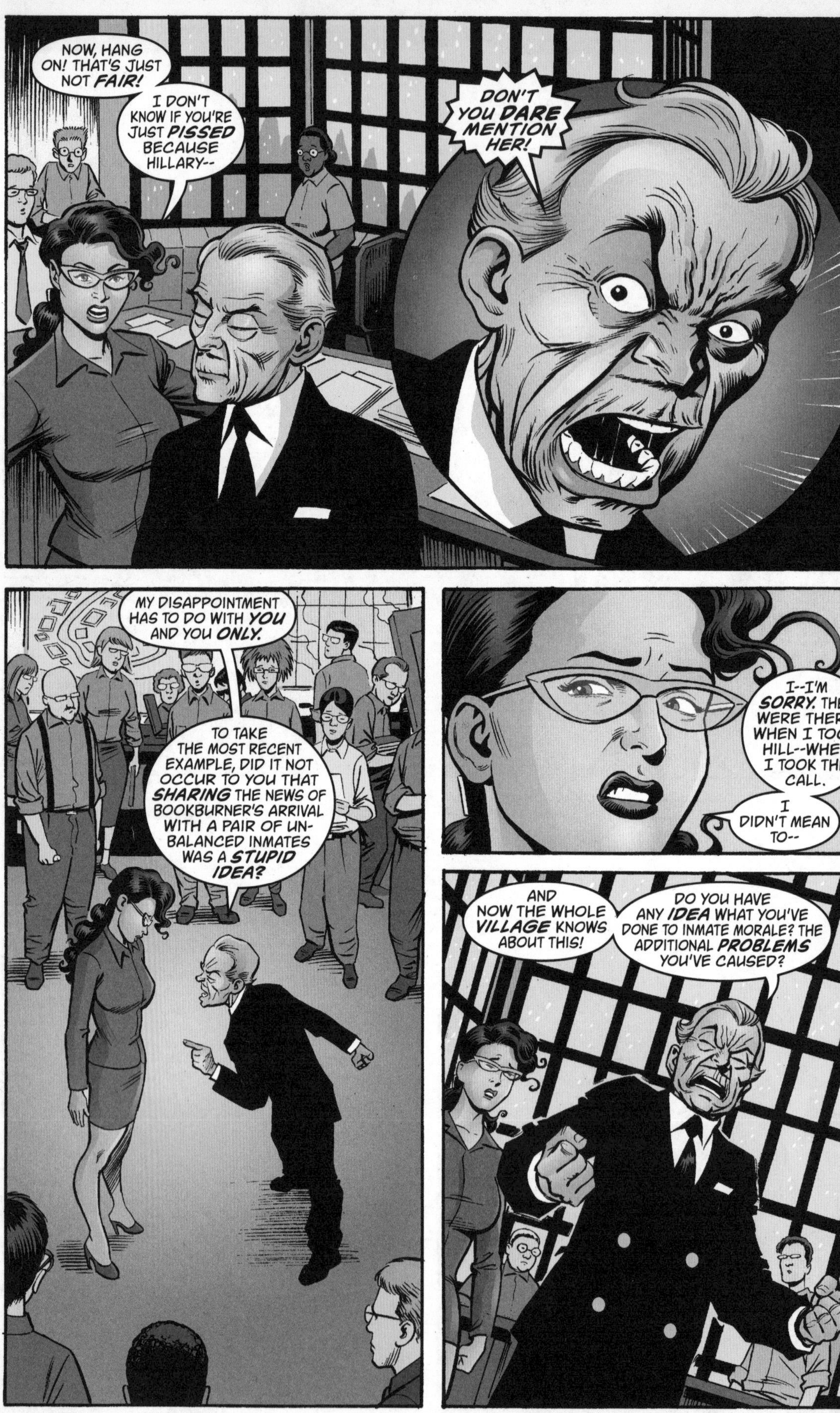
NOW, HANG ON! THAT'S JUST NOT FAIR!
I DON'T KNOW IF YOU'RE JUST PISSED BECAUSE HILLARY--
DON'T YOU DARE MENTION HER!
MY DISAPPOINTMENT HAS TO DO WITH YOU AND YOU ONLY.
TO TAKE THE MOST RECENT EXAMPLE, DID IT NOT OCCUR TO YOU THAT SHARING THE NEWS OF BOOKBURNER'S ARRIVAL WITH A PAIR OF UN-BALANCED INMATES WAS A STUPID IDEA?
I--I'M SORRY. THEY WERE THERE WHEN I TOOK HILL--WHEN I TOOK THE CALL.
I DIDN'T MEAN TO--
AND NOW THE WHOLE VILLAGE KNOWS ABOUT THIS!
DO YOU HAVE ANY IDEA WHAT YOU'VE DONE TO INMATE MORALE? THE ADDITIONAL PROBLEMS YOU'VE CAUSED?

A FEW MILES NORTH OF OGDEN, UTAH.

I JUST DON'T SEE IT, DUDE. THERE'S *NO WAY* YOU'RE GOING TO PULL THIS OFF.

GAS - FIL'R'UP - GAS

FIL'R'UP

YOU WILLING TO *BET* ON THAT, CHIEF SITTING BULL?

I WOULD, BUT YOU'VE GOT MY SHARE OF THE *GOLD* LOCKED IN THAT MAGIC BRIEFCASE OF YOURS. AND THAT THING IS *IMPOSSIBLE* TO BREAK INTO!

UH, OR AT LEAST I WOULD *ASSUME* IT IS.

EMPLOY MUST TO WASH HAND

YOU'RE DAMN *RIGHT* I'VE GOT YOUR MONEY LOCKED UP, AND IT'LL STAY THAT WAY UNTIL YOU CAN SHOW ME THAT YOU'RE ABLE TO MANAGE YOUR FINANCES *RESPONSIBLY.*

WHICH *CLEARLY* ISN'T THE CASE IF YOU'RE WILLING TO BET AGAINST *ME.*

FWOOSH!

MEN

BET AGAINST HIM ON WHAT?

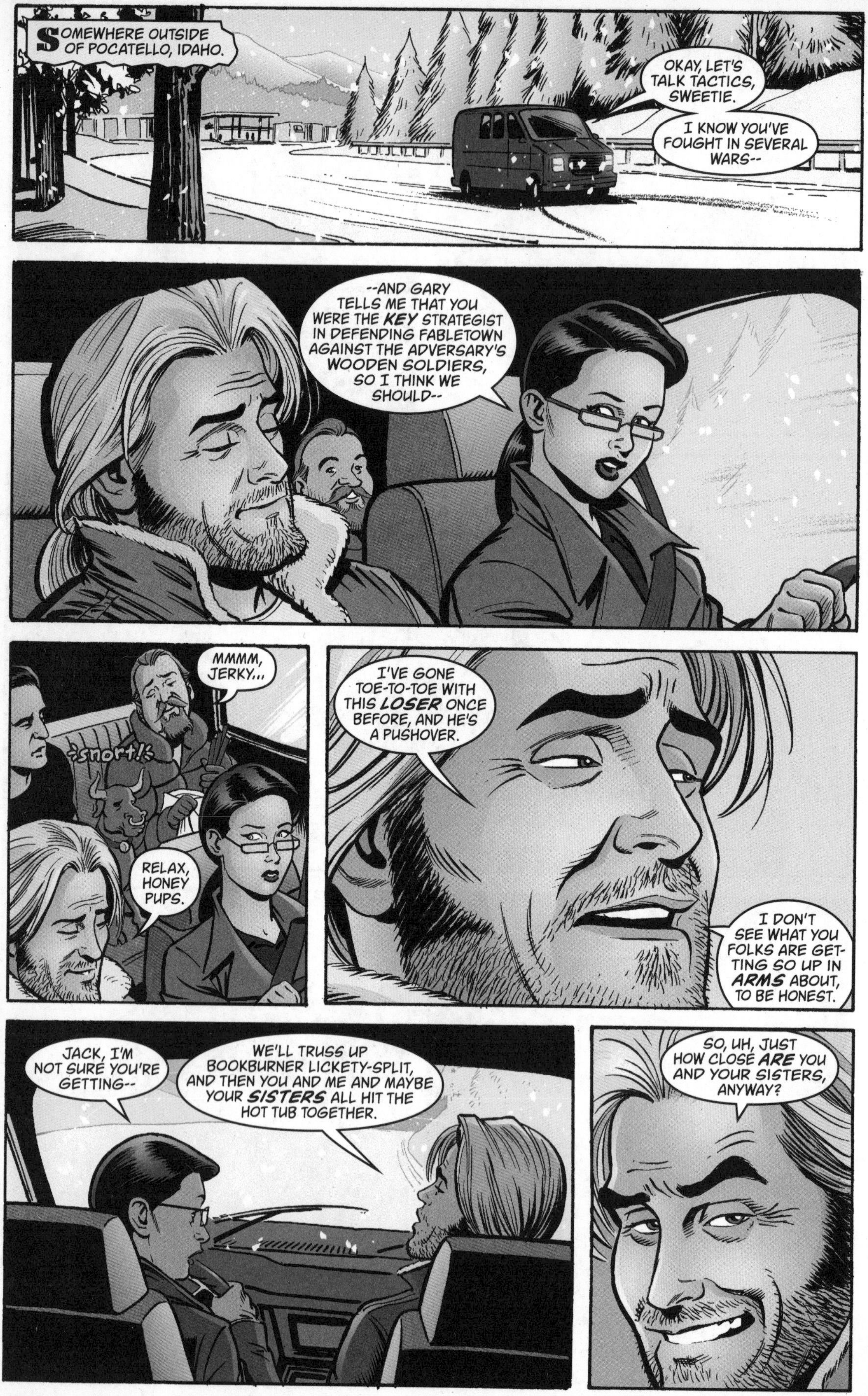
SOMEWHERE OUTSIDE OF POCATELLO, IDAHO.
OKAY, LET'S TALK TACTICS, SWEETIE.
I KNOW YOU'VE FOUGHT IN SEVERAL WARS--
--AND GARY TELLS ME THAT YOU WERE THE KEY STRATEGIST IN DEFENDING FABLETOWN AGAINST THE ADVERSARY'S WOODEN SOLDIERS, SO I THINK WE SHOULD--
MMMM, JERKY...
SNORT!
RELAX, HONEY PUPS.
I'VE GONE TOE-TO-TOE WITH THIS LOSER ONCE BEFORE, AND HE'S A PUSHOVER.
I DON'T SEE WHAT YOU FOLKS ARE GETTING SO UP IN ARMS ABOUT, TO BE HONEST.
JACK, I'M NOT SURE YOU'RE GETTING--
WE'LL TRUSS UP BOOKBURNER LICKETY-SPLIT, AND THEN YOU AND ME AND MAYBE YOUR SISTERS ALL HIT THE HOT TUB TOGETHER.
SO, UH, JUST HOW CLOSE ARE YOU AND YOUR SISTERS, ANYWAY?

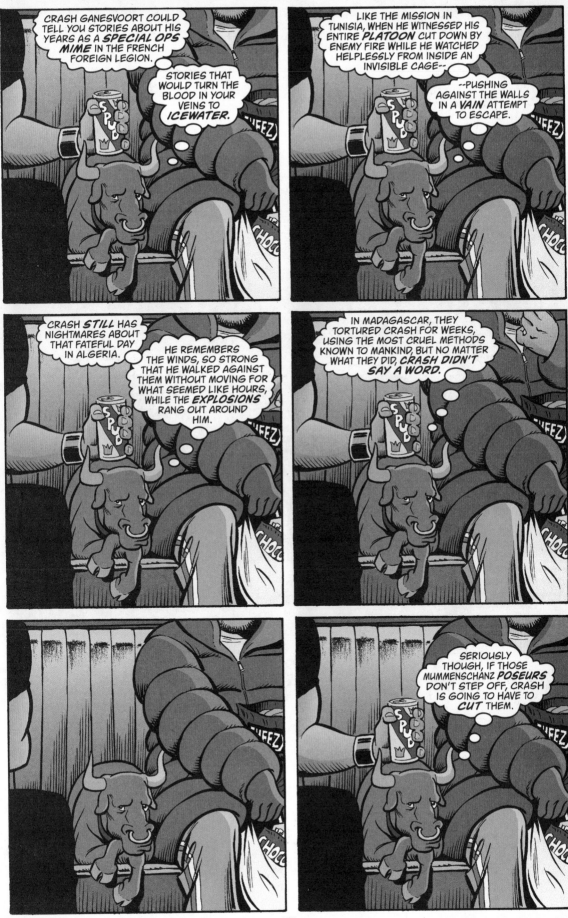

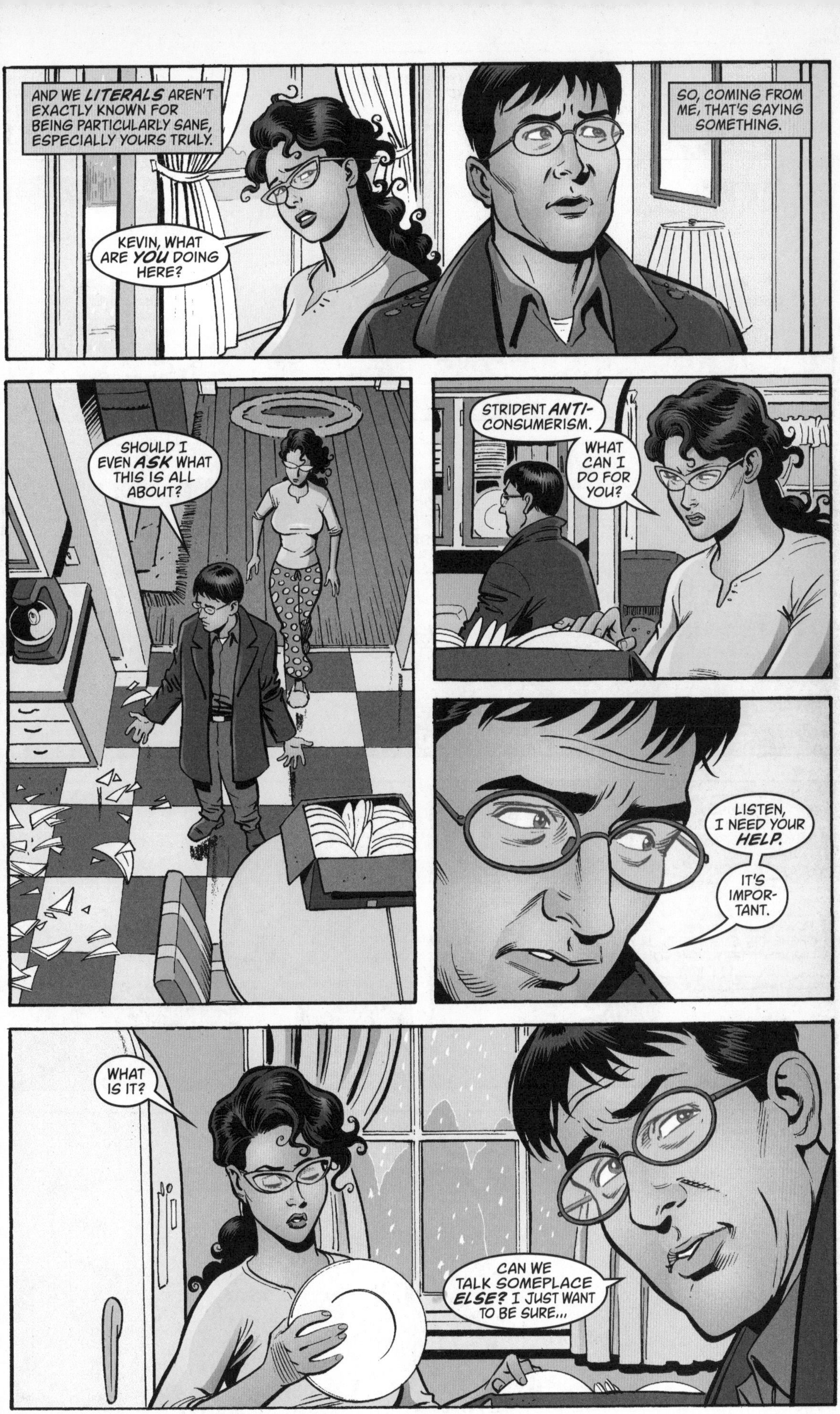
AND WE LITERALS AREN'T EXACTLY KNOWN FOR BEING PARTICULARLY SANE, ESPECIALLY YOURS TRULY.
SO, COMING FROM ME, THAT'S SAYING SOMETHING.
KEVIN, WHAT ARE YOU DOING HERE?
SHOULD I EVEN ASK WHAT THIS IS ALL ABOUT?
STRIDENT ANTI-CONSUMERISM.
WHAT CAN I DO FOR YOU?
LISTEN, I NEED YOUR HELP.
IT'S IMPORTANT.
WHAT IS IT?
CAN WE TALK SOMEPLACE ELSE? I JUST WANT TO BE SURE...

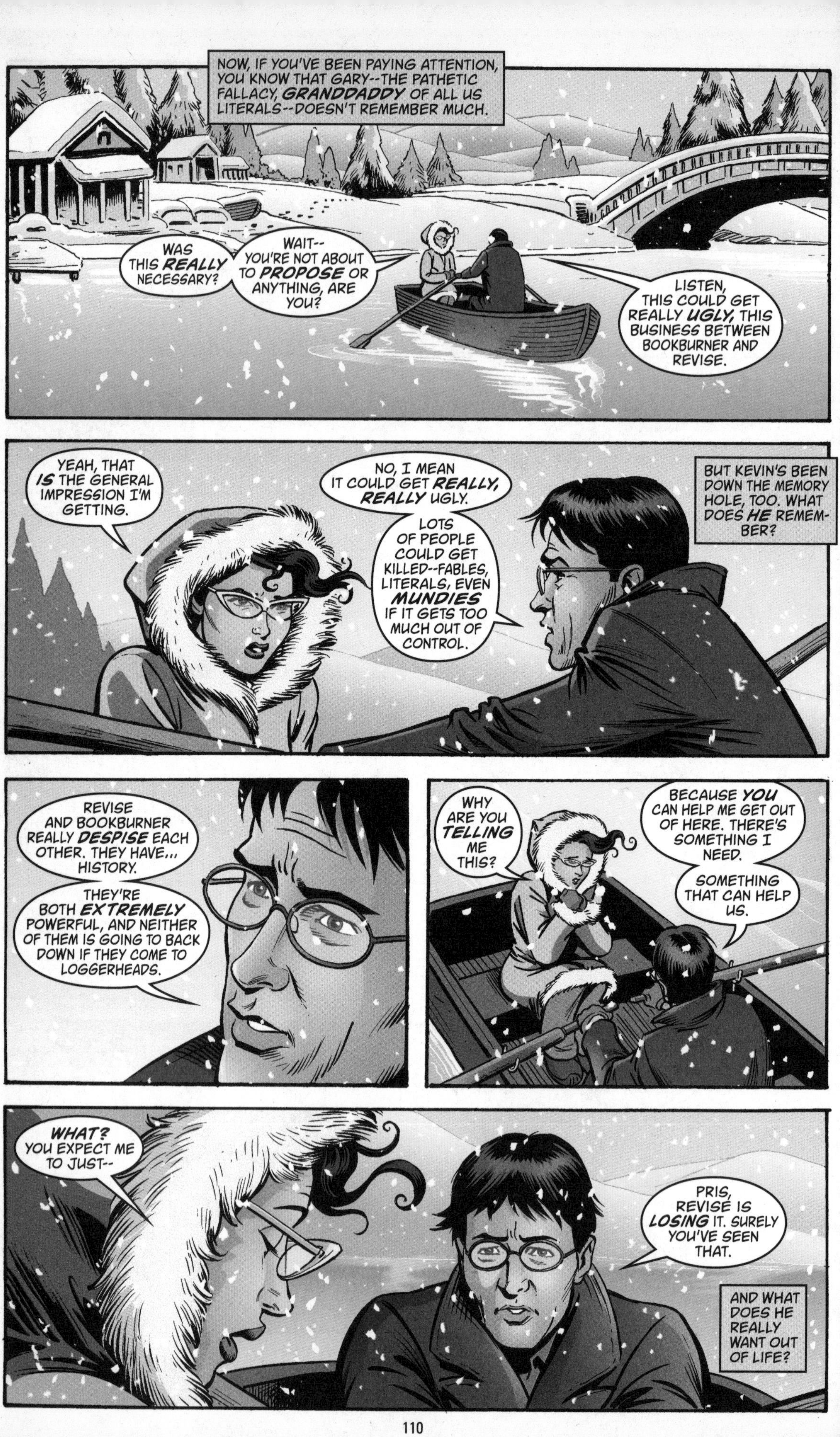
NOW, IF YOU'VE BEEN PAYING ATTENTION, YOU KNOW THAT GARY--THE PATHETIC FALLACY, GRANDDADDY OF ALL US LITERALS--DOESN'T REMEMBER MUCH.
WAS THIS REALLY NECESSARY?
WAIT-- YOU'RE NOT ABOUT TO PROPOSE OR ANYTHING, ARE YOU?
LISTEN, THIS COULD GET REALLY UGLY, THIS BUSINESS BETWEEN BOOKBURNER AND REVISE.
YEAH, THAT IS THE GENERAL IMPRESSION I'M GETTING.
NO, I MEAN IT COULD GET REALLY, REALLY UGLY.
LOTS OF PEOPLE COULD GET KILLED--FABLES, LITERALS, EVEN MUNDIES IF IT GETS TOO MUCH OUT OF CONTROL.
BUT KEVIN'S BEEN DOWN THE MEMORY HOLE, TOO. WHAT DOES HE REMEMBER?
REVISE AND BOOKBURNER REALLY DESPISE EACH OTHER. THEY HAVE... HISTORY.
THEY'RE BOTH EXTREMELY POWERFUL, AND NEITHER OF THEM IS GOING TO BACK DOWN IF THEY COME TO LOGGERHEADS.
WHY ARE YOU TELLING ME THIS?
BECAUSE YOU CAN HELP ME GET OUT OF HERE. THERE'S SOMETHING I NEED.
SOMETHING THAT CAN HELP US.
WHAT? YOU EXPECT ME TO JUST--
PRIS, REVISE IS LOSING IT. SURELY YOU'VE SEEN THAT.
AND WHAT DOES HE REALLY WANT OUT OF LIFE?

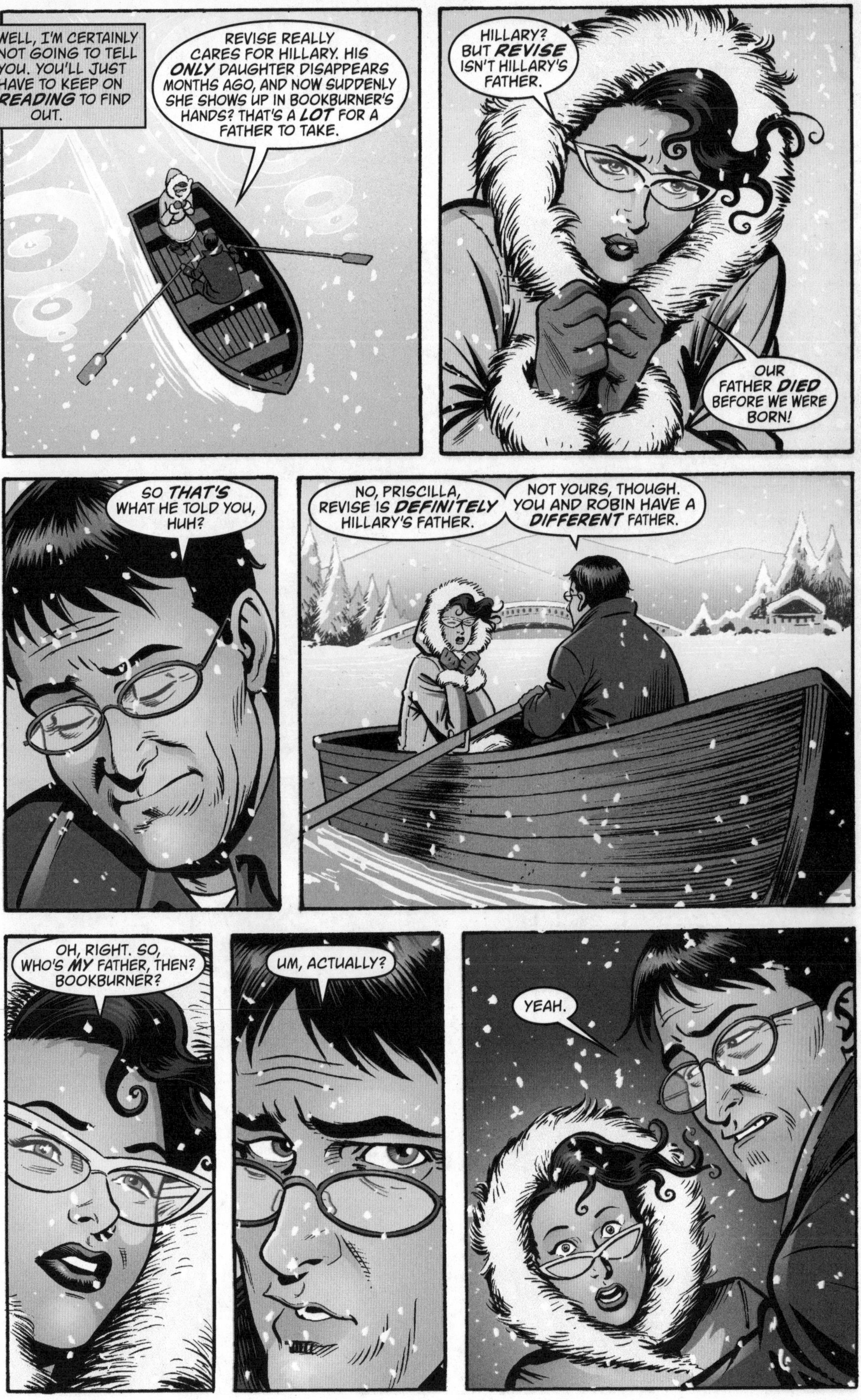
WELL, I'M CERTAINLY NOT GOING TO TELL YOU. YOU'LL JUST HAVE TO KEEP ON READING TO FIND OUT.
REVISE REALLY CARES FOR HILLARY. HIS ONLY DAUGHTER DISAPPEARS MONTHS AGO, AND NOW SUDDENLY SHE SHOWS UP IN BOOKBURNER'S HANDS? THAT'S A LOT FOR A FATHER TO TAKE.
HILLARY? BUT REVISE ISN'T HILLARY'S FATHER.
OUR FATHER DIED BEFORE WE WERE BORN!
SO THAT'S WHAT HE TOLD YOU, HUH?
NO, PRISCILLA, REVISE IS DEFINITELY HILLARY'S FATHER.
NOT YOURS, THOUGH. YOU AND ROBIN HAVE A DIFFERENT FATHER.
OH, RIGHT. SO, WHO'S MY FATHER, THEN? BOOKBURNER?
UM, ACTUALLY?
YEAH.

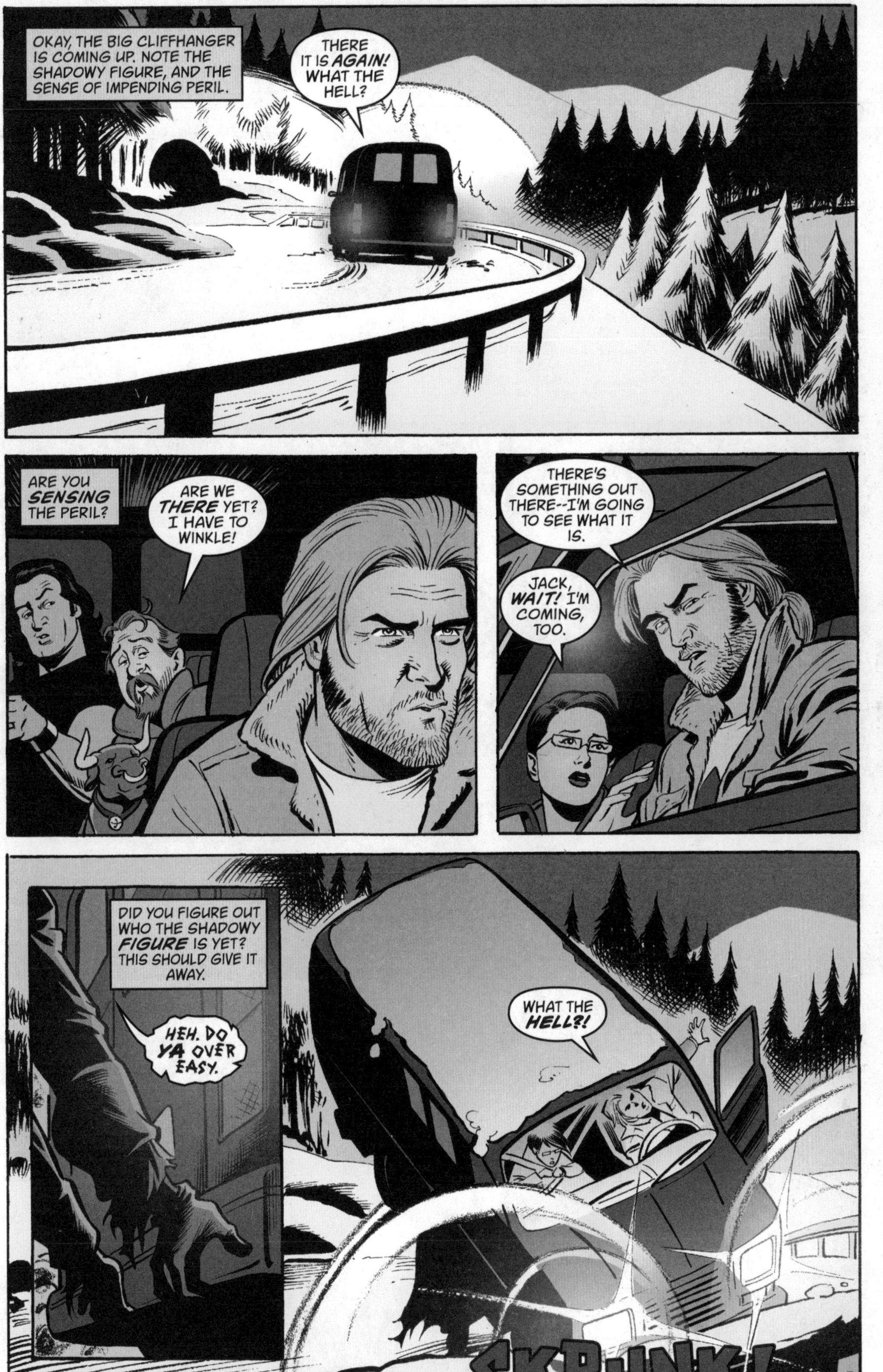
OKAY, THE BIG CLIFFHANGER IS COMING UP. NOTE THE SHADOWY FIGURE, AND THE SENSE OF IMPENDING PERIL.
THERE IT IS AGAIN! WHAT THE HELL?
ARE YOU SENSING THE PERIL?
ARE WE THERE YET? I HAVE TO WINKLE!
THERE'S SOMETHING OUT THERE--I'M GOING TO SEE WHAT IT IS.
JACK, WAIT! I'M COMING, TOO.
DID YOU FIGURE OUT WHO THE SHADOWY FIGURE IS YET? THIS SHOULD GIVE IT AWAY.
HEH. DO YA OVER EASY.
WHAT THE HELL?!
SKRUNK!

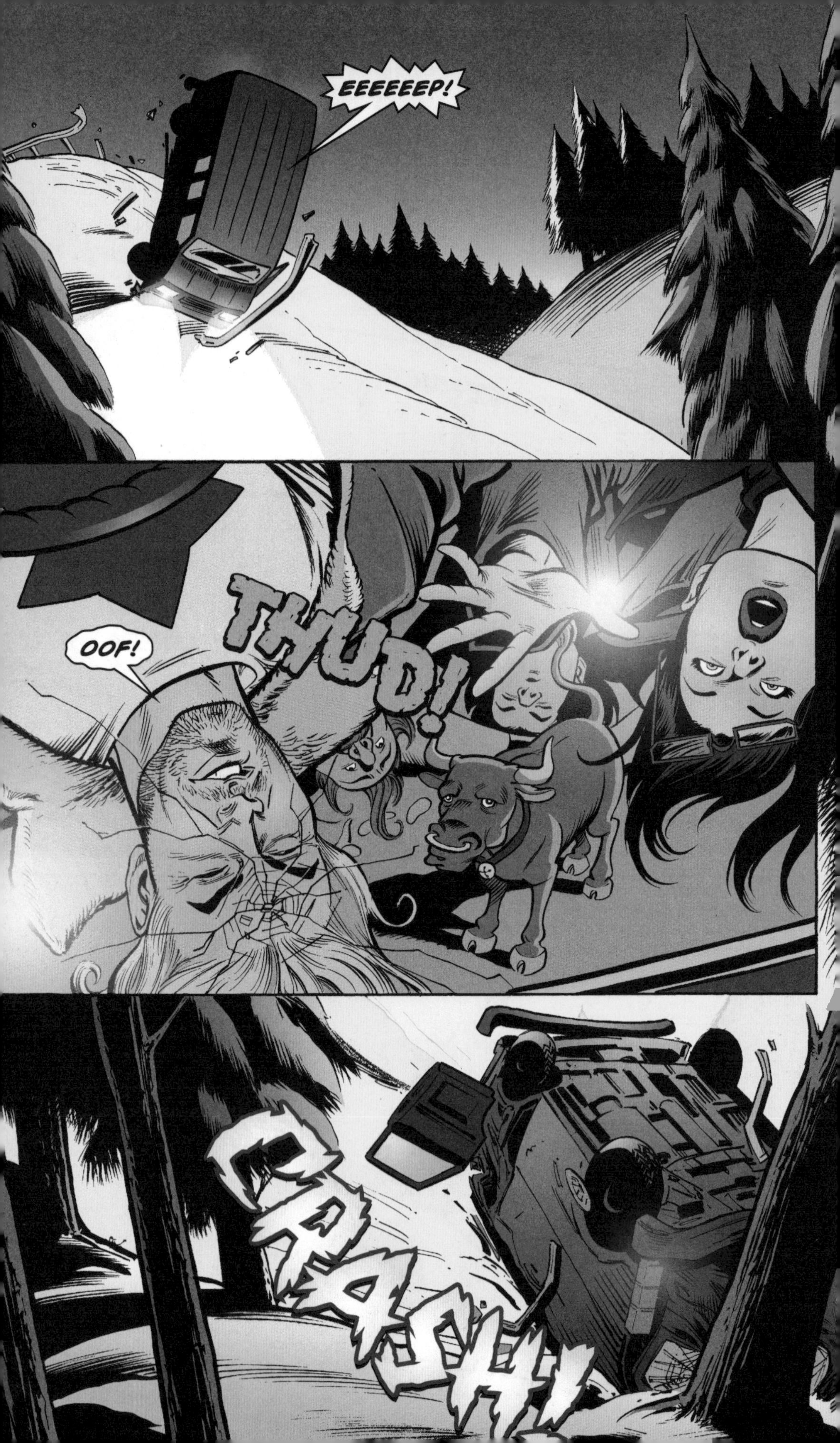
EEEEEEP!
THUD!
OOF!
CRASH!

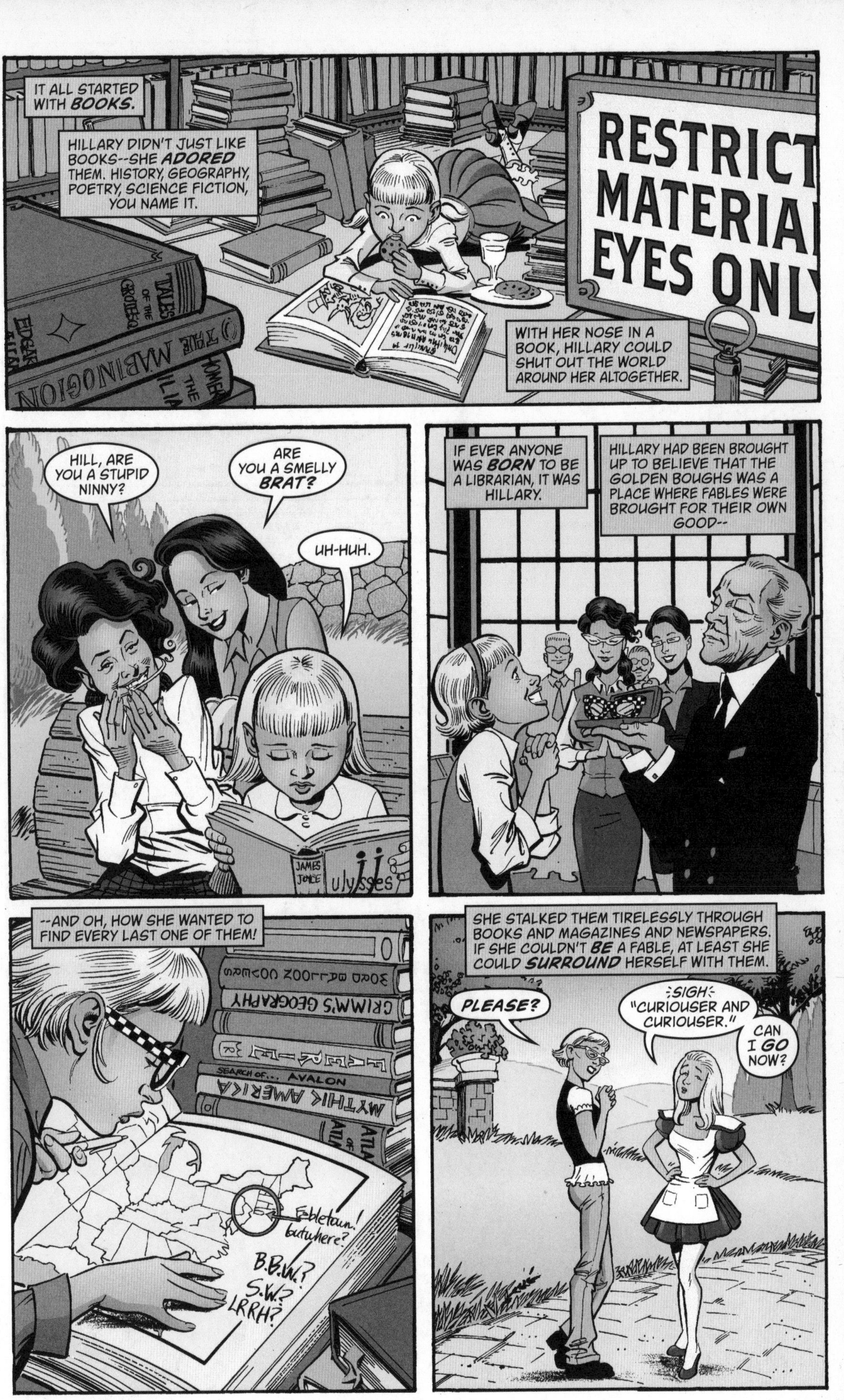
IT ALL STARTED WITH BOOKS.
HILLARY DIDN'T JUST LIKE BOOKS--SHE ADORED THEM. HISTORY, GEOGRAPHY, POETRY, SCIENCE FICTION, YOU NAME IT.
RESTRICT MATERIA EYES ONL
TALES OF THE GROTESQUE
EDGAR
THE MABINOGION
HOMER THE ILIA
WITH HER NOSE IN A BOOK, HILLARY COULD SHUT OUT THE WORLD AROUND HER ALTOGETHER.
HILL, ARE YOU A STUPID NINNY?
ARE YOU A SMELLY BRAT?
UH-HUH.
JAMES JOYCE ulysses
IF EVER ANYONE WAS BORN TO BE A LIBRARIAN, IT WAS HILLARY.
HILLARY HAD BEEN BROUGHT UP TO BELIEVE THAT THE GOLDEN BOUGHS WAS A PLACE WHERE FABLES WERE BROUGHT FOR THEIR OWN GOOD--
--AND OH, HOW SHE WANTED TO FIND EVERY LAST ONE OF THEM!
GRIMM'S GEOGRAPHY
SEARCH OF... AVALON
MYTHIK AMERIKA
Fabletown! but where?
B.B.W.? S.W.? LRRH?
SHE STALKED THEM TIRELESSLY THROUGH BOOKS AND MAGAZINES AND NEWSPAPERS. IF SHE COULDN'T BE A FABLE, AT LEAST SHE COULD SURROUND HERSELF WITH THEM.
PLEASE?
SIGH "CURIOUSER AND CURIOUSER."
CAN I GO NOW?

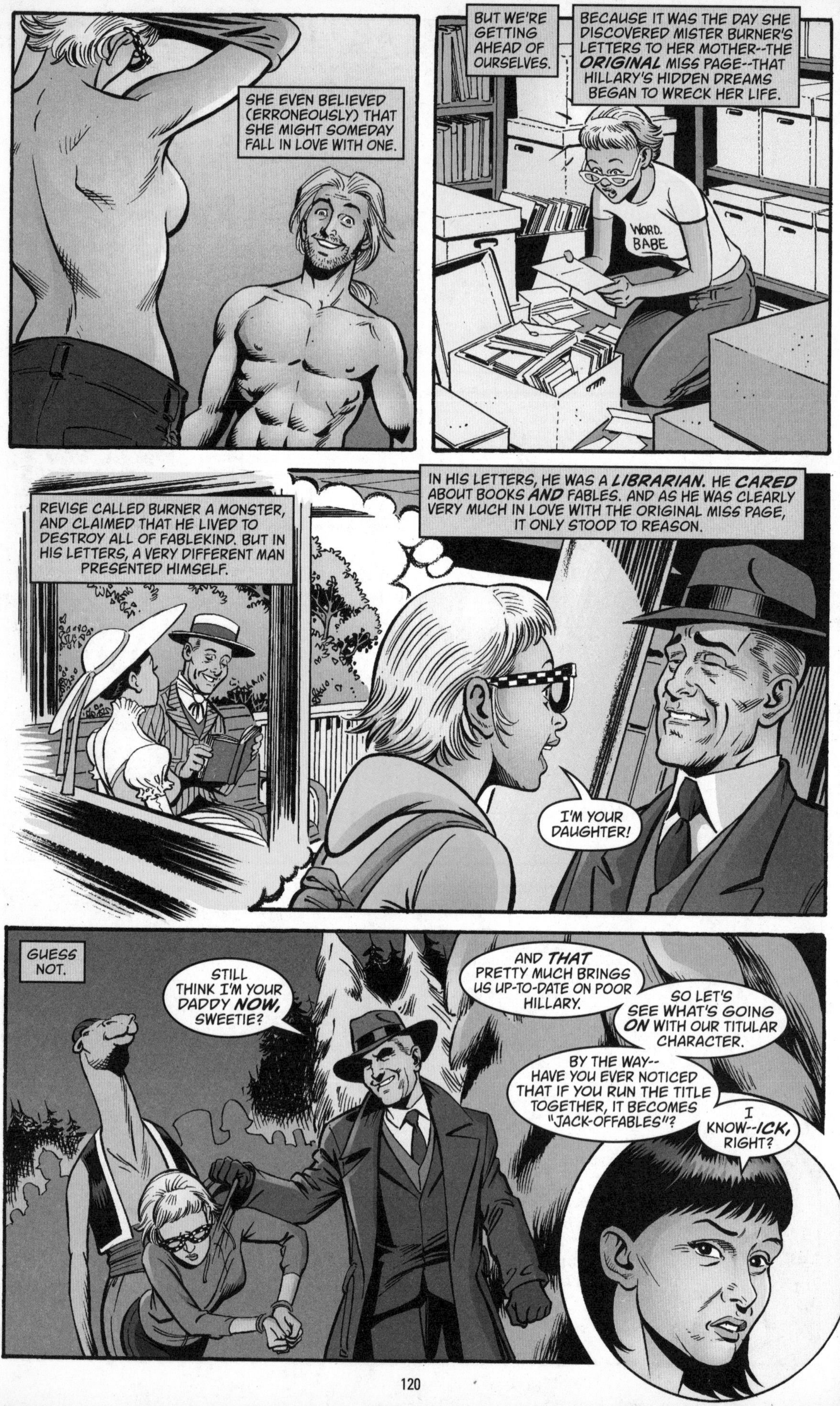
SHE EVEN BELIEVED (ERRONEOUSLY) THAT SHE MIGHT SOMEDAY FALL IN LOVE WITH ONE.
BUT WE'RE GETTING AHEAD OF OURSELVES.
BECAUSE IT WAS THE DAY SHE DISCOVERED MISTER BURNER'S LETTERS TO HER MOTHER--THE ORIGINAL MISS PAGE--THAT HILLARY'S HIDDEN DREAMS BEGAN TO WRECK HER LIFE.
WORD. BABE
REVISE CALLED BURNER A MONSTER, AND CLAIMED THAT HE LIVED TO DESTROY ALL OF FABLEKIND. BUT IN HIS LETTERS, A VERY DIFFERENT MAN PRESENTED HIMSELF.
IN HIS LETTERS, HE WAS A LIBRARIAN. HE CARED ABOUT BOOKS AND FABLES. AND AS HE WAS CLEARLY VERY MUCH IN LOVE WITH THE ORIGINAL MISS PAGE, IT ONLY STOOD TO REASON.
I'M YOUR DAUGHTER!
GUESS NOT.
STILL THINK I'M YOUR DADDY NOW, SWEETIE?
AND THAT PRETTY MUCH BRINGS US UP-TO-DATE ON POOR HILLARY.
SO LET'S SEE WHAT'S GOING ON WITH OUR TITULAR CHARACTER.
BY THE WAY-- HAVE YOU EVER NOTICED THAT IF YOU RUN THE TITLE TOGETHER, IT BECOMES "JACK-OFFABLES"?
I KNOW--ICK, RIGHT?

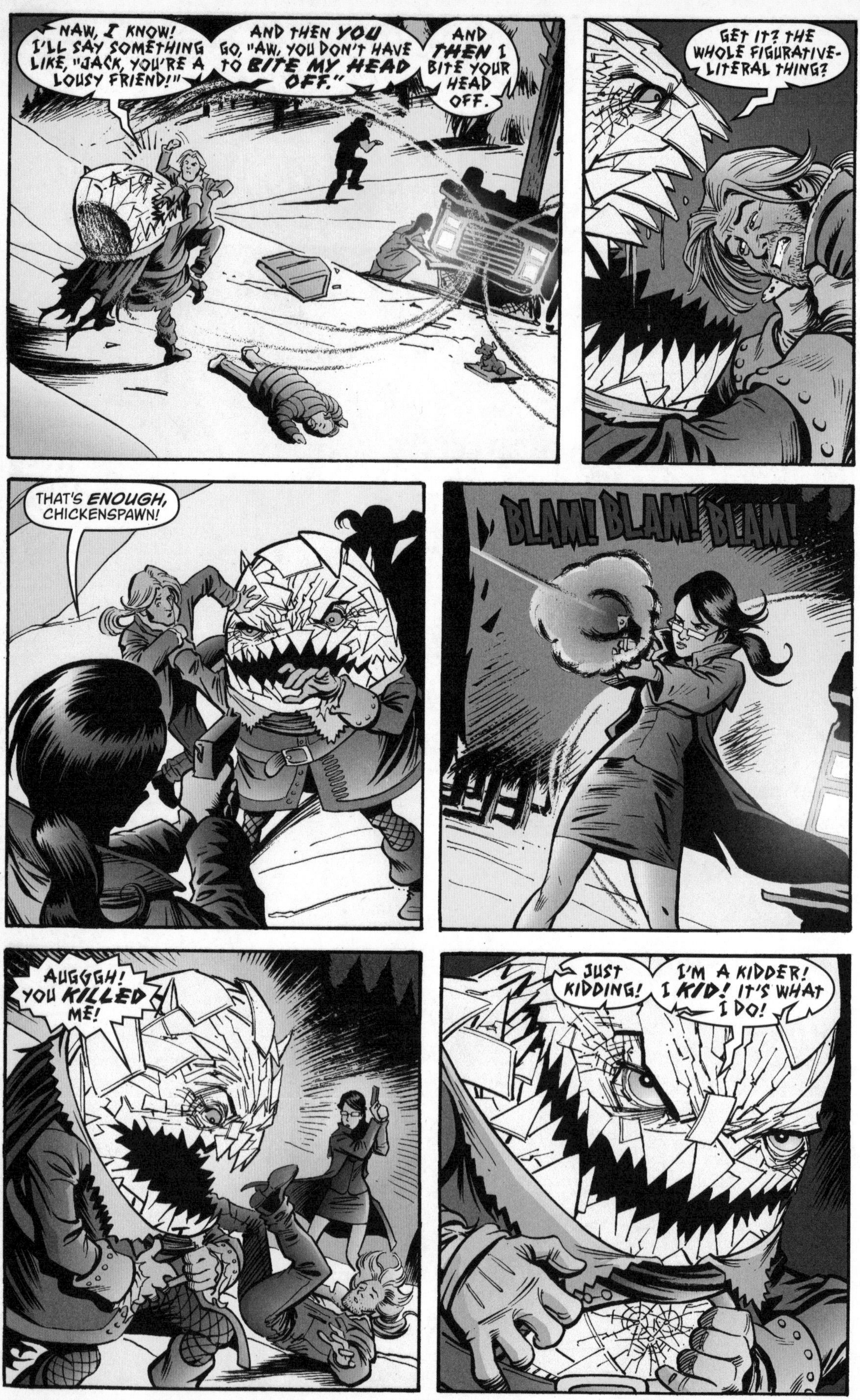
NAW, I KNOW! I'LL SAY SOMETHING LIKE, "JACK, YOU'RE A LOUSY FRIEND!"
AND THEN YOU GO, "AW, YOU DON'T HAVE TO BITE MY HEAD OFF."
AND THEN I BITE YOUR HEAD OFF.
GET IT? THE WHOLE FIGURATIVE-LITERAL THING?
THAT'S ENOUGH, CHICKENSPAWN!
BLAM! BLAM! BLAM!
AUGGGH! YOU KILLED ME!
JUST KIDDING!
I'M A KIDDER! I KID! IT'S WHAT I DO!

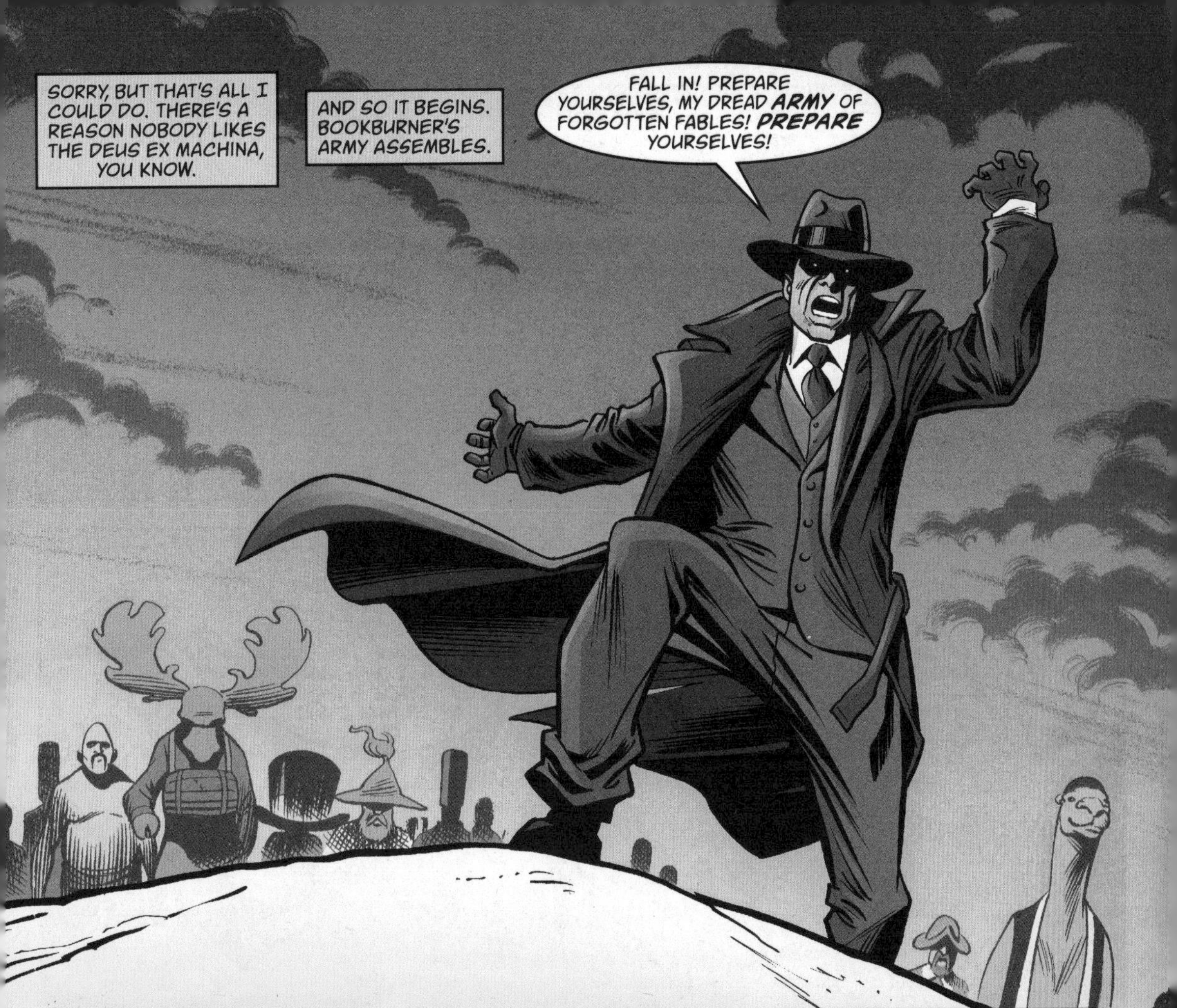
SORRY, BUT THAT'S ALL I COULD DO. THERE'S A REASON NOBODY LIKES THE DEUS EX MACHINA, YOU KNOW.
AND SO IT BEGINS. BOOKBURNER'S ARMY ASSEMBLES.
FALL IN! PREPARE YOURSELVES, MY DREAD ARMY OF FORGOTTEN FABLES! PREPARE YOURSELVES!

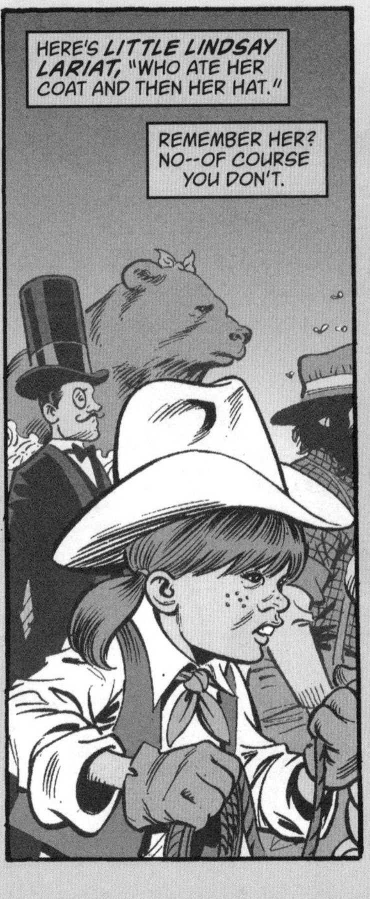
HERE'S LITTLE LINDSAY LARIAT, "WHO ATE HER COAT AND THEN HER HAT."
REMEMBER HER? NO--OF COURSE YOU DON'T.

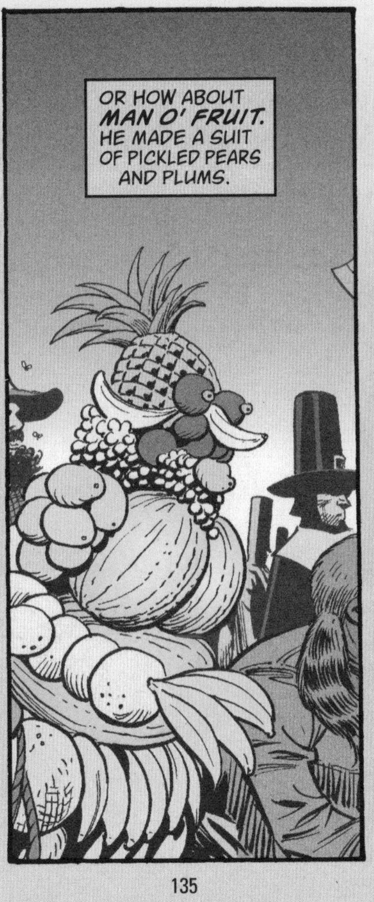
OR HOW ABOUT MAN O' FRUIT. HE MADE A SUIT OF PICKLED PEARS AND PLUMS.

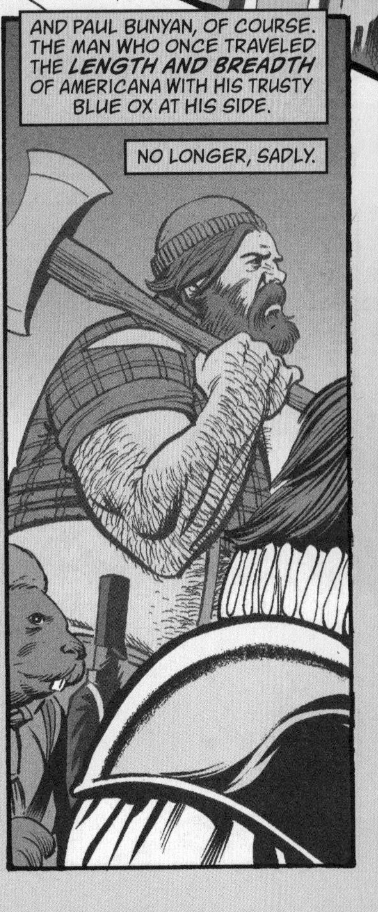
AND PAUL BUNYAN, OF COURSE. THE MAN WHO ONCE TRAVELED THE LENGTH AND BREADTH OF AMERICANA WITH HIS TRUSTY BLUE OX AT HIS SIDE.
NO LONGER, SADLY.

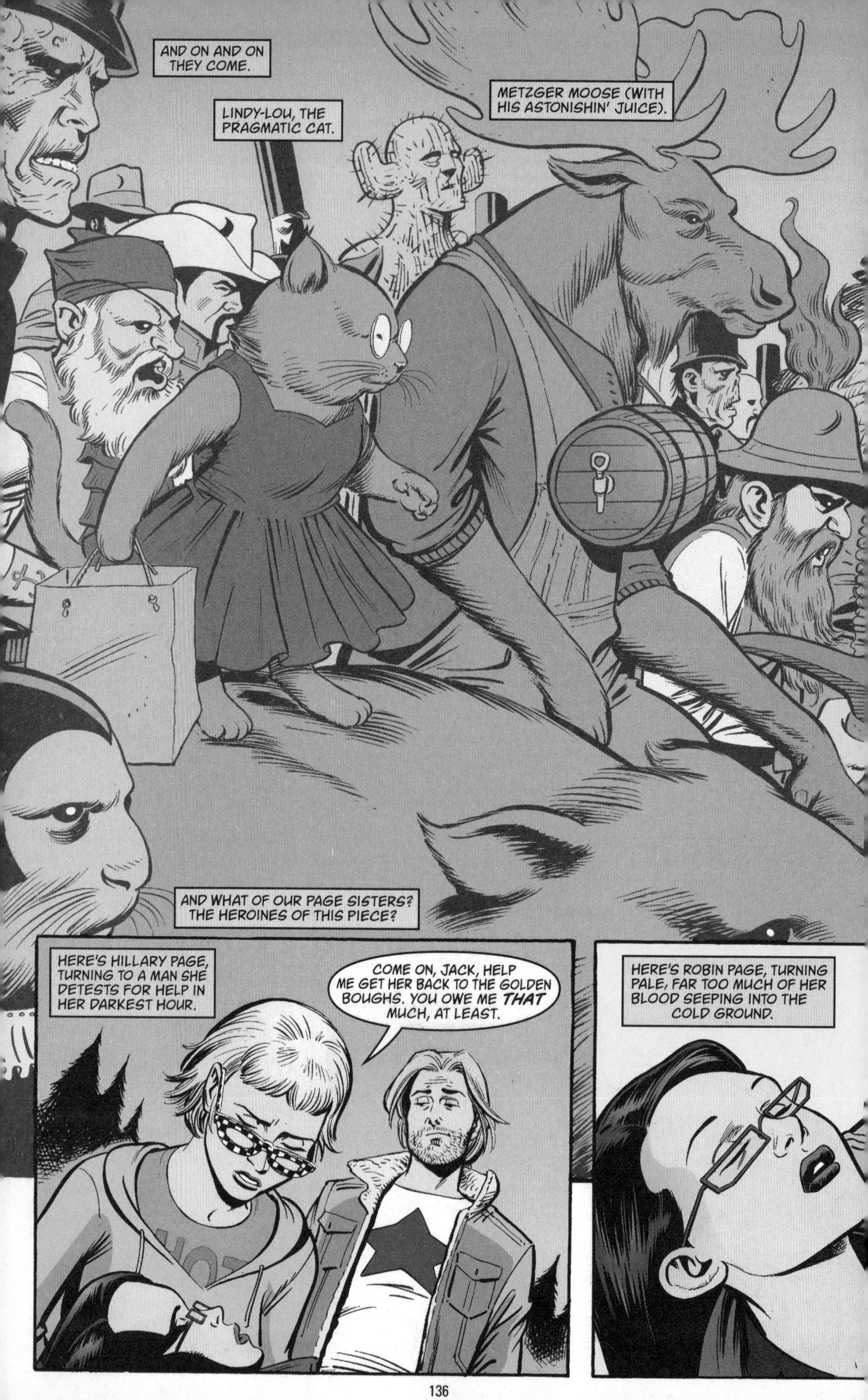

AND ON AND ON THEY COME.
LINDY-LOU, THE PRAGMATIC CAT.
METZGER MOOSE (WITH HIS ASTONISHIN' JUICE).
AND WHAT OF OUR PAGE SISTERS? THE HEROINES OF THIS PIECE?
HERE'S HILLARY PAGE, TURNING TO A MAN SHE DETESTS FOR HELP IN HER DARKEST HOUR.
COME ON, JACK, HELP ME GET HER BACK TO THE GOLDEN BOUGHS. YOU OWE ME *THAT* MUCH, AT LEAST.
HERE'S ROBIN PAGE, TURNING PALE, FAR TOO MUCH OF HER BLOOD SEEPING INTO THE COLD GROUND.

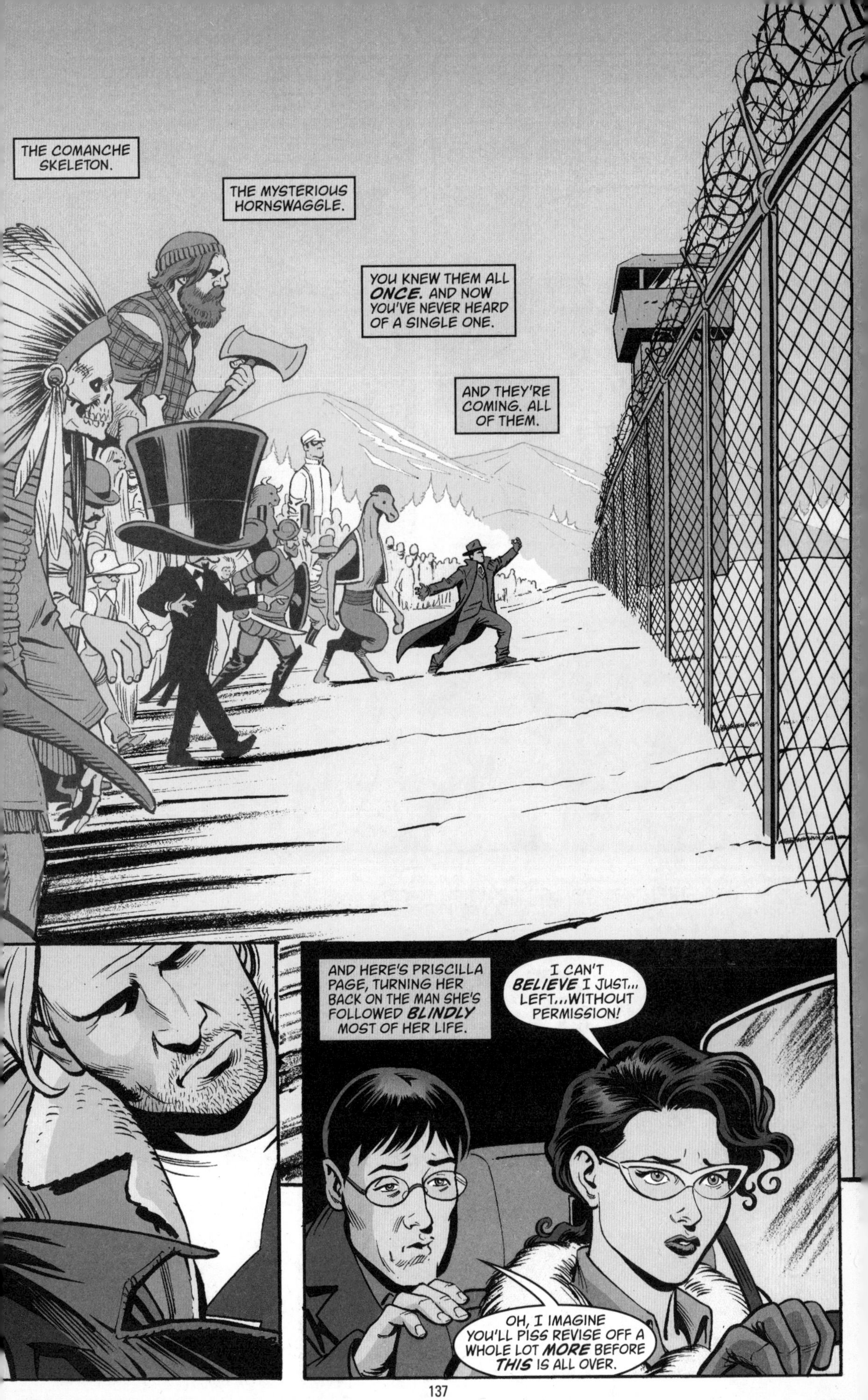
THE COMANCHE SKELETON.
THE MYSTERIOUS HORNSWAGGLE.
YOU KNEW THEM ALL ONCE. AND NOW YOU'VE NEVER HEARD OF A SINGLE ONE.
AND THEY'RE COMING. ALL OF THEM.
AND HERE'S PRISCILLA PAGE, TURNING HER BACK ON THE MAN SHE'S FOLLOWED BLINDLY MOST OF HER LIFE.
I CAN'T BELIEVE I JUST... LEFT...WITHOUT PERMISSION!
OH, I IMAGINE YOU'LL PISS REVISE OFF A WHOLE LOT MORE BEFORE THIS IS ALL OVER.

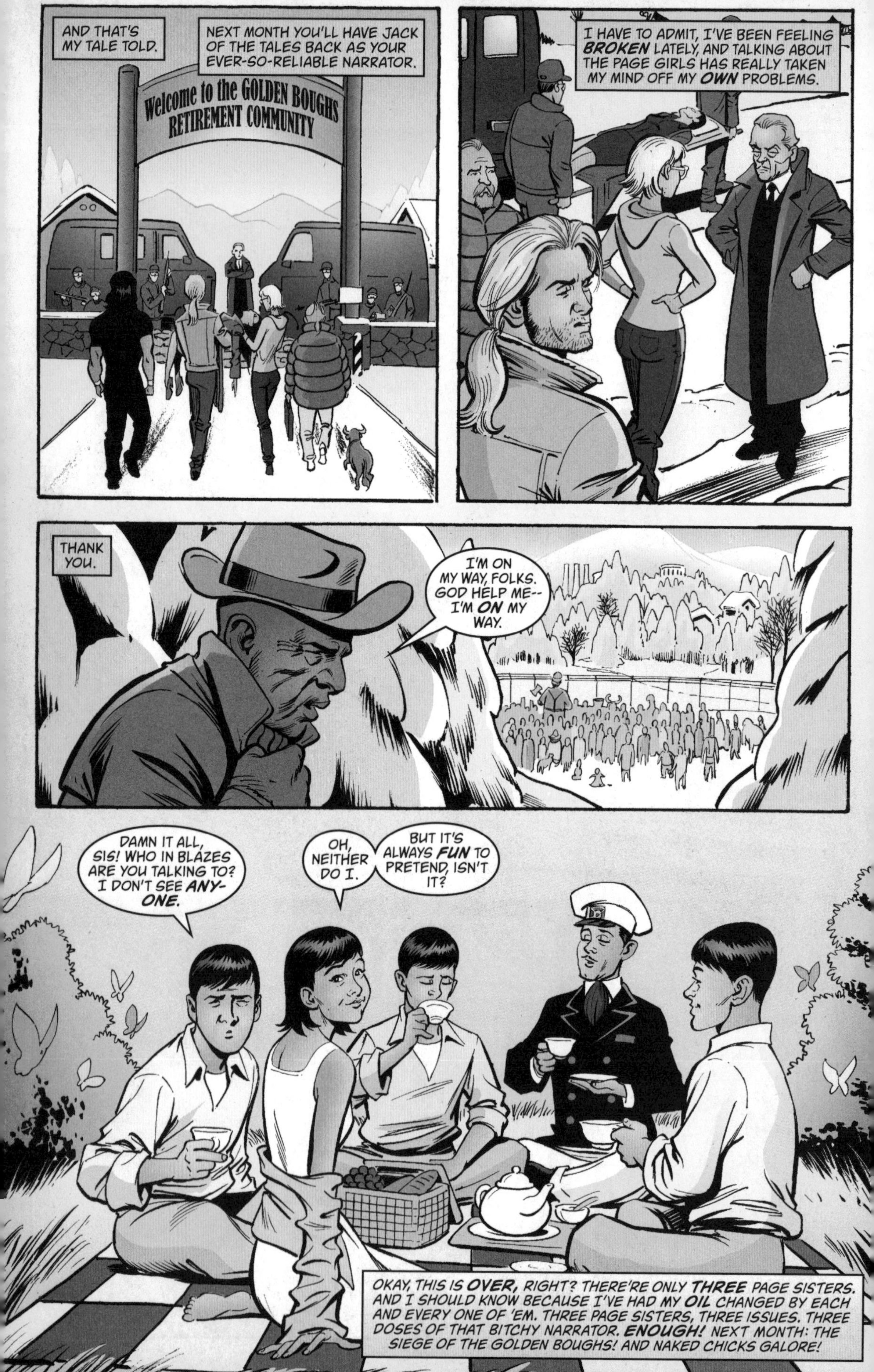
AND THAT'S MY TALE TOLD.
NEXT MONTH YOU'LL HAVE JACK OF THE TALES BACK AS YOUR EVER-SO-RELIABLE NARRATOR.
Welcome to the GOLDEN BOUGHS RETIREMENT COMMUNITY
I HAVE TO ADMIT, I'VE BEEN FEELING **BROKEN** LATELY, AND TALKING ABOUT THE PAGE GIRLS HAS REALLY TAKEN MY MIND OFF MY **OWN** PROBLEMS.
THANK YOU.
I'M ON MY WAY, FOLKS. GOD HELP ME-- I'M **ON** MY WAY.
DAMN IT ALL, SIS! WHO IN BLAZES ARE YOU TALKING TO? I DON'T SEE **ANY-ONE**.
OH, NEITHER DO I.
BUT IT'S ALWAYS **FUN** TO PRETEND, ISN'T IT?
*OKAY, THIS IS **OVER,** RIGHT? THERE'RE ONLY **THREE** PAGE SISTERS. AND I SHOULD KNOW BECAUSE I'VE HAD MY **OIL** CHANGED BY EACH AND EVERY ONE OF 'EM. THREE PAGE SISTERS, THREE ISSUES. THREE DOSES OF THAT BITCHY NARRATOR. **ENOUGH!** NEXT MONTH: THE SIEGE OF THE GOLDEN BOUGHS! AND NAKED CHICKS GALORE!*

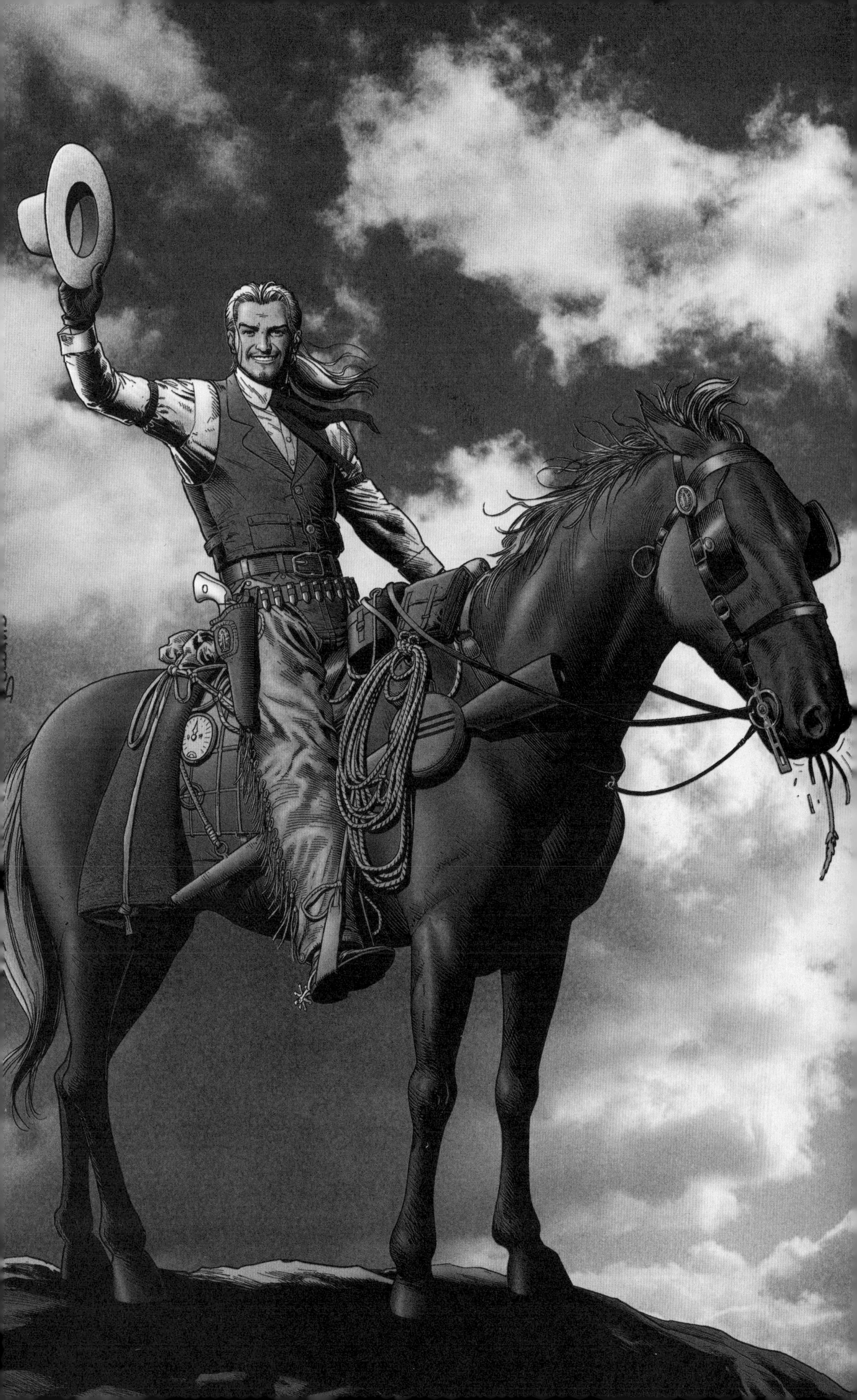

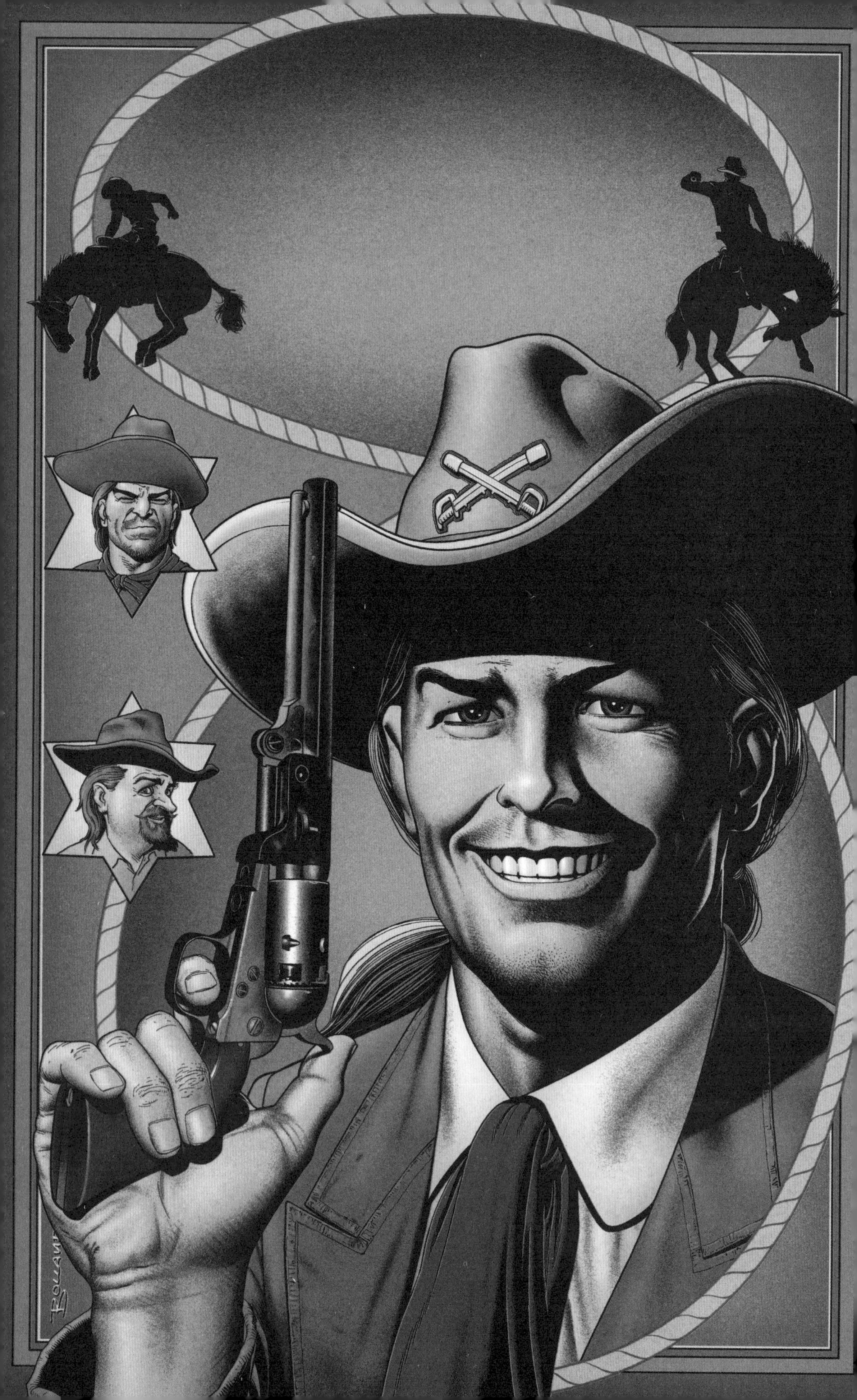

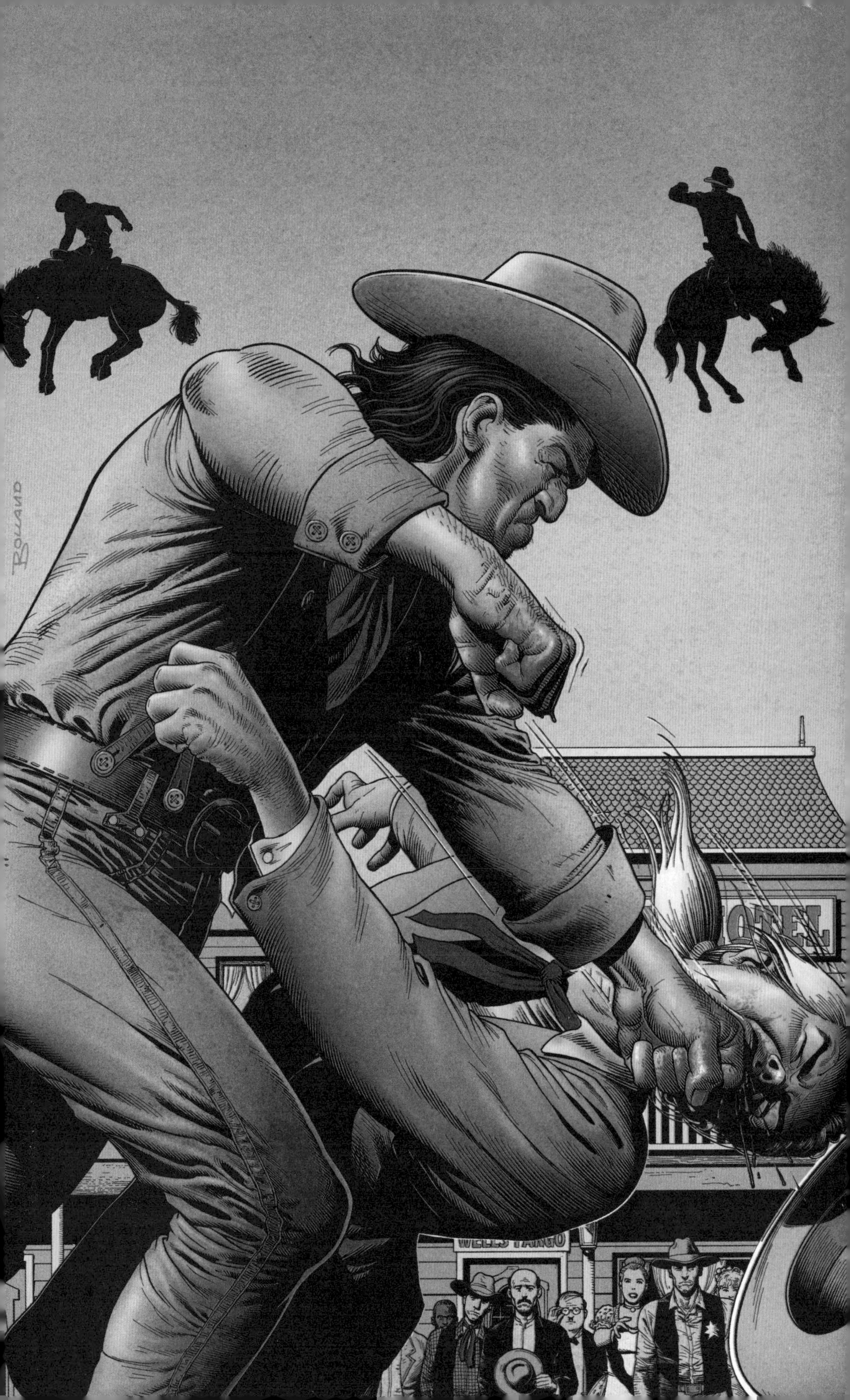
BOLLAND
WELLS FARGO

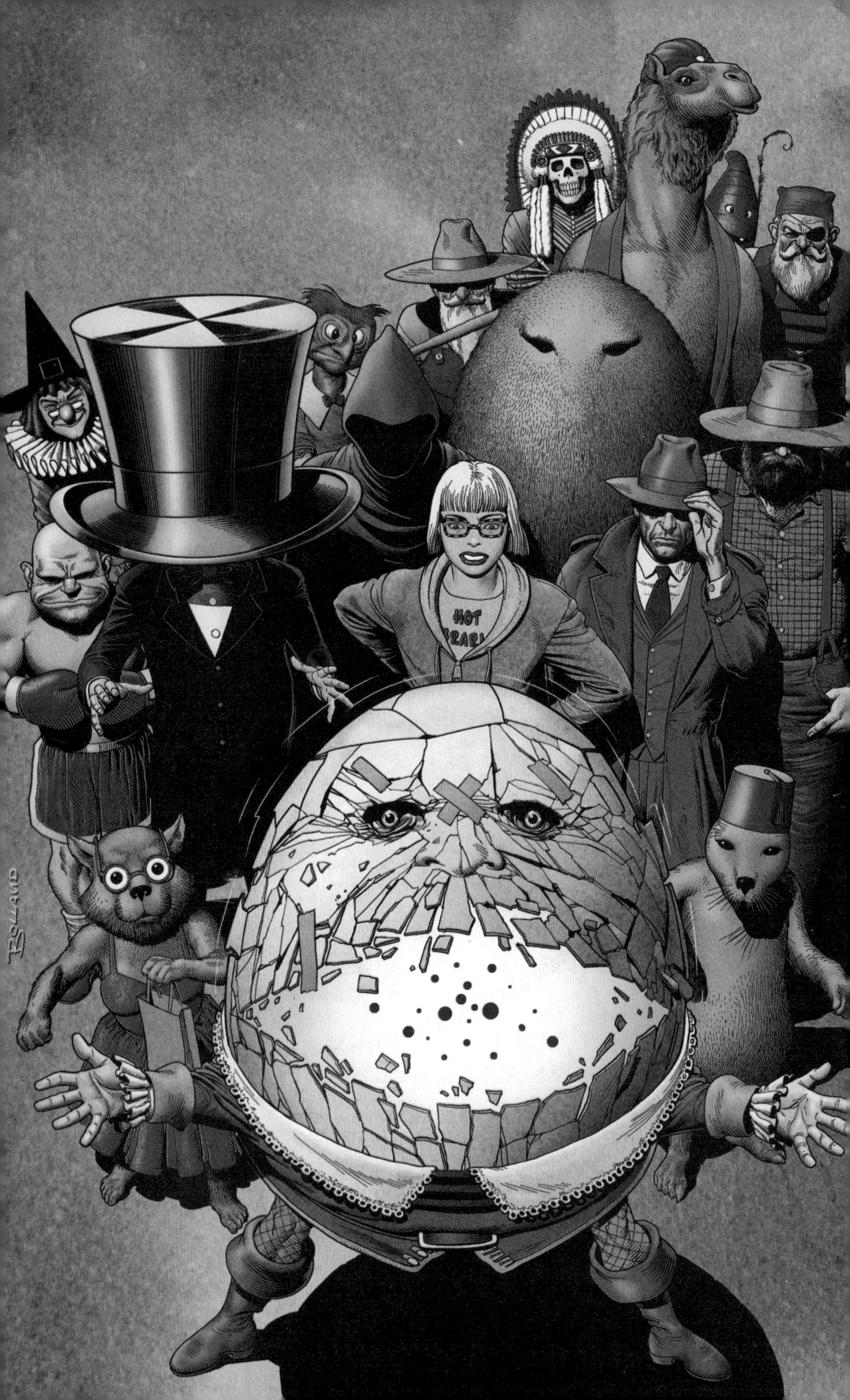
HOT
BOLLAND

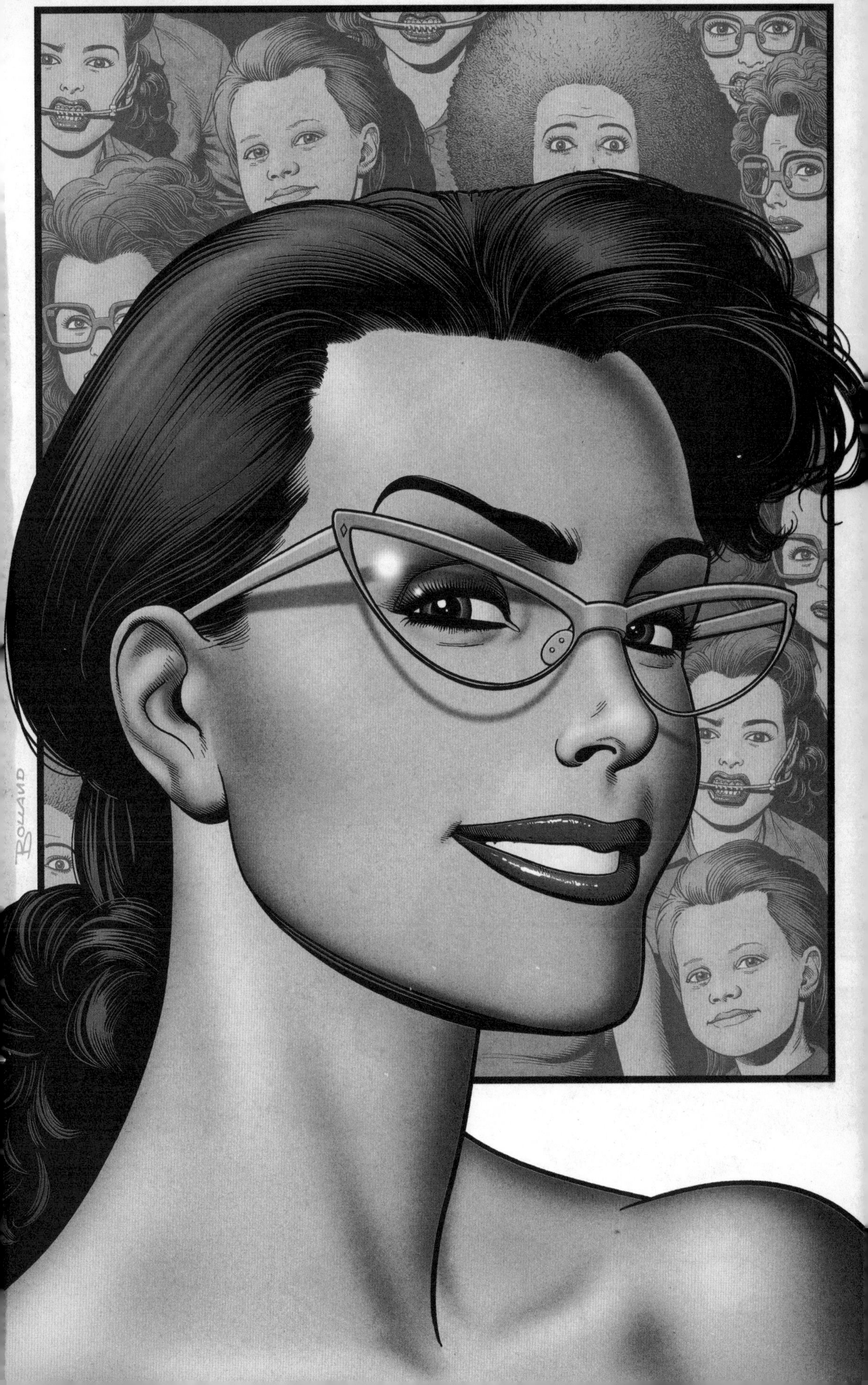
BOLLAND

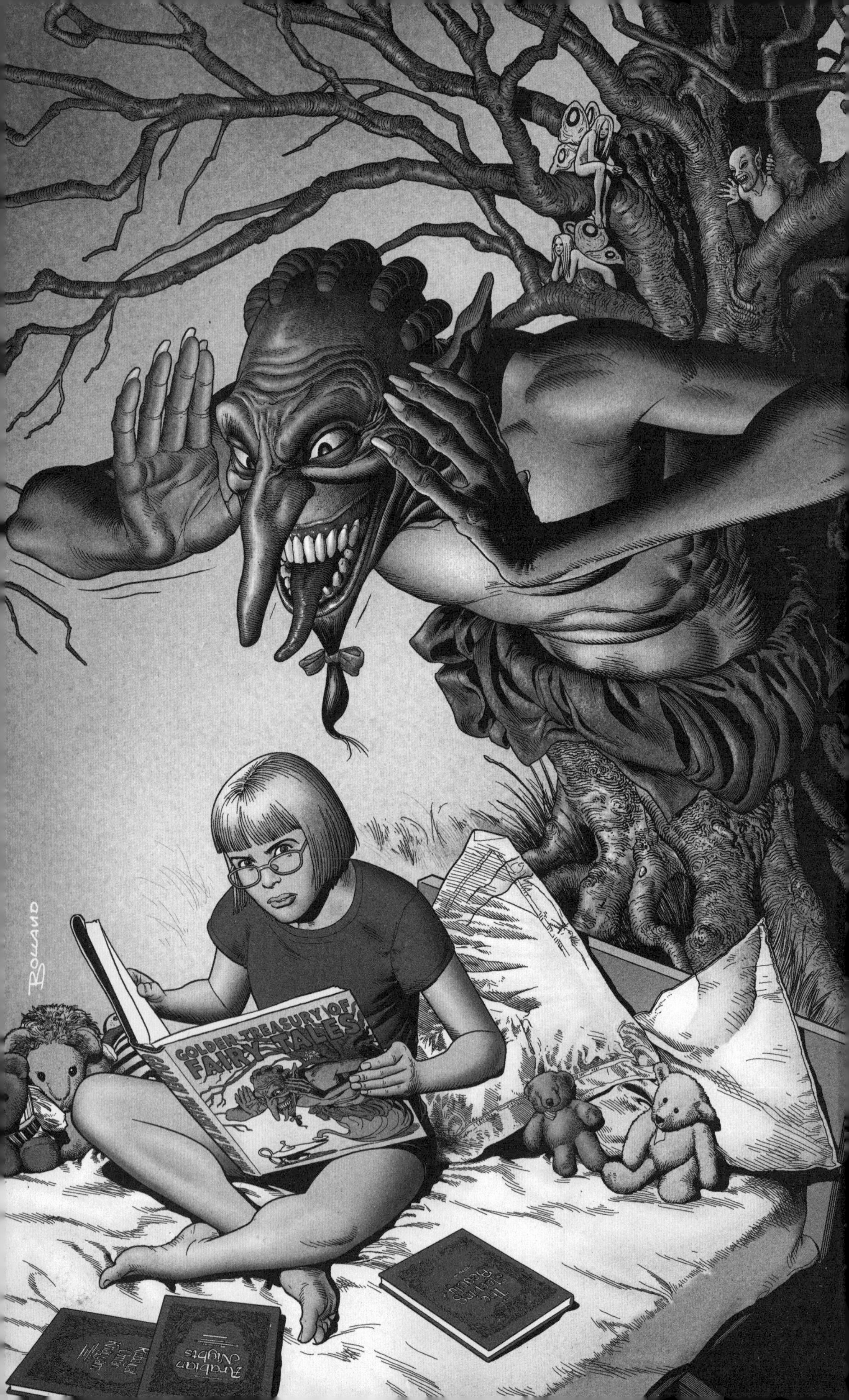
GOLDEN TREASURY OF FAIRY TALES
The Sleeping Beauty
Arabian Nights
BOLLAND